THIEVES
IN
HIGH PLACES

JIM HIGHTOWER

THIEVES

IN

HIGH PLACES

THEY'VE STOLEN OUR COUNTRY—

AND IT'S TIME TO

TAKE IT BACK

VIKING

VIKING
Published by the Penguin Group
Penguin Group (USA) Inc., 375 Hudson Street, New York, New York 10014, U.S.A.
Penguin Books Ltd, 80 Strand, London WC2R 0RL, England
Penguin Books Australia Ltd, 250 Camberwell Road, Camberwell, Victoria 3124, Australia
Penguin Books Canada Ltd, 10 Alcorn Avenue, Toronto, Ontario, Canada M4V 3B2
Penguin Books India (P) Ltd, 11 Community Centre, Panchsheel Park,
New Delhi - 110 017, India
Penguin Books (N.Z.) Ltd, Cnr Rosedale and Airborne Roads, Albany,
Auckland, New Zealand
Penguin Books (South Africa) (Pty) Ltd, 24 Sturdee Avenue, Rosebank,
Johannesburg 2196, South Africa

Penguin Books Ltd, Registered Offices: 80 Strand, London WC2R 0RL, England

First published in 2003 by Viking Penguin, a member of Penguin Group (USA) Inc.

3   5   7   9   10   8   6   4

Copyright © James Hightower, 2003
All rights reserved

Grateful acknowlegment is made for permission to reprint "What the
American Flag Stands For" by Charlotte Aldebron. Used by permission.

LIBRARY OF CONGRESS CATALOGING-IN-PUBLICATION DATA
Hightower, Jim, 1943-
Thieves in high places : they've stolen our country—and it's time to take it back / Jim
Hightower.
    p.   cm.
Includes index.
ISBN 0-670-03141-0
1. Political corruption—United States.   2. United States—Politics and government—2001-
3. Business and politics—United States.   4. Corporate power—United States.   I. Title.
JK2249.H54 2003
973.931—dc21   2003047958

This book is printed on acid-free paper. ⊚

Printed in the United States of America

This is dedicated—
To the one I love

Don't agonize, organize.

ACKNOWLEDGMENTS

Thank you, DeMarco, thank you, thank you, thank you!

And thank you, Laura Ehrlich and Sean Doles, for such terrific work under duress (remember, in time those ulcers will heal). Thanks, too, to Adrian Zackheim and Rafe Sagalyn for your support.

Also, thanks to all the fine folks I met in some of Austin's great coffee joints where I took up space, quaffed java, soaked up the ambience, and wrote this book: Bouldin Creek Coffeehouse (official motto: "Caffeine Dealer"), Cippolina, Little City, Mad Bird Café, Mozart's, Schlotzsky's Bakery, and Texas French Bread on South Congress.

CONTENTS

Kleptocrat Nation

klep·to·crat na·tion (klep′te krat na′ shen), *n.* **1.** a body of people ruled by thieves **2.** a government characterized by the practice of transferring money and power from the many to the few **3.** a ruling class of moneyed elites that usurps liberty, justice, sovereignty, and other democratic rights from the people **4.** the USA in 2003

The Kleptocrats have taken over. Look at America's leadership today—not just political, but corporate, too. Tell me you wouldn't trade the whole mess of them for one good kindergarten teacher.

Forget George W for a moment (we'll get to him soon enough) and sneak a peek at practically any big-deal CEO, congressional heavy, media baron, talk-show yakker, pompadoured TV preacher, and the other pushers of America's new ethic of grab-it-and-go greed. Sheesh! In a crunch, would you want to be tied at the waist to any of these people? When I look at any one of them, I can't help mumbling to myself: *100,000 sperm and you were the fastest?*

Yet, they're in charge! Here we are, living in the wealthiest country in history, a country of boundless possibilities, a country made up of a people deeply committed to democratic ideals, a country with the potential for spectacular human achievement—but we find ourselves ruled (politically, economically, culturally, and ethically) by a confederacy of Kleptocrats.

When did you first realize or at least begin to suspect that America was lost? Not physically, of course—we're right here.

Lost its way, is what I mean, having wandered from the brave and true path first pointed out by Tom Paine, T.J., Jimmy Madison, and several other good thinkers back around 1776—a path toward a society focused not on empire, but on enlightenment and egalitarianism.

We've never reached that glorious place, of course, but the important thing is that in our two-century sojourn we've been steadily striving to get there . . . and making progress. If any one thing really characterizes this big boiling pot of diversity dubbed "America" it is that we're a nation of strivers. Unfortunately, the cultural elites want to minimalize this powerful virtue by reducing it to nothing more than individuals striving for material gain—*Who Wants to Be a Millionaire, How to Get Rich in the Next Half Hour!, You Might Already Be a Winner.*

Then they wonder why there's such a gaping hole in America, an emptiness that can't be filled by nonstop shopping, prepaid elections, more bunting, and reality TV. When the Powers That Be started defining a person's value by the value of his stock portfolio, they lost America, for that's not who we are. These Powers are as clueless as the doomed husband in this divorce case:

ATTORNEY: What was the first thing your husband said to you when you woke up that morning?
WITNESS: He said, "Where am I, Cathy?"
ATTORNEY: And why did that upset you?
WITNESS: My name is Susan.

Don't go calling us names like "Consumer" or "Stakeholder" when who we are is full-fledged, dyed-in-the-wool, unbridled, rambunctious *citizens*—indeed, we're the ultimate sovereigns of this great land. We don't strive merely for material gain, but also for the spiritual satisfaction of building community and reaping the deeper richness of the common good.

The idea of belonging to something larger than our own egos and bank accounts, the idea of caring, sharing, and participating *as a public,* is the BIG IDEA of America itself. As a boy growing up in Denison, Texas, I was taught this unifying, moral concept by hardworking, Depression-era parents who ran a small business in our small town. They knew from experience and from their hearts what America is all about: "Everybody does better when everybody does better" is how my old Daddy used to put it.

The unforgivable transgression of today's leaders is that they've abandoned this common wisdom of the common good and quit striving for that world of enlightenment and egalitarianism that the founders envisioned and that so many throughout our history have struggled to build. Instead, whether from the top executive suites or from the White House, the people in charge today are aggressively pushing a soulless ethic that shouts: "Everyone on your own, grab all you can, and if you've got enough money, secure yourself in a gated compound."

Whoa there, greedbreath. That's not a society, it's a cockfight! And it's damned sure not the proud country that we thought we were living in—the land of Liberty and Justice for All.

Not only are the Kleptocrats stealing our country from us, they're stealing our democratic ideals—*the very idea of America.* And it's time to take it back.

SAPSUCKERS

How far have the elites moved from us? So far that even the moderates have lost their way. Take Sherwood Boehlert. He's a Republican congressman, but despite that, not a bad guy. Sherwood thinks of himself as "part of the enlightened middle."

From central New York, he's been in the House of Representatives for twenty-one years now. A long time. Maybe a tad too long. He says he loves the job, calling it the "ultimate aphrodisiac." Hmmmm. OK, I understand that people who shovel muck for a living come to love the smell, so everyone to his own.

But Sherwood said something not long ago that made me think that maybe he's been sniffing the perfumes of high office longer than is good for him:

"It's the people's house," he gushed about his side of the Capitol, *"the one institution in the whole wide world that's the personification of this great democracy of ours."*

Uh-oh. Quick, someone dial 9-1-1. We need to rush an EMS Reality Crew over to Congress, grab Sherwood, strap him down, and jolt his head with defibrillator pads to shock the poor delusional fellow back to earth.

Think about it: *Congress, democracy.* Do these two words fit together in your mind?

America is a nation of nurses, office workers, cabdrivers, schoolteachers, pharmacists, shopkeepers, middle managers, truck drivers, shift workers, librarians, cleaning people, electricians, fruit pickers, struggling artists—how many of our ilk are sitting next to Sherwood in "the people's house"?

The great majority of Americans make less than $50,000 a year; half make under $32,000. How many members of Congress come from such modest backgrounds? Today's Congress is made up of business executives, lawyers, and former political operatives (which Boehlert was). The Public Interest Research Group reports that nearly half of the people newly elected to Congress last year are millionaires. This is the personification of democracy?

It's time to play "WHO WANTS TO BE A CONGRESS CRITTER?" There are 280 million Americans. To win today's top prize, tell me how many of us are millionaires? BLHAAAAT. Time's up. The answer: 2.1 million. We'll do the math for you. That's about 7/10 of 1 percent of the people.

Not only do the members tend to descend into Congress from the economic heights, but they also spend practically all of their substantive and social time with others from the heights. Congress's real constituency is no longer you and me, but the people who "matter." These are your top-floor corporate executives and the moneyed elites who have full-time lobbyists and who make the $1,000-and-higher campaign donations (only 0.12 percent of Americans are in this class) that grease the wheels of congressional incumbency. They are the privileged few who know members by their first names, who get every one of their phone calls returned—and who get their agendas adopted.

Perhaps this gaping economic chasm between those on the inside and all the rest of us on the outside explains why our strumpets of state never get around to dealing with little matters like assuring health care for all families, passing living-wage legislation, and making sure everyone gets a decent retirement. Members of the congressional club feel no urgency because, hey, it's not *them*—they have no personal anxiety about such matters, because (one) they're well off and (two) they're covered on all this by us taxpayers. Yes, even the multimillionaires in Congress get:

- Full platinum-level health coverage for them and their families, including choosing their own docs, seeing the specialists they need, dental care, and cosmetic surgery for their pets. (Just kidding about that last one—but don't put it past them!)
- A rosy retirement, with pensions that can rise higher than the pay they got while in office. Just the starting pensions are sweet: Phil Gramm, who finally did something for the people of Texas by leaving the Senate last year, starts out drawing retirement pay of $78,534 a year. He'll be paid more for doing nothing than 80-plus percent of us Americans are paid for working full-time.
- Regular cost-of-living pay raises. While Congress has not seen fit to increase the minimum wage (still $5.15 an hour) since 1996, the members did give themselves four $5,000 pay raises during the past five years.

> ### Dick, Call Home
> ### When You Pass Pluto
>
> *"The Congress didn't vote themselves a pay raise. We just simply did not deny ourselves that normal increase in our cost of living that every other worker in America not only expects, but insists upon."*
>
> —House Majority Leader Dick Armey on *Meet the Press* after maneuvering through last year's pay raise, bringing Congress's salary to $155,000 a year.

This $20,000 "adjustment" in each of their own annual pay packets is $8,000 more than the gross pay that a full-time minimum-wage worker would get if Congress ever gets around to the one-dollar wage hike they've been "talking" about for years.

- Excellent job security. *Did you know that a member of Congress is four times more likely to die in office than to lose an election?* This is not only because of the special-interest money they're stuffed with, but also because the GOP and Democrats conspire to divide the turf in each state, gerrymandering districts to assure that 96 percent of them are "safe" for the incumbents. There's not much democracy in a rigged system that now allows only about 20 of the 435 House seats to be competitive in each election cycle.

As a bunch (and, yes, there are important exceptions within the bunch), I think of today's Congress as a colony of cicadas. These are interesting insects with powerful survivalist genes. After hatching from eggs laid in tree limbs, cicadas drop to the ground, immediately burrow deep, and attach themselves to tree roots, where they suck the sap for thirteen years. The major difference is that Congress Critters suck the sap much longer.

ONWARD TO RECLAIM AMERICA!

A couple of years ago, Japanese police discovered more than four hundred pieces of women's underwear in the home of Sadao Ushimura, a fellow who was a prominent official in Japan's finance ministry at the time. Mr. Ushimura proclaimed total innocence of any possible scandal or perversion, explaining: "I picked up all lingerie on the streets by pure chance."

We still have our underwear in America, but we've been stripped of a garment far more delicate and precious: our democracy. On this sprawling continent with its cacophony of voices and unprecedented clash of cultures, we've been able to hold it all together through the years because of our people's instinctive and tenacious belief in the sanctity of democratic principles.

But something has gone terribly wrong in our country. The essence of democracy—our power to control decisions that affect us—has steadily and quietly been pilfered by corporate Kleptocrats. They have collected up our democratic powers piece by piece, hoarding them in the privacy of their own fiefdoms. These elites (fully abetted by the governmental elites they have bought) now effectively control the decisions that affect We the People—everything from public-spending priorities to environmental degradation, from wages to war, from what's on the "news" to who gets elected.

This has taken place not by "pure chance," but through deliberate filching, and the filching now has reached the level of wholesale looting. We can no longer avoid the reality in front of us: The elites have pulled off a slow-motion coup, radically wrenching America's power balance from a people's democracy to Kleptocrat Nation.

This would be terribly depressing except for one thing, which is that one basic has definitely NOT changed in our land: The people (you rascals!) still have that instinctive and tenacious belief in our historic democratic principles. The antidote to kleptocracy is the age-old medicine of democratic struggle, agitation, and organization—and all across our country, the rebellion is on!

As happened in the rebellion of 1776, as happened in the populist revolt against the robber barons of the nineteenth century, and as is already happening in community after community today, America's historic democratic yearnings will not be long suppressed. Despite our present leadership (with their autocratic, plutocratic, and imperialistic ambitions), this is a nation of irrepressible democrats, and their spirit will out.

I think of my country like a rosebush. Many people say roses are fundamentally flawed because they have thorns. But I see it differently—I think it's wonderful that thorns have roses.

America is a thorny bush, for sure, but the ordinary people are its roses, and they are the beautiful story of this book.

I. LOST AMERICA
(The Bad News)

CHAPTER 1

BushCo

Lily Tomlin says she worries that the man who invented Muzak might be thinking of inventing something else.

I'm with her on that, but it ranks only a single "!" on my personal worry chart. Here are some things I find more worrisome, in rising order of alarm:

> **!!** It'll be discovered that the cause of cancer is: Beer.
> **!!!** What if the song is right? What if the Hokey Pokey really
>   is "what it's all about"?
> **!!!!** One word: *BushCheneyRumsfeldAshcroftRidge&Co.*

Aaauuuughh!!!! These people are dangerous. They're also nuts. Here's a small starter package of their nuttiness, just to give you a taste of what's to come:

- The Bushites heard that the economy is wringing out working families like an old worn-out dishrag, so they said: No problem, we'll help you by eliminating taxes paid by rich people.
- They've invented perverse phrases of newspeak, such as "anticipatory self-defense," which give them rhetorical cover to roam anywhere around the globe like Attila the Nuclear Hun to kill people they don't like and take their oil—now, when reporters ask Bush if we're going to war he has to ask: In which country?
- They have an environmental policy that's so polluted they actually tried to designate a California waste dump as a National Historic

Landmark—you know, Mount Vernon, Monticello, Walden Pond, the Frenso Municipal Sanitary Landfill.

• They're so imperious that even when Dick Cheney finally was forced by a court to release some of the documents disclosing the rampant corporate cronyism in his secret energy policy task force, the White House blanked out most sentences in the eleven thousand pages released, including one paper that was entirely blanked out except for this concluding sentence: "I hope this information was helpful."

Imagine what they'd be doing if they'd actually won the election!

I can hear some of you saying, *Hightower, how can you hear what we're saying when you're not in the room with us?* No, no, I don't hear you saying that, I hear you saying, *So what'd you expect, Hightower? It's a Republican administration, for cryin' out loud! Republican presidents have favored big business since the day Abe got shot and they discovered robber barons. So what's new? Besides, bubba, that bunch of Clinton Democrats plays the same footsie with the money bags. Didja forget the Lincoln Bedroom? NAFTA? All the other corporate favors?*

Fair enough. The White House has been the Corporate Feed & Greed Store for some time. But this is much bigger. The Bushites are something else again, a whole other species of political schemers proceeding at an entirely new level of seriousness and sophistication, fully intending to implement an ideological laissez-faire agenda developed during the past thirty years or so in various corporate-funded think tanks and right-wing groups.

They're not merely doing favors, giving payback, dancin' with them that brung 'em, or any of the other colloquial expressions of Business As Usual—giving a subsidy here, a special tax break there, a regulatory twist back over here. This bunch is business-way-more-than-usual.

MEET YOUR GOVERNMENT

Are you old enough to remember when there was no EMS? It seems now as though these no-nonsense professional lifesavers have been around forever, rushing with lights flashing and sirens wailing to get to car wrecks, heart attack victims, and other emergencies. What a terrific job these men and women do. We all benefit by having them at the ready—including many a corpulent old hater of "Biggummint" who's lived to thank his or her lucky stars that this chunk of public spending was available to haul their carcass to the hospital in time.

Until about thirty years ago, though, EMS didn't exist. Instead, funeral homes ran the ambulances. Yes, the undertaker! Talk about a conflict of interest. Wreck on the highway? Call the boys over at the Kingdom of Eternal-Slow-Motion Funeral Home to head on over. (Owner: "OK, Joe Bill, we've got a blood splotch out on 390 West, but don't you go running red lights and such, you hear?") People died, not from the crash, but because the ambulance didn't get there in time, or when it did, the driver didn't know any lifesaving procedures, so . . . plunk . . . another body for the undertaker's slab.

Not since those days have I seen such a big oozing conflict of interest as we now have in the White House. BushCheneyRumsfeld and the rest are not simply dutiful servants trying to please corporate interests, as previous administrations have been, THEY ARE THE CORPORATE INTERESTS.

I believe they should have to wear those peel-off greeting badges that conventioneers stick on their lapels: "HI! I'm Dick from Halliburton." "I'm Rummie from Searle & Company and General Instrument." "I'm Norm Mineta from Lockheed Martin." "Ann Veneman from Calgene, Inc." "Andy Card, here, from General Motors." "Mitch Daniels from Eli Lilly." "Donnie Evans of Brown, Inc." "I'm Elaine Chao with Bank of America, Northwest Airlines, Dole Foods, Clorox, Columbia/HCA Healthcare, and—golly, they just don't give you enough room on these badges, do they?"

Don't forget George himself, who hails from the executive suites of Arbusto Energy, Spectrum 7, Harken Energy, and Texas Rangers, Inc.

From the start and by design, this was Bush Incorporated. Of course, Bush's handlers ran it through their spin cycle so it wouldn't seem like what it was, instead focusing on the cabinet's physical diversity: "It's America," they cried as the cabinet was introduced. Looky there: four women (count 'em, four!), two African Americans, a Japanese American, a Lebanese American, a Chinese American, and—omigosh—even a Democrat American!

What strings all of this apparent diversity together, however, is the corporate connection. Practically every cabinet member has spent a lifetime advancing the interests of corporations over those of working families, consumers, small farmers, the poor, the environment, and ordinary taxpayers—the *people's interests.* With one yank of the string, all that diversity snaps taut with corporate homogeneity. Looking at the cabinet's four CEOs, two corporate lobbyists, and a flock of loyal corporate board members, one business newsletter hailed it as "an all-star boardroom."

Swell. Except that this is supposed to be the cabinet of a democratic country, not of a corporation, and such a country dangerously restricts itself if it's guided by people whose experiences and outlook do not go beyond the bottom line of self-serving, profit-seeking corporations. As we've learned the hard way from Enron, WorldCom, Bush's own Harken Energy, and many more, the boardroom is not even good at governing a corporation, much less a bustling, sprawling, rambunctious, ornery, restless, fluid, *truly* diverse, and determinedly democratic nation like ours.

Tell me if I'm out of line here, but shouldn't there be at least one cabinet member who actually needs the job? And how about choosing three or four from among those of us whose only corporate connection is that we get monthly bills. Two-thirds of us Americans get paid less than $50,000 a year. Where's our seat? This is a job that pays $171,000 a year, yet virtually every cabinet appointee goes out of his way to say that taking "government pay" is a personal sacrifice for him, a step down, as though he's a little embarrassed. I'd like to hear one appointee shout, "Zowee! Order that new dress, momma, we're in the high cotton now."

And what about these people?

Instructive quote from no less an authority than Milton Friedman, the business guru who's the Jesus of the laissez-faire, free-market religion:

*"The corporation **cannot** be ethical, its only responsibility is to make a profit."*

Amen

- 33 million Americans now live in poverty—8 million more than twenty-five years ago.
- 41 million Americans have no health coverage—6 million more than a decade ago.
- 9.6 million Americans have no jobs—2 million more than when Bush came to office.

How about this: If they won't give working families and poor folks a seat at the big table, maybe they could set up a small table on the side. My parents did that when I was just a little scamp. When company came over for supper, there wouldn't be enough room for us kids at the dining table, so my folks would set up a card table. It was *something*, which is way more than we're getting now.

The cabinet was only the beginning. Bush & Co. also have looped their corporate string throughout the government, posting corporate

NICK GOES HOME

How can you not feel sorry for Nick Calio? He's a guy with T-bone tastes, but for the first years of the Bush Administration, he was having to settle for Spam—relatively speaking.

He was W's top White House lobbyist, paid a scant $145,000 a year (plus a chauffeured limo, a wining and dining expense account, full health plan, platinum pension, etc., but let's not get picky). Just before last Christmas, however, Nick left government service. Too little money, he said.

Well, you've got to understand where he's coming from. Before joining Bush, he was pulling down about a million a year as partner in a boutique lobbying firm, carrying water for the likes of Arthur Andersen and ARCO. He wears monogrammed, tailor-made, French-cuffed shirts that cost more than your monthly rent. He's got a $1.5 million Washington home, with a private wine cellar that he likes to keep stocked with the good stuff.

Nick lives large, and, well, you just can't make those ends meet on

$145K. So, he went back home, back to his beloved K Street, the avenue of the big-time corporate lobbyists. He's now the "senior vice president for global government affairs" for Citigroup, the financial conglomerate that finds itself under congressional and SEC investigation for its hanky-panky with Enron, as well as for other pecadillos.

Citigroup needs a friend who has friends in high places, and Nick's just the man. As White House lobbyist, for example, not only did he rub elbows with the prez and all the top agency heads, but he also was in charge of parsing out coveted favors to key members of Congress—things like invitations to state dinners, trips with George aboard *Air Force One*, and use of the presidential box at the Kennedy Center. He won't say how much Citigroup is paying for his "experience and advice," but he'll have no worries about stocking that wine cellar.

Asked if he thought it was ethical for a corporate lobbyist to swoosh through the revolving door into government service, then swoosh right back out to private lobbying, profiting from his government connections, Nick got huffy: "I think that's a silly criticism. What do you want? People going into government who know nothing about it? You need people going in who know the issues." And the game.

executives, consultants, and lobbyists to practically all of the key operational positions in every agency. You hear about the cabinet officials, but these are the faces that rarely surface, the people down in the inner works of our government who wield the monkey wrenches, grease cans, crowbars, drills, and power saws to jury-rig the system. There are scores of them, and their corporate bias thoroughly permeates and dominates the machinery of public affairs.

Are there no talented consumer, labor, environmental, and other public representatives to fill these posts? Well, yes, of course. But somehow or other, the Bushites haven't gotten around to appointing any of them. Instead, it's an all-corporate cast.

Here's just a few of the corporations that now have their very own executive or trusted hireling wearing the hat of an undersecretary, general counsel, assistant secretary, director, or some other powerful government official:

Aerospace Corporation	GTE/Verizon Communications
American Airlines	Huntsman Corporation
British-American Tobacco	IBM
Carnival Cruise Line	Integrated Systems
Charles Schwab	Interwest Mining
ConAgra	Lockheed Martin
Edison Electric	Monsanto
Energy Corporation of America	Northrop Grumman
Energy West Mining	Occidental Petroleum
Enron	Raytheon
Ernst & Young	Sensis Corp.
ExxonMobil	Tesoro Petroleum
General Electric	Union Pacific

What say we meet a couple of these corporately connected public servants?

John D. Graham

Here's a fellow who might already have touched you personally, though he wouldn't have left any fingerprints. John heads a nerdy operation called the Office of Information and Regulatory Affairs of the White House Office of Management and Budget. Let's see, the acronym of that'd be OIRAWHOMB, which can be rearranged as an anagram to spell BIG KIBOSH. That's what Graham is—the guy in charge of putting the kibosh on regulations designed to protect our health from things like asbestos poisoning, toxic emissions, and whatnot.

Gosh, why would he do that? Because he wakes up every morning and takes a couple of lids of LSD, which has turned him into a dangerous, hallucinogenic freak. (Just kidding! Call off the lawyers! I was only seeing if you were paying attention!) Actually, the LSD explanation is not one dot weirder than the reality, which is that Graham is besotted with an antigovernment, antipublic ideology and has found a way to convert his political extremism into a profitable career fronting for corporations that sicken and kill us with their products and carefree sloppiness.

What hole did Graham crawl out of? A place called the Harvard Center for Risk Analysis, which he directed, doing reports on the health risk of everything from secondhand smoke to the dioxins that spew from chemical plants. Well, that sounds pretty academicky, like he's a legitimate independent research scientist. He's not a scientist at all, just another doctrinaire policy geek. As for his independence, Graham's center is funded by more than one hundred corporations, including these specimens: Aetna, Alcoa, Amoco, ARCO, Bethlehem Steel, Boise Cascade, BP, Chevron, Ciba-Geigy, CITGO, Coca-Cola, Dow, DuPont, Eastman Kodak, Exxon, Ford, GE, GM, Georgia-Pacific, Goodyear, International Paper, Johnson & Johnson, Kraft, Merck, Mobil, Monsanto, Nippon, Novartis, PepsiCo, Pfizer, Pharmacia Upjohn, Procter & Gamble, Schering-Plough, Shell, Texaco, 3M, Union Carbide, and Westinghouse.

The companies contribute generously because Graham delivers reports that almost always support them, usually without bothering to mention that they funded his "research." For example, when the EPA finally reported that dioxin is an extraordinarily potent chemical that can cause everything from cancer to birth defects, Graham rushed out as an "expert" to criticize the EPA and pooh-pooh the risk, declaring to the media: "It's a shame when a mother worries about toxic chemicals, and yet her kids are running around unvaccinated and without bicycle helmets."

No mention to the media that his center is funded by forty-eight different corporations that pollute our environment with dioxin.

This is Bush's choice to be the czar who oversees the entire regulatory process of the government's executive departments. No important health, safety, environmental, or other rule to protect you and me from corporate excess can be issued by the EPA or other executive agency without getting stamped by John's signet ring. Yet, his appointment to head OIRA caused little media stir, and you probably know nothing about it. But the corporate executives and lobbyists knew about it, and their beaming smiles would have lit up the sky on the darkest night of an Arctic winter.

Among those beaming the brightest would have been the honchos of W.R. Grace & Co., the chemical and asbestos giant. They had a problem. Millions of American homes, schools, and businesses—perhaps yours—are insulated with a product named Zonolite, made from a substance containing an extremely lethal asbestos fiber that came from W.R. Grace's mine in Libby, Montana. Hundreds of the Libby miners and their families have died from asbestosis, hundreds more are diagnosed with it, and thousands are sickened by it.

This is nasty stuff—breathing even a little can cause major health problems. The Zonolite insulation poses no problem if it's not disturbed. That's the good news. Bad news is that it takes very little to disturb it. Bumping the walls as you sweep your floor or doing work in the attic can shake loose a mess of fibers. It's such a problem that Bush's EPA administrator, Christine Todd Whitman, who's not exactly a tiger on corporate wrongdoing, was so alarmed that she was prepared in April of '02 to issue a national health warning about Zonolite.

Do you recall getting any warning? You didn't, because just days before Whitman was to go to the media, John Graham and his OIRAWHOMB put the kibosh on her warning. It seems that Graham's obligation is not to us pollutees, who might want to know about Zonolite's danger to our families, but to the bottom line of the polluter, W.R. Grace.

Under what authority had Graham single handedly quashed such an important effort by a cabinet officer to protect the public health? No response from OIRAWHOMB. Had he been contacted by Grace officials? Silence. An agency spokeswoman told an inquiring reporter: "We don't discuss predecisional deliberations."

There you have it—your tax dollars at work, Bush style.

Nancy Victory

What a good name! Sounds like a comic book heroine. But, no, she's for real, and whether you think she's a heroine or not depends on which end of the cell phone you're on. If you're on the consumer end, not. But if you're an executive or lobbyist for Cingular Wireless, SBC Communications, Verizon, or one of the other big sellers of cell phone plans, definitely yes.

Nancy is based these days at the Commerce Department, where she heads an outfit you're not likely to have heard of: the National Telecommunications and Information Administration. Sounds awfully boring. But as administrator of NTIA, Nancy packs some punch, for it makes her the Bushites' point person on telecommunications policy. There's lots of dough riding on the policy decisions she's making—dough that's ultimately going to come out of the pockets of Mr. and Ms. Youknowwho.

Now I know this will surprise you: Guess who Nancy worked for before joining Bush Incorporated? The cell phone makers and marketers! Isn't this fun? Her former law firm, Wiley Rein & Fielding, is one of the biggest in Washington, specializing in communications regulation and representing such clients as Verizon and SBC. Her husband still is a partner there, which puts a nice family touch to the story.

After Bush appointed Ms. Victory, she was feted at a private reception by her old corporate pals. The party was hosted and paid for by the top lobbyists for Cingular, SBC, and Motorola. Asked how much they spent and whether the money came from corporate funds, both the Cingular and Motorola lobbyists said, and I quote them here, "I don't remember."

Ah, but Nancy remembered them. *Only ten days after her gala reception,* she woke up in a gay and generous mood, ate a big bowl of Special K, went to the office, and zipped off a formal NTIA letter to the FCC demanding the immediate repeal of a regulation that had long bothered her friends at Cingular, SBC, and so forth. In essence, what this repeal would do is to let these big players divide the territory and eliminate pesky competitors. *Two weeks after her letter was sent,* the FCC did just as Nancy had asked.

Amazing. Who says government is slow and unresponsive?

Confronted by the curious chronology at play here, Nancy indignantly says that any suggestion that there was a connection is *"ridiculous."* She also declined to identify industry guests who attended her reception, simply saying, "They're my friends."

Exactly. And that's what's wrong—Nancy and her friends are running our government as though it's their private party.

CORPORATIONS "R" US

What we have here is a government that's as thoroughly corporatized as your typical shopping mall. Most malls today have the same collection of stores, dominated by Starbucks, The Gap, McDonald's, Barnes & Noble, Toys "R" Us, CompUSA, Target, Wal-Mart, and other nationally branded names that use their deep-pocket financing, predatory marketing, and raw political muscle to overpower local businesses and communities.

Now, this same assertion of corporate power, this same uniformity, is malling our entire government, branding it as corporate America's own. Such uniformity is bad enough in the marketplace, but it's intolerable in a government that's supposed to represent all of the people.

Some say—in fact, Bush and Cheney did say when they were campaigning—that government ought to operate like a business. Oh, which one? Enron? WorldCom? But it's not just a matter of the disgraced corporations. *No corporation is a model for how government should operate.* Corporations are rigid, top-down, autocratic hierarchies in which executive actions are delivered as fiats to be implemented unquestioningly. Checks and balances are a joke—the board of directors, for example, is a brother-in-law job, handpicked by the CEO. Openness? Corporations are towers of secrecy, in which all information is considered a proprietary asset to be doled out only in approved snippets vetted through the PR department, keeping as much as possible from employees, investors, customers, auditors, regulators, lawmakers, the media, and We the People.

If this way of operating sounds familiar, it's because this has been the mode of the Bushites from day one. We really shouldn't be surprised that they're so determinedly secretive, so bald in their grab for power, so disdainful of Congress and anyone who tries to question them, so astonishingly audacious in their assertion of an agenda that benefits very few people and that few support. Having spent their professional lives within the tightly controlled executive-suite culture, they come to government with the narrowest of outlooks, the most privileged of experiences, and the bottom-line arrogance of executives who want to do what they want—and everyone else should just get the hell out of their way.

THE DISARMING POWER OF GEORGE

Why have the media been so laid-back, so unconcerned or even un-aware that a corporate coup is happening in plain sight? An obvious reason is that the owners controlling today's conglomerated, cen-tralized media are part of the coup, profiting enormously from it. Another is that the media and much of the public have had their eyes diverted from the coup by the sound and fury of Bush's war drums. September 11 and Saddam Hussein have provided ample cover and rationalization for the Bushites' relentless concentration of governmental authority.

But another is the "Power of George." It's stupid to call him stu-pid. True, he doesn't have the brain muscle for any heavy lifting, but that's not why he's there. He knows who he is, knows his role, and he's playing it like a Shakespearean star.

The corporate takeover of the U.S. government is ugly. If, say, Dick Cheney were the face of such an un-American power grab, everyone would see it . . . and shriek! Cheney's got a smile like a landlord who's just evicted another widow.

But George is, well, George. So affable, so "What, me worry?" He comes across not as the pouty, petulant, spoiled frat boy that close as-sociates and family know him to be—the inner child who used to stuff frogs with firecrackers and blow them up for laughs*—but as regular ol' George. If you just casually watch him, you think: He might not have it all together, but he surely means no harm, does he?

---

*No, I'm not making this up. "We were terrible to animals," boyhood friend Terry Throckmorton laughingly said in a *New York Times* profile on George W. Terry noted that a low spot behind Bush's house would fill with water after a good rain, and thousands of frogs would come out. "We'd put firecrackers in the frogs and throw them and blow them up." Ah, the joys of childhood.

Remember his pretzel attack? Just into the second year of his presidency, he was home alone in the White House one day, stretched out on the couch with his dogs, Spot and Barney, taking in a football game on the telly, when—*gckkhkxxx*—he got a pretzel stuck in his throat, choked, fainted, fell to the floor, and got a bright red rug burn on his cheek. Next day, he sent a big bag of pretzels to the press with a note saying, "Chew slowly." You've got to like that.

This is who he's always been. The oilmen who gave him a sweetheart deal at Harken Energy, and the corporate heavies who essentially gave him a partnership in the Texas Rangers, were not bringing him on board for his brain or management acumen. They were buying a front man with a bankable name and a likable personality. Same in politics. He has the persona to soften the blow and distract from the theft. That's why the CEOs and lobbyists were so wildly enthusiastic about a do-nothing Texas governor that they put up $113 million for his campaign.

SNOW JOB

Last December, George gave America a Christmas present: A brand new economic team! I really was hoping for a new bike, but instead you and I and all of us were presented with John Snow, Steve Friedman, and Bill Donaldson. It was like getting socks, belts, and underwear, but George looked into the TV cameras and said firmly that we should be grateful, for these three gifts were going to "fix" the economy.

Yes, but for whom? As a hotel worker once said to me, "I live on a fixed income—and I'm looking for the ones who fixed it." She might check out these three fixers and think about what they'll deliver for her:

> *Donaldson,* chosen to head the SEC, which is supposed to be our watchdog against fraud by Wall Street firms. He was CEO of one of the biggest of the Wall Street firms, Donald-

son, Lufkin & Jenrette—which presently happens to be under SEC investigation for fraud.

Friedman, chosen to be Bush's top economic advisor. He was
cochairman of the huge investment house of Goldman
Sachs, where he was a leader in the merge-and-purge boom
of the '80s and '90s, which cost hundreds of thousands of
workers their jobs, lessened competition, raised prices for
consumers, and hurt shareholders.

Snow, chosen to be our country's top economic official as
treasury secretary. He was CEO of the nation's largest railroad company, CSX Corporation, where he presided over a
53 percent dive in the company's stock price while raising his
own pay by 69 percent, at the same time he was slashing the
health care and life insurance benefits for CSX retirees.

This trio is now making the governmental decisions over all aspects
of our economic lives, setting the rules and rewriting the laws concern-
ing our wages, pensions, taxes, credit cards, mortgages, small-business
loans, bankruptcies, and so forth. Sheesh—two Wall Streeters and a rail-
roader. Thanks, George! I wonder why he didn't just shove an ice pick up
our noses.

I ask you: Whose side do you figure Snow, Friedman, and Donaldson
will be on when it comes to the big decisions affecting you, like whether
Congress should cut the taxes on the super rich by another half a trillion
dollars or put those public funds into something more productive that
you could use, like a cut in your payroll taxes or an affordable health care
plan for all? But we already know the answer to that one—all three were
early and eager endorsers of George W's voodoo, hoodoo, woowoo
trickle-down tax plan for the wealthy, which—SURPRISE!—includes
them.

It's not that they're mean men. I have no doubt that each one loves
puppies, adores his grandchildren, and tears up at Frank Capra mov-
ies. They're probably devout churchgoers, too, and give to the fund for
orphans. But being softhearted or hard has nothing to do with their
views on policy. That's about business, and, well, they don't see the

world from the same perspective as you and I do. We look out at life from the street level. They're always looking down from on high. It's different.

Now I'm hearing you again. I'm hearing you say, *Whaddaya mean they're different from us, Hightower? Give us an example we can sink our teeth into.* Okey-dokey. Take a squint at Mr. Railroad Man.

HIM: John Snow wrote a clause into his CSX contract that would pay him $15 million if he left the corporation to take a position in "public service." Prescient, no? And tacky. It was so stinky that when Bush called him to serve, the threat of media exposure compelled him to reject the 15 mil, magnanimously saying that he certainly didn't want to appear to be getting a corporate subsidy to do government work. Oh? So why'd he write it into his contract?

YOU: It wouldn't occur to you to expect such a payment, and even if you did, you'd be laughed out of the building and pelted with cabbages.

HIM: In 1996, CSX loaned $25 million to Snow so he could buy a big chunk of the company's stock, which he hoped to ride to glory. Unfortunately for Snow, under his guidance of the company, CSX stock began to plummet. So he took the hit, right? Get serious. He's the CEO, so he's bulletproof. In 2000, the board took back its now devalued shares, forgave the $25 million owed by Snow, and gave back his down payment! After Snow's cabinet appointment, a White House spokeswoman was asked about the ethics of this deal. She said curtly that it was "legal."

YOU: You're not an insider, so you don't get it—you neither get a loan nor do you "get" the game they're playing.

HIM: Although he cut back on the pensions of CSX retirees, he got the board to give him pension credit for forty-four years on the job—even though he was there only twenty-five years.

YOU: Rank-and-file workers get only one year of pension credit for one year worked and not a minute extra, you slacker.

HIM: Snow's retirement pay will be based not on his salary alone, but also on his bonuses and on the value of 250,000 shares of CSX stock that the board *gave* to him.

YOU: Are you crazy? You think we're gonna give stock to you? You think this is some charity, you slug? Your pension pay is based on your wages, period.

HIM: Eternal wealth is John's future, for his pension adds up to $2.5 million. A year. Every year. Until he dies. Guaranteed.

YOU: Eternal harassment is your future, for we're not ever gonna stop whacking at your monthly retirement stipend, unless we just decide to loot the entire fund before you croak.

HIM: Snow gets promoted by Bush to be in charge of America's economic policy.

YOU: Good luck, chump.

Thinking about Snow, I thought of the British House of Lords. I'm an aficionado of the pomp, queerness (yes, it's OK to use this word in this context—lighten up!), and general atmosphere of buffoonery in the House of Lords. Assorted officials there wear what look to be pieces of crinoline petticoats thrusting from their throats, they have various medals and fobs hanging from their sixteenth-century garb, and they are given such marvelous official titles as the "Gentleman Usher of the Black Rod." Yep, he does walk around toting a black rod that's about four feet long. I think it would be splendid if the royal lords of our society had such titles. Instead of treasury secretary, for example, Lord Snow could be the Gentleman Usher of the Golden Shaft, and be required to carry it with him wherever he goes.

The Bushites' domination and transformation of the governing apparatus is so antithetical to our democratic values, yet so thorough, that we no longer have The Government of the People of the United States of America.

But, what the hell, I say we go all the way with it. I mean, what kind of name is "The Government of the People of the United States of America" anyway? That's so yesterday. We could use some marketing savvy here, some twenty-first-century identity branding that can connect to the wired, hip, commercial culture that is "today."

Let's get with the times, people! You don't see phone companies, for example, sticking with stodgy old names like Bell Atlantic Telephone Corporation, do you? No—they become "Verizon." Now that's got some zip to it! (Alright, it's not really a word and no one can figure out what it is or what it's selling, and the company's stock price is down by half in the three years since the name change, but let's not fall into the trap of negativity here.)

So let's rebrand. Forget The Government of the People of Yada-YadaYada. Let's call it something consumers can remember, something that'll look good on Washington's marble walls, something punchy and true to the spirit of the Bush government. Let's call it: **BUSHCO!**

CHAPTER 2

Never Have So Few Done So Much for So Few

These days, honesty in politics is about as rare as a rooster laying eggs, but in the 2000 presidential run, there was one wonderfully candid moment.

It came from George W at a fat-cat dinner in New York City. A sea of affluence filled the room—men were dressed in white tie and tails, women in designer gowns. Trying to make a little opening joke about his Big Money support, George said: "This is an impressive crowd. The haves and the have-mores. Some call you the elite. I call you my base."

Oooooo, rich, huh? And true to the core. One thing I like about Bush is that he is unabashed about favoring the rich. The guy is simply true blue! It's refreshing in its own way that he wears class loyalty for all to see, like a flaming red fraternity jacket. Unlike the Democrats (to choose the exact opposite behavior), George never disowns or turns on his base, and he consistently, fearlessly, *gleefully* delivers for them. By the sackfuls. As audaciously as a daylight bank robber.

In 2001, first thing he pulled off after his swearing-in was, what? A bank robbery!

He robbed *our* bank, the public treasury, which holds the money we all put in there to finance the things we need, from schools to roads, libraries to national parks. George rode up on his little pony, darted in, and before we even realized he was in there, he'd heisted $1.3 TRILLION of our public funds and given the money away. To whom? The bulk of it goes to the richest 1 percent of Americans; nearly all of the rest goes to the wealthiest 10 percent. "My base."

To make it look good, he tossed a few coins at some of the rest of us.

A fourth of Americans got nothing out of his bank job, the middle class got a cup of coffee, and George's buddies at the country club are still wallowing in wads of new wealth that'll keep coming their way for the next decade. It was an act of the man we now know as: DOOH NIBOR! Spell that backward, from right to left. No one gets it more backward than George.

Hey, wait a minute, DOOH NIBOR! That was *our* wealth. There were some things we had in mind to do with that money—paying for some basic things we all need, like good health care for everyone, fixing our schools, cleaning up our rivers so we might fish and swim in them again, building a high-speed train system across . . . "Sit down and shut up," DOOH NIBOR shot back at us, smirking: "Money's gone."

After last fall's congressional elections, Bush claimed a mandate. To do what? Make another hit on our bank! He's a serial robber, Clyde Barrow in Dockers, and Dick Cheney is his Bonnie. Instead of a tommy gun, they're whacking us with the presidential seal.

This time he was in our bank demanding another $350 to $726 billion a year. People are hurting, he shouted, so give me all the money they've been paying as taxes on their stock dividends, and I'll give it back to them. People, what people? Well, 89 percent of all stocks are owned by the richest 10 percent of Americans . . . so, *those* people. "The haves and have-mores."

Let's get this clear. The people who really are hurting in our economy are the poor and those working for wages, right? Yes. But they'll not get a dime from George's bank job? Afraid not. Instead, the money is to go to millionaires and billionaires—*people who need the extra money like Michael Jackson needs something else done to his face*? That's the plan.

Where does he come up with this stuff? From his base. Corporate executives, big contributors, right-wing think tanks like Heritage Foundation and Cato, lobbyists, old alums of the Ford–Reagan–Bush I years, and the occasional drift of fuzzy pollen that enters his brain through his nose—these form his network of ideas.

You want an example, don't you? Here's one: **Charles Schwab.** Also known as "Ducky." More on that in a moment. First: The Idea. You might remember the silly "Presidential Economic Forum" that the White House quickly threw together in August of '02. Polls were show-

HELPING THEMSELVES

To hype Bush's elimination of dividend taxes, the White House claimed that "92 million Americans" would get "an average of $1,083" in the first year of the cut.

Let's read between the lies:

- There are 280 million Americans, so by their own numbers, two-thirds of us get nothing from it.
- That $1,083 "average" for those who will get a cut is derived by lumping all of you small shareholders with the big boys, like Bill Gates. You'll get a dime apiece, Bill gets a million, but it averages $1,083. (Averages are like that—put one of your feet in a bucket of boiling water and the other in ice water, and on average, you're comfortable.)

Here's a couple of guys, though, who'd do way better than average on Bush's dividend cut:

George W. Bush. Based on his 2001 tax return, his tax take would be $16,511. Sweet!
Dick Cheney. Sweeter yet is the $104,823 that the V.P. would haul away.

ing Bush doing poorly on the question of "Do you think the president can even spell 'e-c-o-n-o-m-y, s-t-u-p-i-d'?" With congressional elections right around the corner, something had to be done. Not *really* done, as in action to address the problems, but done-up, as in flurry of motion to look like something's being done.

At the time, George wasn't doing anything presidential, having taken August off for a vacation on his new ranchette near Crawford, Texas, where he mostly did daily photo ops posing as a regular rancher-type person. (IMPORTANT MEDICAL ADVISORY: Do not attempt to mimic Bush's choice of vacation venues. It's beyond hot there in the summer. Not for nothing did Civil War General William Sheridan say that "if I owned both hell and Texas, I'd rent out Texas and live in hell." No one who is sane comes to Texas in August. If anyone you love even suggests such a trip, pretend you're going to go with them, but instead drive them directly to an insane asylum.) Suddenly, though, the political heat was on Bush. So, to position him as "engaged" on the economic woes of the little people, Karl "Svengali" Rove yanked George up and zipped him a few miles down the road to Waco for the "forum."

There, some 250 handpicked partisans had been assembled to (1) express their confidence in America, and (2) express their gratitude for the fine job Bush was doing in D.C. In other words, it was a dog and pony show, a Catskills schtick, made all the wackier by staging it in Waco.

JUST DUCKY

Not only is Charles Schwab a New York stockbroker and a quadruple billionaire, but he's also a man of the soil, a yeoman of mega-Jeffersonian scale—Charlie's a rice farmer on 1,500 acres of picturesque wetlands in Northern California.

Not that he raises rice to sell. That's the point. He put his acreage in the federal farm program. Yes, we taxpayers send him some $500,000 a year *not* to market rice. Why did he choose rice over other subsidized crops? Because his place is called Casa de Patos— "House of Ducks." It's not really a farm, but his very own private duck hunting club where he brings friends, clients, bankers, and other associates to—KABLOOIE!—knock a few birds out of the sky.

How does he know there'll be ducks flying across his place when the hunters come? Because ducks are naturally drawn to rice paddies. So, we pay him to grow rice so the ducks will come so his elite associates will have ducks to kill.

Bush would see nothing wrong with Ducky Schwab's grabbing taxpayer cash for his rich man's club from the farm program—a program that delivers zero money to 60 percent of America's real farmers, awarding some of the biggest payments to such corporate giants as DuPont and Chevron . . . and Casa de Patos. Hell, George would give Schwab a little punch on the shoulder and say, "Way to go, Duck Boy." Sadly, it's legal, and it's a fine upstanding example of what George and his base like to call "entrepreneurship."

After the show, straight man Rove declared that "there was unanimity that we've taken the right [economic] steps, that we're going in the right direction."

Not to poop on Karl's parade, but on the very day of the forum, the media reported that American Airlines was slashing another seven thousand jobs, IBM was offing fifteen thousand employees, and the Dow Jones average had fallen another two hundred points. However, Karl was allowing no clouds of reality to darken the klieg lights focused so brightly on his top banana, and he snapped at all the scoffers: "Everyone ought to applaud when the president sits down with ordinary people."

But Bush flubbed it! At the general forum, instead of sitting next to some Regular Joe, George missed his mark and chose a seat next to Charles Schwab! So there he was on national television chatting with a billionaire stockbroker who also was a $400,000 giver to Bush and the GOP. Priceless.

A bit later, George popped into one of the eight panel discussions, and there was Schwab again, offering his "solution" to America's economic woes: Cut the tax on stock dividends. I heard myself shouting into the great vacuum that separates Bush from real life: "Helllooooooo. Charles is a stockbroker. He'll make zillions of dollars in fees from affluent people investing the windfall they'll get from the tax bonanza he's proposing." Too late. Good idea, said George to his have-more friend Charlie. And thus was lodged in the president's mind the plan he proposed this year, yet another way he could serve: "My base."

RIGGING THE RULES

There are three things you never want to see:

- Water coming out of your electrical sockets.
- Flames shooting out of your sock drawer.
- A press release coming out of the White House that begins: "The Bush Administration today announced revised standards for . . ."

It doesn't matter "for what." When you see that eight-word lead you just know it's going to be yet another piece of awful news, yet another revision of the rules that'll let yet another industry or specific corporation have a free hand to clobber us regular folks with. From inaugural day forward, the Bush White House has spewed out a torrent of "revised standards," altering the rules to allow the Powers That Be more leeway to pollute our air and water, restrict our access to health care, invade our privacy, take away our rights on the job, raid our pensions, muffle our freedom of speech, privatize our public resources . . . you name it.

BushCo has quietly, but deliberately, unleashed a handpicked squad of legal beagles, think-tank zealots, corporate henchmen, knaves, demolition experts, hit men, screwballs, and a couple of psychopaths to go deep into the Works of Government, giving them a green light to rip out any and all public protections that corporate interests find inconvenient, irritating, or—especially—*effective.*

I've seen a torrent like this before. I grew up just a couple of miles from where the Denison Dam backs up the Red River to form Lake Texoma. Occasionally, we'd get heavy rains upriver, causing the lake to rise, so the engineers would open the floodgates of this mile-long dam, and oh, God, the roar! We locals would rush out to see it (watching water being one of the more exciting things to do in Smalltown, Texas, circa 1950s). I'd stand just off to the side of the discharge pipes, as wide-eyed and openmouthed as a gap-toothed hick at his first state fair, absolutely awed by the frightening power and sheer volume of water bursting through those massive pipes.

They say you can't go home again, but I've recently felt that same awe at seeing the audacious volume of regulatory revisions ceaselessly churning out of the White House.

Joan Claybrook, as fine a fighter as we Americans have for the public good over private greed, has spent a lifetime monitoring, challenging, and battling industry efforts over the years to control this lever or that of Washington's regulatory process. Since the days of LBJ, she has fought from within the system as well as outside it. She knows it about as well as anyone, and—despite packing her head with painful bureaucratic acronyms and the mind-numbing minutiae of paragraph 6 of subsection E17 (g) of Section XIX of (Help! I'm trapped and can't get out!)—

POLLUTION'S SILVER LINING

Lewis Carroll must be alive and ghostwriting for the EPA. Last year, an environmental group sued the agency, demanding that it enforce its own laws against an outfit that was dumping toxic sludge into the Potomac River, killing fish. Whoa, there, argued the EPA in an internal document, SLUDGE MIGHT BE GOOD FOR FISH, since it could deter them from wanting to eat, thereby saving them from getting caught by people fishing. Say what? Loopy as it sounds, that's their argument. I quote from the document, which says that the toxic discharge *"actually protects the fish in that they are not inclined to bite (and get eaten by humans) but they go ahead with their upstream movement and egg laying."*

Joan's head has yet to explode, though there have been alarming tremors. But now, she says, even her sanity is strained: "There's never in my experience been anything like the breadth, depth, speed and plain gall of the current administration's extremist deregulation agenda—eliminating protective health, safety, and environmental standards and refusing to enforce those that remain. It's sweeping and really breathtaking. If they succeed, people will not be protected against even the most egregious corporate malfeasance."

Yes, presidents have been pushing a de-reg agenda since Nixon, but they were working on this industry or that, merely playing at the fringes compared to Bush II. Allow me to be graphic. (WARNING: If you're underage or easily shocked, read the rest of this paragraph with your eyes covered.) I'm told that sex will sell anything, including a concept, so I'll resort to a risqué metaphor here to try to convey the extent to which these guys have gone beyond the beyond:

In the world of sex, using a feather is erotic.
But using the whole chicken—that's kinky.

BushCo is using the whole chicken.

Still, the only way to grasp the enormity of the changes that they are making in the balance of power between corporations and us citizens is to see a list. It would take volumes to show a full list, so I'll offer only a sample, focusing just on the environment. Even listing environmental changes, however, would take volumes, so rather than kill several small forests to report the full carnage of their chainsaw assault on Mother Nature, I'll limit myself to some of the major lowlights from just two years' worth (March 2001–March 2003) of their Bushwhacking actions to empower their polluter pals at the expense of our earth, our health, and future generations.

For those who don't care to read every dot, I've highlighted a few of the actions so you still can get a sense of what they're doing. Put on a hard hat, a gas mask, and a rubber suit—and wade into this mess:

•Rejected Kyoto global warming treaty •Delayed implementation of mining regulations intended to protect watersheds •Withdrew arsenic-in-drinking-water standard •Sought to roll back "Roadless National Forests" plan •Retreated from campaign promise to reduce carbon pollution •**Tried to shrink boundaries of nineteen national monuments and to allow oil and gas drilling on all public lands** •Delayed and sought to weaken energy efficiency standards for air conditioners •Proposed to open Arctic National Wildlife Refuge (ANWR) to oil corporations •Froze environmental rules finalized by Clinton, including one to minimize discharges of raw sewage •Supported a Florida rule that undermines the Clean Water Act •Defunded program to implement court rulings in Endangered Species cases brought by citizens •**Suspended the right-to-know regulation requiring utilities to inform consumers about arsenic in their water** •Reneged on agreement to protect desert tortoises •Rejected freedom-of-information request for a list of corporate participants in Cheney's energy policy task force •Rejected proposal to increase fuel efficiency of vehicles •Supported nuclear industry's proposal to store waste in Yucca Mountain, despite scientific objection •Okayed plans to let oil corporations drill in the outer continental shelf off the coasts of California and Florida •Proposed to scrap five of the Clean Air Act's toughest pollution control programs, as requested by electric power industry •Rejected appeal of a court decision that denied water rights for a national wildlife refuge in Idaho •**Cut 270 positions from the EPA's enforcement division** •Supported legislation to weaken any president's authority to create new national monuments •Cut by 25 percent U.S. aid to help developing countries curb global warming, and eliminated programs that provided renewable technologies to these countries •Opened eastern Gulf of Mexico to new oil drilling •Backed more reliance on coal-fired power plants to generate electricity •**Announced a plan for recycling radioactive waste into consumer products, from lawn chairs and zippers to spoons and baby cribs** •Proposed to build a missile defense "test bed" stretching from Alaska to Hawaii to California without considering environmental impact •Greenlighted road-building for timber corporations in previously untouched areas of Alaska's Tongass rain forest •Appealed a federal judge's ruling to make it harder for oil companies to drill new wells off California's coast •Stalled implementation of rules requiring utilities to reduce toxic emissions from expanded power plants •Directed that Tongass National Forest be exempted from restrictions on building new timber roads •Proposed letting the U.S. Army Corps of Engineers waive rules protecting wetlands, allowing developers and mining companies to bulldoze wetlands and fill them in •Altered the rule-making process so all agency regulations have to go through the OMB's political wringer of balancing the environment's loss with a corporation's cost •**Directed the Corps of Engineers to expedite development projects on wetlands after September 11, because "the harder we work to expedite issuance of permits, the more we serve the nation by moving the economy forward"** •Proposed to eliminate the public's ability to comment on some important Forest Service projects •Proposed exempting federal facilities, especially the military's, from environmental laws •Adopted arsenic-in-drinking-water standards ten times higher than the EPA's own scientists consider acceptable •**Announced mining rules saying that the Interior Department cannot deny a corporation's permit even if its mining could result in "substantial irreparable harm"** •Stalled cleanup of tons of toxic PCBs dumped into the Hudson River by GE •Reversed a ban on snowmobiles in Minnesota's Voyageurs National Park •Eliminated EPA's ban on doing toxic pesticide studies on humans, at behest of Bayer and the pesticide industry •Shut down the office in Florida that was created to coordinate a thirty-year recovery plan for the Everglades, the largest restoration project in U.S. history •Issued a new policy abrogating the national goal set by Bush I of "no net loss" of wetlands •Eliminated environmental impact reviews that allowed public participation in corporate proposals to develop portions of national forests •**Altered rules so the Energy Department no longer had to prove that Yucca Mountain was geologically safe for storing nuclear waste** •Invited a dozen corporate lobbyists to identify and rank health, safety, and environmental regulations that they wanted killed •Approved oil exploration next door to Arches National Park in Utah's Redrock Canyon •Okayed drilling by a gas company in the spectacular unblemished landscape of Montana's Upper Missouri River Breaks National Monument •Reversed previous scientific ruling that oil drilling in ANWR would harm polar bears •Approved a company's plan to drill fifteen thousand holes in a forty-one-square-mile grid in the Big Cypress National Preserve, detonate dynamite twenty-five feet deep in each hole in a seismic search for oil, and build an access road into the preserve •**Relaxed nationwide permit rules so coal companies, developers, and others can fill in thousands of streams, swamps, and other wetlands, without public notice or comment** •Suppressed a report by the U.S. Fish and Wildlife Service that called the above wetlands policy "scientifically and environmentally unjustified" •Tried to strip the state of California's right to review Bush proposals to allow oil drilling off its coast •Cut the number of criminal prosecution referrals by 53 percent for clean water violations, 54 percent for clean air violations, and 80 percent for toxic substance violations •**Shifted the cost of Superfund cleanups from the polluters to taxpayers** •Sought to reevaluate the "critical habitat" designation that protects half a million Southern California acres from development, asking to subject the protection of the habitat to an "economic analysis" •Opened Missouri's Mark Twain National Forest to lead mining exploration •Proposed a global warming plan based on "voluntary reductions" in emissions of carbon dioxide pollutants—a plan that, even if it works, allows emissions to keep increasing by 14 percent a year •**Announced new targets for power plant emissions, allowing 50 percent more sulfur emissions (acid rain) than current law, three times more toxic mercury emissions, and tons of additional nitrogen oxide (smog)** •Opened Cumberland Island, the country's largest undeveloped barrier island on the eastern seaboard, to motorized tours •Proposed a new concept of "charter forests," modeled on charter schools, that would turn public forestland over to private companies and local trusts to manage •Increased taxpayer subsidy for timber company purchases of trees from our national forests by 35 percent •**Killed funds to support environmental education in public schools** •Eliminated funds for EPA grants for graduate student research in environmental sciences •Sought legislation totally and permanently exempting the Pentagon from environmental regulation, citing the war on terrorism as the rationale, even though the laws already give it emergency exemptions in times of war •Proposed to overturn the ban against oil and gas exploration in Montana's Rocky Mountain Front, and proposed to drill three thousand oil wells and fifty thousand coal bed gas wells in Wyoming's Powder River Basin •Shifted from suing companies that violate the Clean Air Act to a new "Clear Skies" policy of voluntary reductions in pollutants •Notified oil and gas companies that they'll get speedier drilling approvals, easier access to the public's natural resources, reduced royalty payments, and fewer environmental restrictions •Issued permit to BNP Petroleum to drill on Padre Island National Seashore •**Sent an industry lobbyist, representing the country's biggest polluting utilities, to testify for the administration before Congress and defend Bush's cuts in the EPA's enforcement budget** •Proposed to open 140,000 acres of Los Padres National Forest to oil drilling •Gagged Fish and Wildlife officials in Alaska from talking about Bush plans to drill in ANWR •Agreed to an ExxonMobil demand that Bush replace the respected scientist Dr. Robert Watson, who chaired the Intergovernmental Panel on Climate Change •Created task force to streamline the permit process for corporations to get access to natural resources on public lands •**Proposed to end the federal requirement that states test poor children on Medicaid for lead poisoning** •Ruled that commercial overfishing in New England waters can continue indefinitely •Proposed a special "exception" to allow a speedboat maker to test its high-speed boats in a Florida channel designated as a manatee refuge •Proposed to streamline Forest Service rules to speed up development projects by limiting court challenges and outside reviews •Doubled the number of open-pit limestone mines to be opened in the Florida Everglades, eventually creating a thirty-square-mile hole in the middle of this irreplaceable water wonder •**Promoted an increase in production of coal bed methane gas in the Rocky Mountains, a process that pumps fresh water out of the ground and injects contaminated water back into the aquifers, polluting streams and rivers** •Cancelled a two-year ban on destructive gold mining in Oregon's Siskiyou National Forest by corporations that pay no royalties to us for the gold they take and are not required to clean up the toxic mess they leave •Authorized the restart of Alabama's troubled Browns Ferry nuclear power plant •Refused, despite a court directive, to protect 9 million acres of the Tongass National Forest as "permanent wilderness," instead opening it to commercial activities •**Called on a federal judge to suspend his ruling that "Mountaintop Removal" is illegal—a method whereby coal companies simply blow off the top of a mountain to get at the coal, then shove the debris into streams below, killing thousands of miles of waterways** •Reversed a twenty-five-year-old Clean Water rule that flatly prohibited the "disposal" of mining wastes in streams, rivers, and other waters •Cut the Superfund cleanup budget in half •Blamed wildfires on environmentalists •Killed an EPA plan to require developers to reduce the contaminated storm water runoff caused by their projects •Expanded old loopholes so utilities can increase their output without installing pollution equipment •Proposed new standards for polluting, diesel-powered road equipment, but to be enforced voluntarily •**Put industry-backed amendment into Homeland Security Bill that effectively exempts chemical plants, utilities, and other polluters from the public's-right-to-know laws, which require corporations to tell their neighbors what poisons are being spewed on them** •Joined utilities in opposing a Senate energy bill that required power companies to produce 10 percent of their electricity from renewable sources by 2020 •Speeded up the cleanup of old nuclear weapons sites by allowing some of the waste not to be cleaned up •Told Congress it needed up to five years more to study global warming and develop a national strategy • Rescinded the critical habitat designation of 4 million acres that has protected California's red-legged frog—the subject of Mark Twain's celebrated frog-jumping contest in Calaveras County • Approved an absurd water boondoggle allowing Cadiz Inc. to pump water from the aquifer beneath the Mojave National Preserve and sell it to Southern California water districts • Rewrote logging rules to allow timber companies to increase their logging of our national forests in the name of fighting forest fires • **Reversed a scientific finding (after meeting with Peabody Coal officials) that Peabody's proposed 1,500-megawatt power plant, which was to burn Peabody's dirty high-sulfur coal, would pollute nearby Mammoth Cave National Park, allowing Peabody to build the plant** • Weakened protections for whales so oil companies could set off deep ocean explosions to make seismic maps of underwater oil reserves • Scuttled a plan to designate forty-six miles of California coastline north of Santa Barbara as a national seashore, which would permanently have saved it from private developers for public use—a Bush official said simply "land acquisition is not a priority of this administration" • Expanded oil exploration in Colorado's Canyons of the Ancients National Monument • Asserted that federal agencies could not even review the environmental impacts of corporate or governmental actions in the oceans beyond three miles of America's shorelines • Streamlined the survey rules to allow more logging on public land in the Northwest • Surrendered federal water rights on public lands to Western states, letting them take the water for private uses • Issued an executive order speeding up highway construction projects by limiting public participation in the process • **Eliminated scientific committees that disagreed with its policies, stacking new committees with scientists who have ties to regulated industries, including one PG&E hireling who fought Erin Brockovich** • Deleted from its annual report on air pollution the section on global warming, which contained the bad news that carbon dioxide emissions responsible for the warming were up 17 percent • Caved in to the snowmobile industry, whose vehicles can equal the pollution of one hundred cars, by weakening the administration's own emissions standards proposed a year before • Killed a proposal to establish a citizen review panel to oversee the trans-Alaska pipeline • Cut EPA's enforcement staff to the lowest levels since records began being kept • Claimed that virtually anyone working for or assigned to the White House is exempt from the Freedom of Information Act and other disclosure laws • **Sided with America's largest cat-litter manufacturer, Oil-Dri, against local officials in Reno, Nevada, who had ruled that a proposed cat-litter mine would pollute the air and water** • Supported plan to let chemical giants in Louisiana emit more cancer-causing pollutants in exchange for reducing emissions of less dangerous pollutants • Joined Daimler-Chrysler and GM to oppose California's rule on zero emissions from vehicles

•Proposed elimination of public participation in setting standards for forest management, including everything from water quality to hunting to trail maintenance •**Sent memo to all EPA employees urging them to "express support for the president and his program" when off duty** •Stacked the CDC advisory committee on Childhood Lead Poisoning Prevention with industry scientists •Allowed Veritas to begin drilling five thousand sixty-foot holes for seismic explosions in Utah's Book Cliffs region without full environmental impact study •Killed funding for a program to help farmers convert some of their land to conservation •Proposed new rules to give local Forest Service supervisors more leeway to allow logging, mining, etc. on our public lands without having to do an environmental impact statement •Offered a plan to renew commercial trade in the ivory tusks of African elephants •Cut the civil penalties that polluters have to pay by half •Withdrew Clinton rule requiring cleanup of polluted rivers and substituted a voluntary program •Announced that the OMB will "review" more than three hundred federal regulations targeted by industry •**Instructed EPA to discount by 63 percent the value of lives of senior citizens when assessing whether to impose new restrictions on industries that pollute the air** •Ruled that factory farms can write their own rules of operation, be protected from legal liability for their pollution, and keep their rules of operation secret from the public •Sought to eliminate 20 percent of the nation's wetlands from federal protection •Issued a new rule allowing state or local officials, at the behest of commercial interests, to build new roads through federal wildlands without any opportunity for public review or appeal

Source: Various press clips and releases, plus an ongoing tally maintained by the Natural Resources Defense Council on its website at www.nrdc.org/bushrecord

FRIDAY NIGHT MASSACRES AND OTHER GAMES

Bush, who is as polished at practicing the Art of the Photo-Op Presidency as any Oval Office chair warmer has ever been, posed for a beauty just a few months into his tenure. He was on the White House lawn with a bunch of little tykes who'd been invited there to play a game of T-ball. Click! Just as the White House PR team intended, a charming wire-service photo of the prez was snapped, and it ran in papers all across the country the next day, showing George rearing back like Roger Clemens to throw the game's first pitch as kids and parents looked on admiringly.

What's wrong with this picture? I thought to myself. Yes! *There is no pitcher in T-ball!* The ball is simply set upon a tee for the wee batters to swat—hence the name of the game. George's role was a ruse. You could say that this was a small fraud, and it was, but it confirmed my sense that no pretense is too small for this guy, and that what we'd be shown of his presidency would be a whole lot different than what we'd be getting.

The news media, such as it is, not only failed to catch Bush's little T-ball deception, but it has also failed miserably to catch on to the drastic rigging of the rules that's being orchestrated from his White House. Occasionally there are stories about this tax twist or that regulatory revision, but the media establishment has given us no sense of the constancy, of the scale, or of the big picture. Why? Glad you asked:

1. *Gobbledygook:* The White House *doesn't want* these actions covered, so giggling lawyers write the legally required public announcements in Chinese Pig Latin, eliminating all useful and descriptive words, such as verbs. You can hear them cackle as they hit "print": Ha! Let 'em try to decipher this one!

2. *Friday Night Massacres.* The White House releases many of its biggest nasties on Friday evenings, well after the press corps has departed for various bars, beaches, and other amusements. So the press doesn't learn about the regulatory massacre until Monday morn, and by then it's "old news," so it either is tossed or gets a one-paragraph slug buried in Tuesday's paper. Likewise, Saturdays, Sundays, and holidays are favorite times to drop an ugly release—again, no reporters, no news. The final arsenic-in-your-water reg, for example, was dropped on *Halloween.* (What a bunch of tricksters! Surely someone got a raise for that.) Also, the EPA snuck out a package of rules to exempt some seventeen thousand dirty power plants from Clean Air restrictions on New Year's Eve.

3. *Newspeak.* The actions are never couched in straightforward language like: "In another move to shaft the little guy, Bush today . . ." No, no. Instead, every change in the game is expressed in such positive, even soothing phrases as:
   • To *streamline* the process . . .
   • To replace an *archaic* . . . (they often substitute *Depression-era* for *archaic*)

SOLVING THE PROBLEM OF BAD NEWS

What to do, what to do? Bush's team knew the numbers were bad. In 2002 alone, more than 600,000 American manufacturing jobs were lost, including those lost in what the Labor Department calls "mass layoffs."

These are especially embarrassing numbers, because, well . . . they get noticed. When fifty workers or more are escorted out of the factory gates at one time, which defines a mass layoff, it gets in the news—and the Labor Department reported that there were *more than two thousand of these* in 2002. Ouch. That's a lot of bad news . . . and bad politics.

I know! Let's just stop reporting those numbers! Ahh, the simplicity. Clean. So that's what the Bushites did. Last Christmas Eve, with the media home having eggnog, the labor department slipped out a release announcing it would no longer collect or report information on mass layoffs. The Grinches claim they did so to save money.

- To provide greater *flexibility* . . .
- To bring *balance* back . . .

4. *Lies.* From Bush on down, this bunch is shameless about looking you in the eye and telling you that sour is sweet. Example: Late in 2002 the EPA announced new pollution standards for massively stinky hog factories (think overloaded Porta Potti on a 100-degree day, then up the P.U. level of that a hundredfold) that have already polluted thirty-five thousand miles of our rivers. The EPA's Christie Whitman said of the new rules: "This is a major step forward to protect our nation's waters." Solid. Except she was lying through her teeth, eyes, nose, pores, and other orifices. Her "standards" weren't even mandatory. They're simply goals to be wished for. Each hog factory is to develop its own voluntary plan for controlling its pollution, which could be: *"The hog fairy will come here every night, wave her magic wand, and turn our pool of fecal slurry into sweet wine."* We'll never even know what any of the plans are, since the EPA's new "standards" allow each factory to keep its plan secret.

5. *Self-interest.* The media establishment is a hog. NBC (GE), ABC (Disney), CBS (Viacom), Fox (News Corporation), CNN (AOL Time Warner), all *love* George and his de-reg agenda, because it's their agenda, too. Do you think these conglomerate executives want their news departments connecting the dots for you, rousing the rabble, threatening their honey pot? No, sweetie, no. They even have their very own operative ensconced deep inside Bush's bureaucracy doing their bidding—Michael Powell, a former media lawyer named by George to head the FCC. He's another nutball eaten up with corporate theology, declaring "the market is my religion." Fine, take it to a monastery. The FCC is not a corporate church, and it's supposed to *oversee* our public airwaves, not give them away. But this mad media monk is doing exactly that, pushing a plan that will abolish the FCC rules limiting how much control a single media giant can have over our sources of news. Don't look for the networks to broadcast this story to you.

AIR, AS IN *AIRPLANES*

When running for office several years ago, I was being flown from Lubbock to Amarillo by a Panhandle farmer who was a friend and supporter. We were making the hop in his single-engine plane, and, since his farm was on the way, he said we'd pop on down and get a couple of beers for the road. My kind of pilot.

He didn't have a landing strip; instead, this being table-flat West Texas, he always landed on the county road and taxied the plane right up to his house, parking it like a car. As we banked left and lined up to land on the road, I noticed a power line running parallel down our "runway." I said: "You do see that power line, don't you?" And my friend said, cool as could be, "Hightower, the secret to the power line is don't ever look at the power line."

The whole concept of flying—the physics of it—is a mystery to me. I mean, planes are heavy. How do they stay up there? Admittedly, my knowledge of physics rivals that of a turnip, but I think voodoo is involved in flying, so I avert my eyes and mind from what's happening.

One thing I do know, though, is that the air *inside* the plane is important, too, if only for breathing purposes. I mention this obvious fact because those laugh-a-minute practical jokers who run our commercial airlines keep funning us paying passengers over how much air we're entitled to get. Most travelers don't know it, but airlines are required to supply a mix of only 50 percent fresh air in the cabins, with the other half being recirculated air. "Recirculated," for those of you unfamiliar with airline jargon, means "already used" air—as in exhaled, sneezed into, belched up, and so forth. The technical term is: "Icky air."

Flight attendants and we frequent fliers have long complained that this 50/50 fresh/icky split gives us splitting headaches and other unpleasantness, especially on long flights of more than, say, nine minutes. But do they listen to us? (Rhetorical question, forget I asked.)

But the Bush regulatory team is listening—to the industry. When John Graham, Bush's right-wing regulatory czar and corporate butt-kisser (BRWRCCBK), put out his call last year for regulations that corporations would like to change, Boeing Company, the largest maker of commercial planes, was front and center with a request to change the required balance of fresh air to only 25 percent fresh and 75 percent recirculated. Welcome to the friendly skies.

YOU DON'T NEED A BIG NOSE TO SMELL BAD BALONEY

The good news is that despite the failure of the media and the deception of the politicians, the full stench of BushCo's actions and policies are beginning to waft across We the People. Folks are beginning to understand that the White House's efforts add up to something far bigger—and much stinkier—than some cuts in regulations and taxes. Fundamentally, the Bush agenda is to disunite America, to uncouple the few from the many, uncouple their private interest from the common good. The rhetorical rationale is that they are unleashing the great American spirit of entrepreneurship and individual ambition—"Let the eagles soar" is their cry! And what about our society's founding notion that we're all in this together, *e pluribus unum,* as it says on our coins? That's so eighteenth century. BushCo seeks less pluribus, more unum.

A Class Act

Some days when I read the paper, I don't know whether to laugh, cry, or go in for a brain scan. January 3rd of 2003 was one of those days. George W, who was being roundly ridiculed at the time for his proposal to aid the poor rich by eliminating their dividend taxes, was in a pout over the criticism, so he lashed back:

> *"Some would like to turn this into class warfare. That's not how I think."*

No satire writer in history, no borscht-belt comedy writer, no fantasy writer, no *Saturday Night Live* gag writer could possibly have come up with a more hilarious line to put in the mouth of the forty-third president of our United States. What *was* he thinking? Again, I wanted to shout into the vast void that is Bush's brain, *yoooooo-hooooooooooooo:*

> *George,* you *grew up* rich in a family of Bushes and Walkers who have been avid class warriors for generations.
> *George,* you had a C average in prep school, yet *still* you got into Yale through the Rich Man's Affirmative Action Quota System (and perhaps because your grandfather was on the board of trustees).
> *George,* you *escaped* going to Vietnam because of your family connections.
> *George,* you were a pathetic excuse for a businessman, yet *real* businessmen made you a multimillionaire by literally *handing* a fortune to you.
> *George,* these things don't happen to regular people who are on the grunt end of America's longest war—the class

war—waged against them by powerful people like you who fix the system for your own gain.

But of course, he wasn't thinking. It was a mind sneeze, that's all, an instinctive retort from somewhere deep within his recesses. But it snorted out an ugly spot of snot: While the moneyed elites behind Bush are pushing a major new offensive in their class war (make regulation voluntary, void taxation on wealth, hog-tie labor, give global trade sovereignty over other interests, restrict the legal rights of consumers, and so forth), they also are on the defensive about it. Yes, they're making a grab for all the cookies and for the cookie jar itself—yet they want to feel (and, incredibly, want us to feel) that what they're doing is right and good. Moral even! They're *entitled* to it, don't you know?

To get to that warm, feel-good place, they have to twist the language into Orwellian contortions—those who call them on their class war, for example, immediately become the ones resorting to "class war." But more than language is at play here, for they're trying to mess with our heads, trying to tell us that they are the "populists." Their line is that the rules must be "rebalanced" so they (claiming to be our God-sent wealth creators!) can be free to work their magic, enriching themselves and, in so doing, showering prosperity on everyone.

Perhaps you're thinking: Surely you've gone too far, Hightower, no one can be this bent. I wish. But we're dealing here with some people who binge on ego, and right now they're on a real toot.

Take the tax-cut pitch. I could swallow it a bit easier if there was even a tint of honesty to it: *Of course we're giving billions to our Wall Street pals, who the hell do you think paid for our ride to the White House,*

Punchy quote on the beneficence of greed:

"The prosperity of the middle class depends on the good fortune and LIGHT taxes of the rich."

—Andrew Mellon, the millionaire banker who ran the economy as treasury secretary for Harding, Coolidge, and Hoover, 1922–32, the years leading to the Great Depression

Bucko? It sure wasn't you! Instead, believe it or not, their argument is that rich people are the put-upon class and deserve better treatment.

Since late 2002, White House operatives have been torturing the tax numbers and running to the media to try to generate a public sob story about how the rich are simply paying too much of the freight for government. With the zealotry of true believers, they claim that our society has gone overboard with this "fairness" thing (begin to fade in "The Battle Hymm of the Republic" here), and that it's time—nay, way past time!—for the tax burden to be lifted from the soft shoulders of the wealthy and shifted down to the worker bees, specifically including the poor (those scofflaws and ingrates):

> RICH PEOPLE OF THE WORLD, UNITE! RUSH TO THE BARRICADES WITH YOUR GOLDEN PITCHFORKS! YOU HAVE NOTHING TO LOSE BUT YOUR TAX FORMS! 54-40 OR FIGHT! DON'T TREAD ON ME! DAMN THE TORPEDOS. . . .

What a crock. But they're actually pushing this crock into the debate as though it is a matter of deep principle, hoping we won't see it for what it is: a crock of greed. White House policy makers have wept aloud that there is an "increasing reliance on taxing higher income households" and that "the tax burden will have to begin extending backward down the income ladder."

The Wall Street Journal's editorial page, which is the official mouthpiece of The Corporate Nation, wailed about the horrible injustice of "The Non-Paying Class," declaring that the hoi polloi "who pay little or no taxes" must pay more to relieve those at the top. The editors singled out a hypothetical slob who's making $12,000 a year and "pays a little less than 4 percent of income in taxes," dubbing such people as "lucky duckies."

Forget the fact that trying to eke out an existence on $12K a year is the opposite of lucky. It's poverty, which is punishment enough, and it ought not be taxed *at all.* What the *Journal,* George W, and the rest of these well-heeled class warriors aren't admitting is that they're only counting federal income tax in their sob story of the Rich Man's Burden.

Add in such obnoxiously regressive burdens as payroll taxes, state and local taxes, sales taxes, gasoline taxes, fees, and a host of other assessments—and the slobs at the bottom are paying the same percentage or more than the swells at the top.

ALRIGHT, KIDS, LET'S PLAY:
"SPOT THE LUCKY DUCKIES"

Where do *YOU* fit on the State & Local Tax Scale? Maybe you're *low income.* If so, you pay on average more than 11 percent of your income (paltry as it is) for state and local taxes. If you're *middle income,* you pay about 10 percent. But maybe you're part of Bush's oppressed, overtaxed *rich.* What percentage do you end up paying? Give yourself a Ding Dong if you said 5 percent!

For more fun, let's see if you live in one of the "TERRIBLE TEN" states. In these places, the state tax rate on poor people is as much as 550 percent higher than on the wealthy. The rate on the middle class is as much as 350 percent more than the wealthy pay. Are you a resident of the TERRIBLE TEN? Let's see:

Alabama	Pennsylvania
Florida	South Dakota
Illinois	Tennessee
Michigan	Texas
Nevada	Washington

Source: The Institute on Taxation and Economic Policy www.ctj.org/itep

AUTHOR'S MESSAGE, AUTHOR'S MESSAGE

Bush & Co. are systematically rewriting the rules, seeking (and, so far, mostly succeeding) to produce a permanent, structural change in how America operates, and for whom. With thousands of executive orders, budget shifts, regulatory rewrites, omnibus laws, tax perversions, trade agreements, legal opinions, reinterpretations, cabinet directives, policy letters, and such, these clever boys are enthroning the money powers over the rest of us, abandoning 225 years of striving for a society in which egalitarianism counts.

To jettison our nation's ideals for nothing more than the further enrichment of elites is no mere shift in policy—it's a *moral failure,* a betrayal of what the American experiment represents.

A fellow came up to me recently and politely introduced himself. After only a moment of chitchat, he clutched my arm and his eyes urgently sought mine, as though he might find confirmation there of what he instinctively thought to be happening. Leaning into me, almost in a whisper he said: **"They're changing America, aren't they?"**

Bingo. People are made to feel that it's crazy to think such thoughts, crazy to think that what we're seeing in front of our very eyes is really

SHHHHHHH!

Don't tell, but one very special group is faring *extremely* well under today's skewed tax scheme, and will do even better if its president has his way. This group is far and away the richest on the face of the earth, but Bush and the media have been extremely circumspect about calling attention to it, so I'll just whisper it here: *(corporations).*

Corporations have become rank tax dodgers, moochers that benefit more than people from government programs and protections, yet they pay the least. If you're typical, your tax rate is higher—substantially higher—than what the typical Fortune 500 billion-dollar giant pays. Forget the official corporate tax rate of about 35 percent. Their lobbyists have stripped that log down to a toothpick . . . or less.

For example, there's the scandalous (but still legal) tax dodge known as the Bermuda Loophole, which lets corporate sharpies pretend to be headquartered offshore, even though they're physically located right here on Terra Firma Americana—and pay no taxes to the Red, White, and Blue! Here's my thought on this particular scam: Short of killing it and the scums that use it, I SAY THAT

ALL CEOS PLAYING THE ANTI-AMERICAN BERMUDA CARD HAVE TO WEAR BERMUDA SHORTS EVERY DAY, EVERY-WHERE THEY GO, SO WE REGULAR TAXPAYERS CAN KNOW WHO THEY ARE, AND CAN GRAB THEM ON THE STREETS AND GIVE THEM NOOGIES. No long coats, no cover-up. If you're going to use the Bermuda shuffle, dress the part . . . and get your noogies.

SPECIAL BONUS BOX!

Guess who's a champion corporate freeloader? John Snow, who became Bush's treasury secretary this year. Yes, the fellow *in charge of* our nation's tax policy! This is too rich to be true, but there he is.

Before coming to BushCo, Snow was CEO of CSX Corporation. In three of the four previous years, CSX had paid absolutely zero in federal income taxes, even though it had reaped a total of nearly a billion dollars in profit.

Even luckier, Snow's corporation worked the loopholes like an Enron accountant, so CSX was paid $164 million from our public treasury in tax rebates from us taxpayers during those years.

Source: Citizens for Tax Justice www.ctj.org

happening and really does add up to what our deep, democratic sub-conscious is fearing. This fellow is hardly alone in connecting the dots, though he assumed he was. It's the naked emperor syndrome—someone has to say it out loud, then others will say, "Well I thought so!" If you, too, suspect that something is going badly astray in our great country, join the multitudes.

To talk about what's happening, we have to reach back a bit into America's feisty democratic history and resurface some of the old, but newly relevant terms: Plutocracy. Autocracy. Imperialism. These are what the Bush forces are intent on institutionalizing as the governing ethic of *their* America.

But here is another relevant term from our past: Rebellion. Last year in Vermont, I met a person wearing the best button I've ever seen. It said, "Wearing a Button Is Not Enough." I say we engage them head-on in their class war, asserting the deeply ethical belief in fairness, justice, and *equal* opportunity that forms the moral basis for *our* America.

CHAPTER 3

Bad Apples

The reports began to come in before dawn, with the AP wire clicking out its first alert at 3:51 A.M. CST:

> *"A rampaging band of more than one thousand yet to be indicted CEOs of major corporations made a break for the Mexican border shortly after the markets closed yesterday. Calling themselves the CEOnistas, the chief executives apparently have split into several bands, each one incorporated as a secret partnership in the Bahamas and operating with two sets of books.*
>
> *"The first sighting was last evening along the Rio Grande at Quemado, Texas, where one group of the lamsters bought the town's entire population of 320 people by borrowing against pension fund gains. Overnight, they arbitrarily inflated the population to 960, declared a 200 percent profit, and booked the earnings in an offshore tax haven."*

Several sightings of the CEOnistas were reported on the Internet, where disgruntled shareholders, fired employees, and bilked retirees were tracking the executives' desperate flight. Gloria Garcia of Esperanza, south of El Paso, joined an Enron late-night chat room to file this harrowing first-person encounter with the desperados:

> *"They're plundering our towns as they go and writing it off as a marketing expense. They came into my home about*

eight o'clock last night, made me pay for my own TV, then
double-booked the revenues. Right in front of my daughter."

Early this morning, about thirty of the outlaws bought the electric power supply of the city of Laredo, collected a "transmission fee" for selling power back to the city, and sent a bill to California for $4.5 billion.

Law enforcement officials are on a Code Red alert all along the border, but some of the CEOnistas are known to have made it across. The U.S. Border Patrol concedes that a passel of them crossed near Eagle Pass, with one of the outlaws shouting *"You'll never audit me alive!"* as he splashed into the river. Still, authorities have had some success:

"Last night we caught a dozen of them by disguising one of
our female officers as a CNBC anchor. It was like moths to
a flame."

This just in from Reuters news service:

"Several chief executives were captured late this morning
off Highway 375 near El Paso, including Martha Stewart.
They had cut through a chain-link fence, and some slipped
through. Ms. Stewart would have gotten away as well, but
she was stopping motorists to ask for marzipan and food
coloring to make edible snowmen place settings, using cut
pieces of wire for the arms. 'We put her in cell number
seven,' said a Border Patrol spokeswoman, 'because the
morning sun really adds texture to the stucco walls.'"

Meanwhile, the Internet posse has tracked a large group of the fleeing CEOnistas to San Antonio, where they've holed up in the Alamo. *"Not the historic Alamo,"* reports tracker Jorge Baca, *"but the Alamo car rental out by the airport. They're rotating all the tires on the minivans and accounting each switch as a sale."*

Who are these guys, these CEOs who're giving greed such a bad name? Just a PR-second ago, their face-lifted countenances were beaming at us from the covers of *Fortune, Forbes,* and *Business Week,* where they were lionized as financial Merlins who could turn derivatives of nothing into pyramids of gold. They were the infallible demigods of the new culture of perpetual wealth, showering manna for all from their celestial suites. Then, early last year, something happened. Their pyramids were discovered to be made of fuzz processed from lint secretly collected from the exhausts of our clothes dryers. There was no there there, and these guys were exposed as common thieves, bunko artists in Versaces.

"JUST A FEW BAD APPLES, NOTHING TO WORRY ABOUT, WE'LL HANDLE IT, THE FUNDAMENTALS OF THE SYSTEM ARE SOUND, *PAY NO ATTENTION,*" said an unusually nervous power establishment (which happens to be run by CEOs, but we're not supposed to notice that either).

But of course we paid attention! Lots of attention, because the putty had come unstuck on the carefully polished corporate façade, and millions of innocents got their first, mind-boggling, head-on look at the oozing slime and raw fecal matter inside the executive suites of those tall, logoed buildings. In 2002 alone, trillions of dollars in shareholder wealth—POOF—gone. Retirement nest eggs for millions—fried. Eight hundred thousand jobs disappeared—sorry chump, maybe you can catch on as a Wal-Mart greeter, or if you'll move to West Palm Beach, there's a lawn-mower job open at the boss's winter home.

Even those of us who had seen such greed in action many times gagged anew at the looting and pillaging of the Enroners and World-Comers, Global Crossers and Citigroupers. It's not a sight you ever get used to seeing.

I had the same reflexive response to seeing it that I've occasionally had when flicking through the TV channels late at night and unexpectedly coming across that cable show that zooms in for close-ups of doctors doing open-belly surgery. Have you seen this? I kid you not, they're on TV in full color actually slicing away on someone's liver lesions or such. In the fraction of a second before my brain can admit what's happening, zap the synapse, and shout to my thumb *"GO, GO, GO, GO!"*— too late, I've seen it and my body convulses: *Hyyuuuuucchk!*

What was it that gagged you? Bush's buddy Ken Lay, maybe, the Emperor of Enron, who used favors from Republicans, Democrats, Tories, Mugwumps, Locofocos, and any other partisans he could buy to fix the game so he could erect a sham of a worldwide company that essentially made and sold nothing but smoke. By the time the smoke dissipated, Ken had already cashed out for millions and barricaded himself inside his luxury Houston penthouse, beyond the reach of the hordes of employees, shareholders, taxpayers, retirees, and consumers he'd screwed—a goodly number of whom would gladly volunteer to climb to the top of Lay's building bare-handed, grab his scrawny ass off his satin La-Z-Boy, and throw him over the wall of that penthouse. However, at this writing, Lay is still at large.

It's Curtains for Kozlowski

Personally, what rang the bell on my Gag-O-Meter was Kozlowski's shower curtain. I'm not talking about a bad case of mildew, but a huge case of CEO hubris.

If you thought corporate chieftains were levelheaded, regular folks who live on the same earth as you and me, meet Dennis Kozlowski, the now dismissed and disgraced *jefe* of Tyco International. In the three years before his comeuppance, he paid himself $300 million, making him one of the highest paid egos in all of Corporatedom, even while Tyco (which, by the way, he'd incorporated in Bermuda to avoid paying pesky U.S. taxes) was tanking, causing shareholders to lose $80 billion just in his last year of stewardship.

Dennis, however, didn't let bad performance interfere with the effervescence of being Dennis. Let the stock tumble, let employees go . . . Kozlowski was busy buying a shower curtain. Price tag: $6,000.

Come on! Six grand for a six-foot swath of . . . what? What could it possibly be made of? My mind can't get around the concept. OK, I'm a peasant, and I don't expect the gents of the manor to shower behind a six-dollar piece of plastic as I do. I can see sixty bucks, or maybe $160 if you want the tassels and swags, but how's it even possible to get to $6,000? Could you even let the thing get wet? Not me.

Kozlowski's curtain is the least of it, though. He also billed Tyco's shareholders for:

- a $30 million, fifteen-thousand-square-foot waterfront estate he bought in Boca Raton,
- a $25,000-a-month apartment he rented in New York City,
- a $16.8 million second apartment he bought on Manhattan's exclusive Fifth Avenue (plus $3 million he spent to renovate it and $11 million more to furnish it), and
- a third New York apartment he bought, this one a $7 million Park Avenue co-op for Dennis's ex-wife.

WHAT'S REALLY IMPORTANT IN LIFE FOR CEOS?

Jack Welch, GE's retired CEO, rivals the pig Kozlowski in his gluttony for corporate perks. In retirement, this billionaire had GE provide everything from an $80,000-a-month Central Park apartment to his postage stamps . . . and even his toilet paper! That's more than I want to know. But I found a clue to the thinking of these minor Zeuses in an interview Jack did in 2001:

Q: "Did your 1995 heart bypass surgery change you in any way?"
A: "I thought to myself, 'Before the operation, I didn't spend enough money.' Before that I tended to buy inexpensive wine. I would never spend $100 on a bottle of wine. Now, I never spend less than that."

Get that last one? An apartment for his *ex-wife*. Not his Mrs. Now, not a mistress . . . his ex! This doesn't count such gewgaws as an antique traveling toilet box for $17,000, a $6,300 sewing basket, a $2,200 wastebasket, a $445 pincushion, and a $15,000 umbrella stand shaped like a poodle. Nor does it count the $1 million in Tyco funds allocated for the fortieth-birthday bash he threw in Italy for his wife, complete with a life-sized ice sculpture of Michelangelo's "David," which gaily sluiced vodka through the statue's penis into the glasses of astonished guests. Class will out every time.

Now, while we weren't invited to the party, can't get into any of Dennis's fabulous dwellings, and won't be allowed even a quick peek at that shower curtain, there's still a fun role for you and me to play in Dennis's debauchery: We get to subsidize it with our tax dollars. In the real-life Disneyland of CorporateWorld, these expenditures can be written off by Tyco as part of its cost of doing business, thus reducing the taxes it'd otherwise pay as its share of supporting such boring stuff as America's roads, parks, army, education, and those other publicky kinds of things. Wow, Dennis gets the shower curtain and we take a bath. What's not to like about that?

First you gagged, then you screeched: How did this happen? Who did this to us? Where are the regulators? What are we going to do about it? *Get a rope!*

The Powers couldn't ignore this one. Too vivid, too real, too big. The esoterica of corporate finagling was suddenly laid bare, and the finaglers had names, faces, and in a couple of cases, mug shots. Plus, the countless victims of their greed were bleeding all over the daily news. People everywhere got it. "Enron" quickly became a four-letter word; Lay's name was turned into a verb—to be Layed; café chatter was filled with fun new phrases like "off the books"; and the polls flared, with 78 percent of Americans demanding that CEOs be rounded up and fed to the goats. OK, I made that stat up, but not this one: 91 percent of Americans said the spreading scandals were a serious or very serious matter to them.

Oh, what a flurry of motion your outrage stirred! Seven congressional committees at once were investigating the malfeasance, subpoenaing glum executives, holding televised hearings, and generally foaming like a washing machine that'd had a whole box of Tide dumped in it.

Then came the perp walks. Prosecutors put a few of the miscreants in handcuffs and paraded them before the TV cameras, starting with five executives of Adelphia Communications. This stunned the Comfortable & Cozy Club:

> *"Our clients are calling with concerns about the breadth of the government's reactions."*
>
> —A corporate lawyer with the Holland & Knight firm

"There are more elegant ways to arrest someone than under the eyes of a camera. The CEOs I know are absolutely appalled, because even drug dealers aren't treated this way."

—A partner in the executive search firm of Spencer Stuart

"Do this too much, and you start frightening the public."

—Chief executive of medical malpractice insurer SCPIE Holdings

"When it affects someone you play golf with, it strikes home."

—CEO of John Hancock Financial Services

BUSH IN TIGHTS

The outrage grew so hot that even George W momentarily doffed his everyday CorporateMan suit and sprang forth in a Ralph Nader costume, posing as ReformerMan! This was a hoot to watch. You might as well try squeezing a walrus into pantyhose as to try fitting Bush into reformer tights, and at first he balked, showing no heart for the task of criticizing the corporate brotherhood that had gotten him where he is. His first effort was to downplay the seriousness of the issue, rolling out White House mouthpiece Ari Fleischer to do a little dance of dissemblance: "*If* there are any bad players in our free-enterprise system, they will be held accountable by this administration."

If? If! It sounded like J. Edgar Hoover in the sixties denying there was such a thing as the Mafia, even while he was dancing around in a pink tutu at secret midnight parties arranged by the Mafia. It sounded like Cardinal Law in Boston saying, "I don't know nothing about no pedophiles." It sounded stupid.

It also didn't work. The log had been lifted, and ugly squirmies were all over the place, so George's handlers decided they had to move him to the front of the public outrage (even as White House lobbyists swarmed into the back rooms of Congress to sidetrack, limit, and water down assorted bills that threatened to compel slightly less corruption in the system).

Finally, when Congress passed a weak bill to restrict some of the worst boardroom practices, George climbed on it like he was Teddy Roosevelt wearing jodhpurs and carrying a riding crop to whip the bad boys: "No more easy money for corporate criminals," he bellowed as the cameras rolled and he signed the bill, "just hard time." Trying to sound serious, he added, "The era of low standards and false profits is over."

You could almost hear the guffaws coming out of the executive suites. Hard time? What a kidder! A few of these guys might do a little easy time at Club Fed, but forget Ken Lay, Bernie Ebbers, our boy Kozlowski, or the rest ever going into lockdown and having to shower with guys named Ice Pick, Big Booger, and Lovie. Nearly all of the malefactors will keep the bulk of their booty, their mansions, and even their pensions, because George W was winking as he was scolding.

As for "low standards and false profits," say hello to Harken Energy, the failed oil company that counted the Bush boy as a paid board member ($100,000 a year) and a member of its audit committee. In 1990, just two months before Harken reported a $23 million loss that caused the stock to drop from $4 a share to $1, George sold all of his holdings for the top price, cashing out with a tidy $848,000. He took the money and ran while regular shareholders took the hit, getting no warning from their future president.

On George's watch, Harken also cooked its books à la Enron—hiding losses of millions of dollars by secretly selling a subsidiary to a group of insiders, thus deceiving investors about the true financial health of the company. In addition, Harken created its own Cayman Island tax dodge and, on a motion from George himself, pulled a slick off-the-books end run around creditors that would make an Enron auditor's head spin with envy. But Bush the Reformer gets all testy and squinty-eyed on the rare occasion that a reporter has the effrontery to question his good old Harken days: "Everything I do is fully disclosed. It's been fully vetted. Any other questions?" he snapped to an impudent questioner about it last year.

There was an SEC investigation in 1991 of George's cash-out from Harken, and he and his henchmen have flatly insisted several times since that the agency completely exonerated him of wrongdoing, so case closed. If books had neon, I'd put a flashing sign right here screaming: BIG BALD LIE . . . BIG BALD LIE . . .

What the SEC said was that it could not get enough information to nail him. One reason for this is that its inquiry was at best perfunctory, including the curious fact that investigators never even interviewed the suspect! Imagine yourself skipping away so pleasantly. But your daddy wasn't POTUS at the time—the President of the United States. And the head of the SEC wouldn't have been a personal pal of your daddy's as he was of Bush's. And it's unlikely that the general counsel of the SEC, who oversees such cases, would previously have been your personal lawyer, as he had been for George.

You now can see why the current SEC hierarchy, handpicked by George, refuses to allow anyone so much as a peek at File No. MHO-3180, containing the records of the Bush "investigation." I can just hear George telling the SEC chairman, "You can turn loose that file when they pry your cold dead fingers from it." Assuming that there's anything left in the file other than the hairball of the cat burgler sent by the White House to purge it.

Say hello, too, to Uncle Dick. Maybe you noticed that V.P. Cheney was not making a lot of public appearances during the hot season of the corporate scandals. In fact, it was when the corporate shinola really began to hit the fan that we learned about the secretive underground government that Bush had set up in two fortified bunkers somewhere along the East Coast, with Cheney supposedly in charge. Like a skittish mole, Dick didn't surface for weeks. Excuse my lack of charity, but I suspect that one reason for Dick's disappearance can be spelled H-a-l-l-i-b-u-r-t-o-n.

Better to put the veep in the deep than to let reporters ask why this giant Pentagon contractor had not paid any taxes during four of the five years Cheney headed it, or why he had increased from nine to forty-four the number of Halliburton's offshore tax havens, or why the SEC is investigating the shady accounting practices that Cheney implemented when he was Halliburton's honcho, including a probe into the company's Enron-style shell game of booking cost overruns as income. E-m-b-a-r-r-a-s-s-i-n-g.

CIRCLE THE WAGONS

Things were bad for CEOs. *Your line:* How bad were things, Hightower? *Me again:* So bad that CEOs were forming support groups so they could share each other's pain and read Ayn Rand novels together.

I wish I was making that up, but here it is in no less of a lifestyle authority than *USA Today* (and we know they don't make up things). Headline, 9-20-02: "Scandals Lead Execs to 'Atlas Shrugged.'" This book, along with *The Fountainhead* and other 1950s novels by Rand, who was a Russian immigrant and Hollywood scriptwriter, exalted successful businessmen as heroic, laissez-faire capitalists who battle government, unions, do-gooders, and all the other "moochers" who feed off those who "achieve"—i.e., them.

The reporter tells us that there's been a recent surge in purchases of *Atlas Shrugged,* with executives reading and rereading the 1,075-page novel "to remind themselves that self-interest is not only the right thing to do from an economic standpoint, but it is *moral* as well." Executive support groups have sprung up in various cities, allowing the beleaguered CEO class to discuss the book and be reassured that "they are not the greedy crooks they are portrayed to be in today's business headlines, but are *heroes* like the characters in Rand's novels." The reporter notes that corporate executives view themselves as "real-life achievers who do far more to lift the world's standard of living, cure disease, and end starvation than *Mother Teresa.*"

Whew! Moral. Heroes. Mother Teresa. Let's all take a deep breath right here. These guys aren't just full of themselves; they have the kind of big-shot egos that see lightning and think it's God snapping pictures of them. It's a little unnerving to think that these are the people running our world these days.

Things truly were bad for them in 2002. Bush and Cheney, their dream team, were *personally* and directly tied to the overall corporate scam and were in trouble; domino after corporate domino was falling and there was no telling how many more down the line were ready to fall; the media was actually reporting this stuff, and prosecutors were on a hot-

THRILLS AND SPILLS!

One of the wildest rides at the Corporate Scandal Amusement Park is aboard the red-hot Executive Rocket. The insiders ride this baby up to the zenith of its reach, powered by the investment dollars you outsiders have paid to be passengers. Then comes the stomach-turning part of the joy ride—when the E-Rocket sputters and begins to plummet, the executives parachute out with hundreds of millions of your dollars, without telling you that you're going to take the fall and lose everything!

Thousands of you have ridden the E-Rocket in the past couple of years, and maybe you'd like to know exactly who took you for that ride. Thanks to *Fortune* magazine, I can provide the following list of what *Fortune* calls "the twenty-five companies with the greediest executives." These are the big-time companies whose stock had plummeted by at least 75 percent in value while their CEOs, CFOs, COOs, and other top dogs climbed out of a secret hatch at the top and serenely parachuted to the ground, clutching the most loot. In all, 466 insiders from these twenty-five corporations walked away with a cool $23 billion since 1999 as their companies (and you) crashed. Ready. Set. Leap!

Corporation	Total Loot Taken by Executives	Top Looter in the Corporation
Qwest Communications	$ 2.26 billion	Phillip Anschutz
Broadcom	$ 2.08 billion	Henry Samueli
AOL Time Warner	$ 1.79 billion	Steve Case
Gateway	$ 1.27 billion	Ted Waitt
Ariba	$ 1.24 billion	Rob DeSantis
JDS Uniphase	$ 1.15 billion	Kevin Kalkhoven
i2 Technologies	$ 1.03 billion	Sanjiv Sidhu
Sun Microsystems	$ 1.03 billion	Bill Joy
Enron	$ 994 million	Lou Pai
Global Crossing	$ 951 million	Gary Winnick
Charles Schwab	$ 951 million	Charles Schwab
Yahoo	$ 901 million	Tim Koogle
Cisco Systems	$ 851 million	John Chambers

Corporation	Total Loot Taken by Executives	Top Looter in the Corporation
Peregrine Systems	$ 818 million	John Moores
Sycamore Networks	$ 726 million	Gururaj Deshpande
Nextel Communications	$ 615 million	Craig McCaw
Foundry Networks	$ 582 million	Bobby Johnson
Juniper Networks	$ 557 million	Scott Kriens
Infospace	$ 541 million	Naveen Jain
Commerce One	$ 531 million	Thomas Gonzales
AT&T	$ 475 million	John Malone
Network Appliance	$ 470 million	David Hitz
Inktomi	$ 431 million	Paul Gauthier
Priceline	$ 417 million	Jay Walker
Vignette	$ 413 million	Ross Garber

breath tear; blood was on the moon and the hounds were baying. Something had to be done—so the establishment circled, then rumbled out its media arsenal to limit the damage, rephrase the debate, and preserve business as usual.

Yes, mistakes were made, goes their soothing line, *and some bad people did some very bad things, and we're just sick about them—but, oooooh, look, those few bad apples are already being plucked out of the barrel, so, see, the system is working perfectly, taking care of its own all natural-like—so let's not make too much fuss over what boils down to so little, and for sure let's not tamper with the rules of the system itself, I mean we don't want to get in the way of innovative arrangements that help our corporate leaders be competitive in today's dog-eat-dog global economy, and, after all, a lot of the corporate practices that the liberal, I-hate-America media has tried to tarnish as illegal or even immoral (can you believe the gall of those witch hunters!) is the very kind of push-the-envelope executive initiative we must reward, not punish for goodness sake, so to avoid confusion and better explain what our corporate executives are doing we're introducing some new language, such as "aggressive accounting" to replace that vulgar phrase "cook the books." Can you say "aggressive accounting"?*

Yes, I can. But I won't. That's the same as saying that robbing 7-Elevens is "aggressive consumerism." Is that OK? Should we ignore the thievery, let the robbers keep the loot, and give them their own show on Fox Financial News?

What the soothing-phrase coiners don't want us focusing on is the reality that the scandal is not about a few bad apples, but about a whole system that's become rotten. The *illegalities* are the least of it—the deeper horror is that rottenness has been made legal. At Enron, for example, the core of the rot was not in the crimes that were committed—there were very few crimes, it turns out, and they had almost nothing to do with Enron's collapse. Rather it was those off-the-books partnerships (2,832 of them!), secretly set up by the top executives to enrich themselves, that toppled this giant. These things were stinky as could be . . . but they were legal. "Enron was following the letter of the law in nearly all of its deals," says finance professor Frank Partnoy, an expert who analyzed the partnerships.

This is the secret the corporate elites are protecting. For the past twenty-five years, they've worked diligently in the White House and Congress, in the courts and regulatory agencies, in state capitols and city halls, in politics and the media, in think tanks and universities—in our heads—to change the rules and pervert the governing ethos so selfishness is favored over fairness, property over people, expediency over loyalty, private over public.

Think about the overarching political message in both parties and throughout our culture for the past quarter-century. Forget the common good. Instead, from Carter, Reagan, Bush I, Clinton, and especially Bush II, the relentless mantra has been "ation"—as in privatiz*ation,* deregul*ation,* no tax*ation,* globaliz*ation,* anti-union*ization.* . . . These have become the governing principles of America, and under their ideological banners have come the sneaky amendments, regulatory rewrites, court interpretations, executive orders, trade arrangements, tax rulings, loopholes, revolving doors, subsidies, and other actions to rewire the system and separate the corporate powers from accountability to anyone but their god Mammon.

- Want to lock your employees' 401(k)s into the company's plunging stock price, which will smash their 401(k) to an 001(k)? Go ahead, perfectly legal.
- Want to urge Uncle Elmer and Aunt Elvira to buy shares of BigHonkingStupid.Com, even though you think the stock will sink like an anvil, but BHS.Com has hired your firm at a sweet consultant fee, so . . . tough luck, Uncle and Auntie El? Not nice, but not illegal.
- Want to reincorporate your Old American Values Inc. in Barbados by simply paying a little fee to open a mailbox there, then run a profit-shifting game through that mailbox so—*alakaasham!*—Old American pays no taxes to the good ol' USA? Hug your lobbyists because they fixed it so this is as legal as flying the American flag on July 4th.

The problem with putting the Wall Street perps in the pokey is that the Congress Critters who pounded the gavels and screeched the loudest about Enron, WorldCom, and the rest in 2002 are the very ones who had taken their campaign contributions earlier, then taken out the legislative wire cutters and monkey wrenches to fix it so corporations are able to do their dirty deeds legally.

Joe Lieberman is one luminous example. Remember the senator's display of moral indignation, wagging his finger and expressing disgust at Enron's fast-and-loose accounting practices? But Joe Baby, did you forget? You helped loosen them! You remember Ken Lay, don't you, Joe? He's one of your campaign contributors, along with all those other Wall Street pals of yours who put a quarter-million bucks into your campaign pockets over the years.

Remember that bill that Ken and a bunch of other high-flying CEOs from the "new economy" wanted? They were running a little "stock options" scheme that let them take tens of millions of dollars each out of

GARY GIVES BACK

CEOs may have overactive egos, but Gary Winnick is living proof that they also can be people of good heart.

Gary, a former junk-bond salesman and protégé of the light-fingered King of Junk, Michael Milken, became one of the shooting stars of the telecommunications boom in the '90s. While he knew nothing about telecom, he certainly knew the art of the deal, which he parlayed into an outfit called Global Crossing, which of course he incorporated in Bermuda to avoid being bothered with having to pay income taxes to Uncle Sam.

At the zip-a-dee-doo-da height of the '90s investment boom, Gary attracted a mountain of capital. The stock price soared and several people made spectacular hauls in a hurry—Daddy George Bush, for example, took an $80,000 speaking fee from Global Crossing and, on the advice of a winking company official, put it right into GC's dazzling slot machine. In only weeks—Sweet Jesus!—the ex-president came up all cherries, walking away with $14 million. Also, in a bipartisan spirit, Winnick let Bill Clinton's close buddy Terry McAuliffe (now chair of the Democratic Party) put $100,000 in the slot and—Come to Papa!—out came an $18 million payoff in only one year.

Alas, not everyone did so well, especially little investors with no power connections. The market wasn't buying what Global Crossing was selling, and the company's stock went down faster than Britney Spears's singing career. Shareholders lost $90 billion on GC stock in 2001–2002, and tens of thousands of workers lost not only their jobs, but also their retirement money, which was mostly parked in company stock.

Naturally, Gary took the hardest hit, since his fortune also was tied up in the stock. HA HA! Just kidding. What—you think there's some ethic about the captain going down with the ship? Not in CEOland, pal. Gary took the early boat off his Titanic. As the people in steerage class were drowning in Global's red ink, Gary rowed away with $734 million before the whole company finally sank into Chapter 11.

Here, though, is where you'll want to reach for a tissue to dab your eyes as I tell you about the stunning generosity of this extraordinary man. Called before Congress late last year to testify about his company's collapse, Gary verged on tears as he told the committee that he felt just awful about crushing his employees' 401(k)s. Then in a Sally Struthers moment of spontaneous, heart-tugging compassion, Gary announced that he personally would write a $25 million check to the depleted pension funds of fourteen thousand workers—amounting to about $1,800 each. It's hard to retire on that, but Winnick said he wanted to make a gesture to "those who worked hard for this company."

Gary's gesture reminded me of when my friend Studs Terkel was robbed in his home a couple of years ago. Studs, who's deaf as an iron pipe, had gone upstairs to go to bed and had removed his plutonium-powered, megawatt hearing aids. As he turned back the bedcovers, he was confronted by a man making threatening gestures—but Studs couldn't hear a word. So he told the guy to just hold it while he fumbled around to put the hearing aids back in his ears and crank up the volume.

The robber was demanding cash, and it just happened that Studs had been to the bank that day, so he had $400 in his wallet and he had no choice but to give it to the thief. But as the robber was leaving the room, Studs hollered to him: "Hold on there! Now you've got all my money. Gimme $20!" he demanded, pumped up by anger. The guy did! Studs says it's a metaphor for the system—they take 400 from us and give back 20.

But this thief's 1-to-20 payback is better than what Global's workers got from Winnick, who wants a pat on the back for lifting $734 million, then returning $25 million—about a 1-to-30 advantage for Winnick, who still netted $709 million in his mugging.

Interestingly, the FBI reports that bank robbers make off with only about $70 million a year in our country.

their companies in annual pay, yet not report this to shareholders as a cost to the corporation. Mind you, these millions are in addition to their salary, bonuses, and other cash payments. (CEO pay packages are like a salad bar. First comes the base salary, which is the plain lettuce. Then they add on a dipperful of blue cheese dressing, plus a rasher of bacon bits. Then they say, oh, what the hell, go ahead and put a cheeseburger on it, too. The stock options are the cheeseburger.)

But those tiresome, regulatory nitpickers over at the SEC thought investors had a right to see this sizeable shift of their corporate funds going into the CEO's pockets, so the SEC was going to require that stock options be accounted for on the books.

Fearing that investors (those pesky busybodies) might balk at such lavish outlays for CEOs if they saw them in black and white (or red), Kenny Boy and the rest came running to you, didn't they, Joe, shrieking that such disclosure would stifle executive ingenuity, would drive a stake through the heart of entrepreneurship, would cause the new economy to collapse, and would mean that they'd be so poorly paid they'd have to buy next year's Escalade *without* the sunroof. So you came to their relief, didn't you, Joe, by sponsoring a bill that forced the SEC to back off, letting CEOs keep getting their cheeseburgers without accounting for them. Yes, you did.

Ken Lay is gone and Enron is in deep bankruptcy. Yet the stock options pay scheme is still there, the gift that just keeps giving, now being used by practically every major corporation. It's what they call being "morally modern."

A few bad apples? Enron is cited as the baddest of them all, but wait—did it do its financial shimmy-shimmies alone in a dark room? Hardly. Its accountants, lawyers, bankers—some of the most upstanding peers of the business establishment, with names like Arthur Andersen, Vinson & Elkins, Citigroup, and many more—were right there alongside Enron's connivers, wearing their green eyeshades and working their calculators to build the Rube Goldberg contraptions that caused money to flow uphill, into the pockets of all involved. The Wall Street analysts and the business media also said they were watching Enron closely, yet, until it imploded, none said anything bad about the baddest, instead using accolades like "greatest."

WHAT'S IN A NAME?

As a fresh-faced CEO, Ken Lay used to wish that his company would someday become a household word, like Coca-Cola, IBM, or Ty-D-Bol—and boy, did that dream ever come true!

"Enron" became a vulgarity—so ugly that the Houston Astros baseball team paid $2 million to the company in February of 2002 to get the "Crooked E" logo off its stadium. In that same month, the caretakers of the now-bankrupt company announced that even they were looking for a new moniker because, as the interim CEO so delicately put it, "there's something of a taint with the Enron name."

On my radio show (for info: www.jimhightower.com), I held a "Name That Enron" contest, inviting listeners to do their damnedest to come up with an appropriate name. Hundreds of suggestions poured in from as far away as Tokyo and Saudi Arabia. Here are the Top Ten Winners:

bEnwrong	Enrot
401-deron	EnYours
Emroid	Robenron
EnDeep	Scamron
Enfamy	Takethemoneyandron

Two special awards were also given: The Plain Speaking Award went to the disgusted lady who suggested "just plain old Greed," and the Best Twist Award went to the fellow who revealed that if you turn Enron's "Crooked E" logo all the way back on its side, it becomes the "Crooked W." And George thought he could avoid being connected to the scandal!

Governors, members of Congress, presidents—all were elbowing each other to get closest to Ken Lay and his deep political pockets, hungrily accepting not only his checks, but also his outline for deregulating derivatives, subsidizing his power project in India, or protecting the hundreds of subsidiaries his company had set up in the Cayman Islands tax haven. Like frolicking dogs trying to get a treat from the master, both parties licked the hand of Lord Lay. Ken was tight with W, as we know, but he was also one of the privileged ones who enjoyed an overnight in the Lincoln Bedroom during Clinton's tenure, and more than two-thirds of the Congress were recipients of Enron money.

What we have here is not a conspiracy, but a Fraternity of Greed that can be called: The System. Enron, WorldCom, and the other "bad apples" flourished in an interconnected system that doesn't merely wink at their corrupt actions, but aggressively fosters them . . . and wants a piece of the same action.

Today most corporations are Enron—booking phantom assets, hiding losses, manipulating prices, looting pensions, running funny-money partnerships, milking government subsidies, crafting tax-avoidance scams, hiring see-no-evil auditors, appointing brother-in-law compensation committees, et-cetera-to-the-tenth-power. Enron didn't game the system, it gleefully embraced it, perfected it, *became* the system.

Indeed, in 2002, after the SEC announced its intention to review the financial statements of the largest corporations, hundreds rushed forward to—ahem—"restate" their earnings, meaning they had been lying about how well they were doing. Lying is wrong, as Momma told us from our first little fib onward. But among today's gentlemen of business, it's technically not illegal, it's richly rewarded, and it's practiced by nearly all of the apples, not just the "bad."

REFORMS? WHAT REFORMS?

So much scandal, so much outrage, so much motion . . . so little action. Oh, there were pretensions aplenty, including a three-act farce called the Public Company Accounting Oversight Board, starring Groucho, Harpo, and Chico.

Prelude. As you're probably aware, the first rule of do-nothingism is: Create a board. Hence the PCAOB, created by the one law Congress did pass in response to the public's clamor for action. Fear not, said Bush, surrounded by a gaggle of grinning lawmakers as he signed the law, this will be the new watchdog America needs to stop accounting fraud in its tracks. Grrrrr . . . sic 'em, boy!

Act One: The Murder. John Biggs, a splendid chap who headed a large pension fund and had long advocated tougher oversight of Wall Street's flimflammers, was in line to head the PCAOB. He was the choice of reformers and, reform being all the rage at the moment, Biggs was girding himself to take the new job, when BAM! Dead man. The big accounting firms and some of their corporate clients had scurried to the White House when they learned Biggs's appointment was imminent, crying, "Holy moly, you're not really going to be serious about this reform marlarky, are you, unleashing a guy who could mess with our money, the American way, and your campaign contributions?" How many nanoseconds do you think it took Karl Rove and that covey of conniving corporate bloodsuckers to say: "Uh . . . no!"

Act Two: A Botched Cover-up. Biggs was gone, but the demand for reform was not, so they had to make this look good. Who could they install at PCAOB who could generate public trust, but who could also be trusted not to, you know, interfere? Of course: William Webster, the former federal judge, former head of both the CIA and the FBI, a recipient of the Presidential Medal of Freedom, now a corporate lobbyist, and, most important, a regular on Washington's social circuit. The seventy-eight-year-old peer of the Order of Insiders had sloshed martinis with all the key players at one cocktail reception or another, and he would be unassailable. Big Bonus Point: He also knew less about accounting oversight than a pig knows about the libretto of *Aïda.* So Webster got the nod. To keep him on track, the four other PCAOB members were named, including a lawyer who represents corporate executives charged with insider trading, a former accountant for Arthur Andersen, and a lobbyist for big insurance companies. There, all safe for the industry . . . except that—*CRASH!*—before Webster could convene a meeting, it was revealed that only recently he had headed the audit committee of a corporation that was now practically insolvent and being investigated for fraud. And when this company's outside auditors had raised questions about its accounting practices, Webster abruptly fired them. Oops. Webster was soon slipped out the back door.

Act Three: All Fall Down. Six months after it was created to reinstill public trust in corporate ethics, PCAOB finally had its first meeting, still without a chair, a budget, or staff directors. Nonetheless, it got down to business. Its very first decision was on a proposal to rotate the board's own auditors every five years to assure their independence, thus setting a positive example for the industry it oversees. No, ruled the board. Then, demonstrating a complete cluelessness about the value of symbolism, the board voted to locate its offices on Washington's K Street corridor of corporate lobbyists, choosing to lease the very space that had belonged to Arthur Andersen, the accounting firm that went kaput because of its finagling. Finally, as pleased as punch with this jolly start, the board members voted themselves annual salaries of $452,000 each—$52,000 more than the president gets and more than double the pay of cabinet officers.

Meanwhile, the same bill that created the PCAOB also authorized 77 percent more funds for the SEC so it could hire more investigators and upgrade its antiquated computers (which, I understand, are so old they were powered by wind-up springs taken from old clocks). Bush made a big political flourish of signing the bill, bragging that the new money would provide the policing tools needed so "corporate misdeeds will be found and be punished."

Tough stuff. Except that the W in George W stands for Weasel. Little-known fact. Three months after signing the bill, he slashed the SEC's 77 percent budget increase. No press conference on this one. He now says he'll ask Congress for more money in the 2004 budget. Even if he does, though, and even if he pushes to get it—two very iffy ifs—that's yet another year before the agency would get the money and begin staffing up,

WHAT DOES IT SPELL?

Like a Monet, Renoir, or other Impressionist painting, it helps to stand back from all the oily dots on the canvas of corporate crashes so you can comprehend the full picture. Here's a listing of some of the corporations that were named in 2002 for financial shenanigans—bilking investors, stock-rating scams, insider trading, and such. Stand back and see what the artist is trying to say:

Kmart, Priceline.com, **T**yco, Waste Management, Inc., **H**alliburton, Adelphia, Aon, **O**racle, CDW Computer Centers, **S**unbeam, Xerox, Lehman Brothers, **E**rnst & Young, **G**oldman Sachs, KPMG, Ford Motor Co., General Electric, CSFB (Credit Suisse First Boston), Wells Fargo, **R**eliant Resources, U.S. Technologies, **E**l Paso Corporation, MBNA, eBay, Advance PCS, McLeod USA, WorldCom, Arthur Andersen, **E**nron, CMS Energy, Metromedia Fiber Network, **D**uke Energy Corporation, Cigna Corporation, ImClone, **H**omestore.com, Inc., Citigroup, Merrill Lynch, **E**dison Schools, PricewaterhouseCoopers, Global Crossing, **A**OL Time Warner, JPMorgan Chase, **D**ell Computers, Computer Associates International, **E**MC, Qwest Communications International, AT&T, Microsoft, Williams Companies, **D**eloitte & Touche, Duke Power, **B**rocade Communications, National Century Financial Enterprises, **A**t Home, Danaher, Plum Creek Timber, **S**iebel Systems, **T**rump Hotels, PNC Financial Services Group, **A**quila, Mirant Corporation, Winstar Communications, **R**aytheon, Veritas Software, **D**onaldson, Lufkin & Jenrette, Dynegy, Inc., Charles **S**chwab, IBM Corporation pushing any enforcement possibilities into 2005, when the weasel hopes to be in a second term and can quietly quash any action his corporate pals oppose. Not exactly the commitment to reform that people were led to believe they were getting.

More than a year after Bush and the other politicos swore a blood oath at high noon to track down every scammer, cheater, and finagler in corporate America, the SEC remains strapped for the foreseeable future. It's unable even to review more than a few of the vast number of corporate documents filed with it every day, much less do anything about any funkiness it spots. It's a joke that this outgunned agency is the public's protector against the wolves of Wall Street—in fact, one firm alone, Merrill Lynch, has a bigger legal staff dealing with regulatory matters than the entire enforcement division of the SEC.

BUSINESS AS USUAL

New York Times business columnist Gretchen Morgenson writes, "Denial is a powerful thing. And entrenched business practices, especially those that are immensely profitable, will always be hard to change. But it is nonetheless remarkable how deep the resistance to change is in the upper echelons of business and on Wall Street, even after trillions of dollars have been lost by investors."

Exactly. Too much money is being made by powerful people for the corrupt system to change itself. Take the matter of tax evasion. *WOO-WHOOP, WOO-WHOOP!* HALT! WORD ERROR! WORD ERROR!

Sorry, I misspoke. Tax "evasion" is illegal. Of course I meant to say "aggressive tax avoidance," the euphemism that Wall Street's accounting, legal, and consulting firms actually use when packaging and selling their "Why Pay Taxes?" schemes to corporations and grossly rich people. Evasion is what bad people do. Aggressive avoidance is what good people do—people with gumption who're merely seizing the opportunities presented to them. Avoidance is treated as legal by the authorities, even though it's essentially the same thing as evasion—either way, those who do it get to skate on paying their taxes.

However, avoidance is complex, which is why avoiders need professional help. The schematic of the electrical wiring of the space shuttle is not as dizzying as these hide-the-profit tax schemes that the pros sell. Suffice it to say that Point A does not lead to Point B, which is the whole purpose of the game—in fact, Point B doesn't even exist, at least not on paper.

It was not until last year's corporate exposés that most of us rubes first heard that such screwy wire jobs existed. It was revealed that accounting giants like Ernst & Young, PricewaterhouseCoopers, KPMG, Deloitte & Touche, and the since-defunct Arthur Andersen had done much of the wiring for the Enrons—but they were also doing exactly the same thing for the entire Fortune 500 and the swells who live in Park Avenue penthouses, Beverly Hills, River Oaks, and other posh zip codes. And guess what? They're still doing it.

Ernst & Young, for example, is presently marketing a cute package that helps someone selling a business "avoid" Mr. Taxman. Say it's you, you lucky dog. Of course, you have to be a very rich dog even to get into this game, but let's say you are and that you sell your business, pocketing $100 million in profit. You would owe $20 million in capital gains taxes, leaving you "only" $80 million. But, look—swooping down in a pair of gold lamé tights and a platinum cape is some slick from Ernst & Young with a deal you won't refuse. Instead of $20 million, you pay only $5 million—and this money doesn't go to the government, it goes to E & Y. Five mil is its fee for zeroing out your taxes, plus a little more you pay to the law firms, bankers, and currency traders who make the "arrangements."

Could you get into trouble? Perfectly legal, says the Ernst wiring crew. Besides, this deal is run through several partnerships, a couple of offshore banks, a charitable trust, and a fruit stand in Arkansas before coming to you. One financial analyst, terming the scheme "brilliant," told *The New York Times*: "You would have to have the most suspicious and thorough and intelligent auditor in the world to find this, and he would have to peel back several layers to find the real stuff." Even then, Ernst & Young would have provided an opinion letter for you from one of its tax lawyers (who gets $50,000 for writing it) vowing to you that the deal is legal—sort of like getting a note from your mom saying it's OK for you not to pay your taxes.

How different is this from the straightforward tax dodging of Lucky Luciano, the old-time New York Mafia boss? In a 1936 trial, Luciano was being mocked for his farcical tax returns, which showed he never made more than $22,500 a year. "You just picked those figures on your income out of the sky, didn't you?" grilled the prosecutor. Luciano replied: "I just thought it was the proper amount I should give the government." (JUICY MORSEL: In 1998, *Time* magazine named Lucky Luciano one of the 100 "most influential business geniuses of the century.")

Like in a magic show, reform was right in front of us one moment, then—*whoosh*—gone. What happened? Three things. One, Bush wagged Saddam, that dog, and the media, which only yesterday was full of fury over the corporate crime spree, jerked its nose out of that real news and went running off with George to cover his unreal story that Iraq had, overnight, become an imminent threat to us. News judgment aside, apparently the multibillion-dollar behemoths that own our media are incapable of covering more than one big story at a time.

They failed us. The hot issue that the public cared passionately about—the systemic corruption of America's corporate system—has since been relegated to occasional snippets back in the business section about the "few bad apples" being prosecuted. All the better for Bush, who obviously needed to shift the media's focus, for he didn't want last fall's congressional elections to be a mandate on corporate ethics, including his own. But even he must have been surprised that the media could have its leash jerked so easily.

Two, Congress reverted to type. When the scandals were breaking, the public outcry blew the top off Congress's Rage Detector, telling our Congress Critters that they had to start flapping their arms and loudly squawking, which they did until around Labor Day. That's about when the corporate lobbyists got most of the congressional feathers smoothed, cooing sweetly to them:

There, there, what a good job you've done! You really told off those creeps at Enron and Arthur Andersen, didn't you, and how about that neat new oversight board you created? You must be so proud. But you've got an election coming up in—what?— gosh, it's only two months away, isn't it! So, here, we took up a little collection back at the office, and we want you to have this. It's our way of thanking you for the way you dealt with this spot of ugliness, and we're just glad we can put it all behind us now.

Here are the campaign contributions given to finance last year's congressional candidates by just a few of the corporations under investigation at the time:

Corporation	Amount	Democrats	Republicans
Microsoft	$3,532,605	40%	60%
Goldman Sachs	$3,003,581	68%	32%
AT&T	$2,763,769	46%	54%
Citigroup	$2,742,279	47%	53%
Deloitte & Touche	$1,969,406	18%	82%
AOL Time Warner	$1,650,239	72%	28%
Ernst & Young	$1,641,156	29%	71%
KPMG	$1,451,914	15%	85%
El Paso Corporation	$1,422,201	15%	85%
Global Crossing	$1,217,970	65%	35%
PricewaterhouseCoopers	$1,190,678	18%	82%
Credit Suisse First Bank	$1,120,698	36%	64%
WorldCom Inc.	$1,020,561	46%	54%
Qwest Communications	$ 969,575	41%	59%
General Electric	$ 879,116	39%	61%
JPMorgan Chase	$ 874,693	58%	42%
Merrill Lynch	$ 767,932	41%	59%
Lehman Brothers	$ 660,119	7%	93%
Arthur Andersen	$ 610,288	31%	69%
Enron	$ 547,225	29%	71%
Wells Fargo	$ 467,852	32%	68%
Reliant Resources	$ 466,623	25%	75%
Dell	$ 462,252	16%	84%
Kmart	$ 374,939	37%	63%

Corporation	Amount	Democrats	Republicans
Waste Management, Inc.	$ 318,779	23%	77%
Tyco	$ 271,297	23%	77%
Dynegy	$ 254,182	45%	55%

Source: The Center for Responsive Politics www.opensecrets.org

Three, you could just hear Bush and his political gnome, Karl Rove, yelping with glee: Thank God for the Democrats! Dick Gephardt, Tom Daschle, Terry McAuliffe, and the other deep thinkers who were directing the so-called opposition party's fall election strategy made this absolutely astonishing decision: Let's not talk about that corporate stuff (remember, we need their campaign contributions, too). Instead let's say that we're in full support of the president's Iraq attack. Yes, instead of going after Bush's glaring weakness, the Democratic leaders ran at his strength, and they did so by agreeing with him!!! It just leaves you whopperjawed.

After the election, the political pundits were unanimous in heaping hosannas on Rove's election strategy, but he didn't even need a strategy when he had the hapless trio of Gephardt, Daschle, and McAuliffe opposite him! Obviously, this bunch was operating from what the Firesign Theatre comedy troupe calls the "Bozone"—the invisible layer that surrounds stupid people and prevents any smart ideas from penetrating.

DON'T GET DOWN, GET MOVING

The corrupt system rolls on, as though Enron never happened, as though the people never spoke. The message from the reigning corporate powers is clear: You don't count. We're untouchable, so don't even bother trying to stop us.

But I have a message for you, too: *YOU DID NOT FAIL.* As much as the Powers That Be want you to believe otherwise, your outrage at what has now been revealed as the *death of ethics* at the top of our society is not the end of the story, but the beginning.

Do they imagine that our outrage simply disappeared—as the media, the Congress, and the Democrats did?

Do they imagine that there's no price to pay for this further breaking down of people's faith (especially among young people) in the honesty of our governing institutions?

Do they imagine that we can't see this for what it is: their attempt to displace our democracy with their plutocracy and kleptocracy?

Do they imagine that we're just going to go away?

The beauty of America . . . is Americans! We're a nation of mavericks, rebels, mutts, and agitators. We've been kicked by better greedheads than these in our two-plus centuries of trying against all odds (and some of the evens, too) to build a society that practices our democratic values. King George III kicked us in the 1700s and thought he had us down for good. The robber barons kicked us in the 1800s and thought they'd rule forever. The barons of Wall Street kicked us in the 1920s and thought we wouldn't get up.

Today, if you look at Washington and Wall Street, you have to be filled with despair, for there is no balm there. But I'm fortunate—I've been able to travel all across our great land the last few years and see, in place after place, people just like you who are fighting, organizing, and succeeding (!) against the very corporate powers that smugly think they've already triumphed over us. What I see fills me with hope, inspiration, and even (yes, I know this is a big word, but it fits what I feel and want to convey to you) *awe* at the resiliency of our democratic spirit.

I think of the rambling travels that Woody Guthrie made in the '30s and '40s, of the strength he found in people, and of the stories he told in song about that strength. "I hate a song that makes you think you're not any good," he said on a radio show he hosted in the 1940s. "I hate a song that makes you think you're born to lose." Instead, said Woody:

> *I am out to sing songs that will prove to you that this is your world and that if it has hit you pretty hard and knocked you for a dozen loops, no matter how hard it's run you down nor rolled*

over you, no matter what color, what size you are, how you are built, I am out to sing the songs that make you take pride in yourself and your work. And the songs that I sing are made up for the most part by all sorts of folks just like you.

Our story has just begun.

CHAPTER 4

The Super-Duper Empire of King George the W

The surface of American Society is covered with a layer of democratic paint, but from time to time, one can see the old aristocratic colors breaking through.

—ALEXIS DE TOQUEVILLE, *Democracy in America*

What a happy-go-lucky guy we've got in the White House. He wasn't the choice of the people in the election of '00 (also known as "oh-oh!"), but "What, Me Worry?" Not George. Not his merry band of CheneyRumsfeldAshcroftRidge&Co., either. Grab power and go! And they haven't looked back since grabbing the keys to the White House, instead pushing themselves forward as the supreme executive, enrobing George the W as our War King, and demanding that you, me, and the world follow them to . . . where, exactly?

To a place our country hasn't been since the redcoats were running things and we Americans were chafing under the restraints of King George III's empire. Already, our Land of the Free has fallen down Bush's rabbit hole into a place of permanent war, homeland security agents, militarized budgets, executive secrecy, trade *über alles,* and other antidemocratic grotesqueries that are going bump in our long, restless night.

Did we vote for this? Even if you voted for Bush-Cheney in '00, is this what you had in mind?

To get a grip on the situation, I thought it might be helpful to seek out the wisdom and insights of some Bush predecessors, former Republican presidents:

> WARREN G. HARDING. "I don't know much about Americanism, but it's a damn good word with which to carry an election."

Hmmm, Bush & Co. already seem to have figured that one out. Never has so much bunting been used to cover so many bad ideas.

> CALVIN COOLIDGE. "Four-fifths of all our troubles would disappear if we would only sit down and keep still."

Good Yankee common sense there from Silent Cal, but not likely to be heeded by a group as pumped up on thrice-daily testosterone injections as the Bushites are. Keep still? They say they've got sixty countries on their "bad guy" list, and we're only to number three or four so far. So much evil, so little time.

> RICHARD NIXON. "Politics would be a helluva good business if it weren't for the goddamned people."

We hear ya, Dick. What a loveable guy, huh? Nixon thought Poppa Bush was a fatuous, preppie, New England pansy, but he probably would've liked the boy, for W seems able to spit out the word "democracy" in a way that squeegies those goddamned people right out of it. Admirable.
    Speaking of Poppa,

> GEORGE HERBERT WALKER BUSH. "I'm conservative, but I'm not a nut about it."

There you go! Now we're getting to the nub of it. This bunch of Bushites is nuts about implementing imperial executive authority and its dreams of empire. To quote one more Republican ex-prez, Gerry Ford, about yet

AMERICA'S BEACON

Our Empire-Builder-in-Chief sometimes trips on his own vision. Just before his inauguration, Bush said:

> "Redefining the role of the United States from enablers to keep the peace to enablers to keep the peace from peacekeepers is going to be an assignment."

Whatever. Instead of seeing America's mission in terms of a sword-rattling colossus bestriding the world, George would have done well to reflect on the profound yet simple thought of Benjamin Franklin, who saw America's historic promise in different terms than empire:

> *"America's destiny is not power, but light."*

The light he referred to is the idea of our democracy, illuminated by our deep belief in fairness, equality, and justice for all.

That's who we are, and that's the beacon of idealism that truly makes us strong.

another: "If Lincoln were alive today, he'd be turning in his grave." A little twisted, Gerry, but good point.

So must all of the founders be turning over in their graves, for they rightfully abhorred empire, autocratic executives, and military power. That abhorrence, expertly crafted into our founding documents and governing ethos, defines what is unique about America, what makes our people's democratic aspirations possible to achieve. They fought a war to free us from empire, autocracy, and militarism—but in only a couple of years, Bushite zealots embraced what the founders abhorred and put our America on course to become the very thing that we rebelled against in 1776.

"THE BULLY ON THE BLOCK"

Just before moving into the White House, George W said: "I hope I'm viewed as a humble person." Good start! Where'd that guy go?

Well, you might say, September 11 kicked the humility right out of him. That's a neat theory, and it's certainly the present rationale of Bush & Co., but it has one big hole in it: They never had any humility. Despite the fact that only 24 percent of eligible voters cast their ballots for George in 2000, despite losing the popular vote, they seized power through the Supreme Court and immediately began to act as though they'd won a landslide mandate. Bush's hand was barely off the Bible before they began to issue executive edicts, impose unprecedented secrecy to cloak their actions, jack up the military budget, and ram through an elitist agenda that the vast majority of people don't support. They came in more juiced up than a herd of bulls on jimson weed. How soon we forget:

- Cheney's secret energy task force,
- the revival of the multibillion-dollar Star Wars boondoggle,
- Bush's decree that the presidential papers of Reagan and his father (including the incriminating Iran-Contra documents) were not to be made public,
- the agenda to privatize Social Security . . .

and so much more, *all in the first days of his presidency!*

Then came September 11. Sure, those despicable and horrific terrorist acts required a powerful presidential retort, and the nation genuinely rallied behind Bush's pledge to get Osama bin Laden "dead or alive." But endless war? Rewriting the Bill of Rights? Suppressing dissent? A secret Pentagon agency to spy on Americans? A grandiose assertion that America is the world's new high sheriff and by-damn you'll do it our way or feel the full fury of our righteous might? September 11 warranted a measured response, not a wrenching of American values and purpose—but it provided the Bushites the excuse they needed to impose their already-existing autocratic vision on the world and the "homeland."

The Bush Doctrine

I hear some of you mumbling, *Come on, Hightower, that's a lot of conspiracy crap. What are you saying—that BushCheneyRumsfeld and all had some big secret scheme to rule the world? I guess next thing you'll be flapping your gums about is that—ooooooo, there's some X-file containing this madcap plan!*

Yes. Yes, I am; yes, I will; and yes, there is. Bush wasn't part of the planning, but Cheney, Colin Powell, and Rumsfeld's top deputy, Paul "Howling" Wolfowitz, were. The plan had nothing to do with September 11. It was first put together way back in 1992, when Daddy Bush still wore the presidential jacket, Cheney was defense secretary, Powell headed the Pentagon's joint chiefs of staff, Howling Wolfowitz was a Cheney underling, and George W was a goof-off doing PR for the Texas Rangers baseball team.

Let's relive those days. It was the fading months of Bush I's term, and the greatest threat to the U.S. military machine was: The American People. The Soviet Union had gone kersplat, the worldwide commie bugaboo that had kept the military's coffers overflowing had been reduced to Fidel Castro, and people rather sensibly were saying that some of those Pentagon billions might be put to work on our domestic needs.

Aiieeeee! shrieked the generals and the corporate contractors who had fed at the Pentagon's trough for so long. Clearly a bold plan was needed to defend the budget trough. Hence: "DEFENSE PLANNING GUIDANCE," a classified policy paper outlining a radical new military role for our country.

Drafted by Wolfowitz, and backed by Powell and Cheney, the DPG declared that while the U.S. could easily crush any military in the world, our force must be made even stronger, indeed *much stronger* (requiring beefed-up budgets), so the U.S. can dominate all other militaries for all time, becoming so absolutely powerful that we would prevent any other nation or group of nations—friends or foes—from rivaling our world authority. Furthermore, said the DPG, the U.S. military must have the swat and clearance to go it alone in the wicked world, intervening when

PUSHING THE ENVELOPE

Just before the 2000 election, a right-wing think tank called the Project for a New American Century prepared a policy paper for Cheney, Rumsfeld, Wolfowitz, and other Bushites, updating the DPG. This paper called for Bush II, nearly three years before his invasion of Iraq, to take military control of the Gulf region, calling our armed forces "the calvary of the new American frontier." It also took on our allies, declaring that the U.S. must "discourage advanced industrial nations from challenging our leadership or even aspiring to a larger regional or global role."

and where it was deemed necessary.

Powell put the rationale of the DPG most succinctly in testimony before Congress in '92: "**I want to be the bully on the block.**" And he's considered the dove among the Bushites!

The plan went into cold storage, however, after Bush the Elder lost the presidency to Clinton. But only eight years later, the Bushites were back— and so was the Bully. It didn't immediately kick in the door and present its full hairy hulk to us, but all the key members of the DPG team were now in even more powerful positions under Bush II, and various other elements of the plan suddenly began to appear as policy. Unilateralism, for example, surged into play as George W blithely reversed years of bipartisan policy focused on playing nice with others in the global school yard:

- The Anti-Ballistic Missile Treaty? *Cancel that baby, 'cause we're gonna build our Star Wars scheme.*
- The Kyoto global warming agreement? *Do you think we're going to put a cap on our oil-guzzling economy? You gotta be kidding.*
- The ratification of a nuclear test ban pact? *Don't mess with our nukes.*
- Approve an international plan to ban biological weapons? *Nyet. We don't want Saddam to have these nasties, but don't tie us down.*

- Allow an international criminal court to prosecute war crimes? *Hold it, you're talking about Henry Kissinger there—and maybe us! So forget it.*

Then came al Qaeda's crash bombings into our buildings, and Cheney, Rummy, Powell, and Wolfowitz had all the rationale they needed to unleash the BullyBeast in full howl. Now George W could be brought into the DPG plan and turned loose to flog it publicly. It even got a new moniker when he unveiled it as official policy in a June 2002 speech at West Point: "The Bush Doctrine."

More like the Bush *dictate.* Formally published last fall as "The National Security Strategy of the United States of America," it says that the U.S. now asserts its military right to go where it wants, when it wants, to do what it wants, including:

1. acting alone to intervene anywhere, even in defiance of the international community;
2. making "unwarned attacks" (Pearl Harbor, for example, was an unwarned attack);
3. making "pre-emptive strikes" against nations that pose no imminent threat to us but are deemed by a president to be a potential threat sometime on the misty, distant horizon of hypothesis;
4. deploying an "effects-based" military force, which is to say overwhelming firepower, specifically including nuclear weapons (George had earlier authorized what he cutely called "baby nukes"—maybe they'll be the His & Hers special in the Neiman Marcus Christmas catalog this year, the perfect accessory for your twin Hummers);
5. aggressively using U.S. economic aid, the World Bank, the IMF, and free trade (which George has labeled a "moral principle") to compel nations to adopt "pro-growth legal and regulatory policies to encourage business investment," as well as "lower marginal tax rates that improve incentives" for foreign investors; and
6. doing all of the above on whim, without having to explain to anyone, much less prove, why such actions are warranted. As Bush told the National Security Council: "I do not need to explain why I say things. That's the interesting thing about being the president . . . [I] don't

feel like I owe anybody an explanation."

Golly, sort of takes your breath away, doesn't it? This is imperialism dressed as anti-terrorism and delivered with Bush's squinty-eyed, moralistic piety. (A PSYCHOLOGICAL ASIDE: The world is divided into two kinds of people—those who *think* the world can be divided into two kinds of people, and those who think it *juuuust might be* a little more complicated than that. W doesn't do complexity, so there are no mental bungee cords to pull him back from such absolutes as: You're either with us or against us, it's the good guys versus the bad guys, I'm right, you're wrong, and on and on. But I digress.)

Where, pray tell, is the media? And the Democratic Party? Why has no one in leadership cried bloody hell and hoisted up this rancid perversion of America's principles for all the people to see, discuss, and rebuke? King George the W proclaims aloud that he's imposing a Pax Americana on the whole wide world, and his roundtable of autocratic knaves have even committed it to print, but . . . silence.

How to drag a country into war

"Why of course the people don't want war. Why should some poor slob on a farm want to risk his life in a war when the best he can get out of it is to come back to his farm in one piece? Naturally, the common people don't want war: neither in Russia, nor in England, nor for that matter in Germany. That is understood. But after all it is the leaders of the country who determine the policy, and it is always a simple matter to drag the people along, whether it is a democracy, or a fascist dictatorship, or a parliament, or a communist dictatorship. . . . Voice or no voice, the people can always be brought to the bidding of leaders. That is easy. All you have to do is tell them they are being attacked, denounce the pacifists for lack of patriotism and exposing the country to danger."

—Hermann Göring, Luftwaffe commander. Interview, April 18, 1946. From *Nuremberg Diary* by Gustave Gilbert.

Even with the eerie silence, however, people do sense that something basic has abruptly turned topsy-turvy and that it won't end well for us or the world. Read the letters-to-the-editor columns, and you'll find them filled with thoughtful, distressed, logical questioning, such as: If our government proclaims the unilateral right to impose "regime change" through sheer might, where does that leave us when, say, China asserts its full strength in another decade or two?

"Lord help me to be pure," prayed St. Augustine, "but not yet." Our country's history is hardly pure (the Spanish-American War being one especially ugly blemish), but our tendency is against empire, and we've put ourselves on the line against British royalists, German fascists, Soviet totalitarians, and others who've sought global domination. Now we've got to fight our own goofy president, who's saying to the world in our name: Empire? I are one.

BUST THE BUDGET

Richie Ashburn, a great hitter and Hall of Famer for the Philadelphia Phillies, once ripped a screaming foul ball into the stands, hitting a woman square in the face and breaking her nose. They stopped the game for a few minutes to tend to her, then, as they loaded her onto a stretcher and were carrying her out, play resumed. The pitcher reared back and threw, Ashburn took another mighty cut at the ball, and again he ripped a screaming foul into the stands—hitting the same woman as she was being carted out, this time smacking her on the leg.

I feel like that besieged woman every time I read about yet another Pentagon budget hike coming at us, yet another new weapons boondoggle, yet another screaming cost overrun or missile system that doesn't work—all smacking us square in the public wallet.

Empire is expensive. It takes a lot of troops, equipment, and weaponry to police the world, enforce your will, and pursue permanent war. The annual Pentagon nut is now at $400 billion. That's $4 *trillion* over the next decade, even if there are no increases (which of course, there will be—Bush already plans for the Pentagon outlay to top $500

HOW MUCH IS 1,000,000,000,000?

You have not lived a trillion seconds. Our Western civilization has not been around for a trillion seconds. One trillion seconds is 31,688 years. A trillion seconds ago, Neanderthals stalked the earth.

billion a year by 2010). That's the amount we taxpayers have to cover just to have the war machine idling. It does *not* cover putting the machine in gear.

Wars are extra. As are "skirmishes," "actions," "engagements," "excursions," and other euphemisms the Pentagon uses for war. Bush's Iraq Attack and subsequent "nation building," for example, is figured to cost between $75 billion and $200 billion (depending on who's counting), on top of the $400 billion annual budget.

Toys are extra, too—like Star Wars, the "anti-missile missile" that Reagan first fantasized about. The fantasy also dances in George's head, so we taxpayers are on the hook for a multibillion-dollar payout for a silly system of sky darts that has been proven a failure and isn't needed. But the boy wants his toys, so in 2003 an extra billion and a half is being added to the $8 billion a year already allocated for this boondoggle, good money being thrown after the $95 billion already wasted during the past twenty years.

The money that Bush added will fund the initial setup of the Star Wars system. Yes, they're going ahead with building something that they admit doesn't work. Rumsfeld: "The reason I think it's important to start is because you have to put something in place

MISSING IN ACTION

A staggering amount of military spending is sheer waste. The Pentagon's inspector general conceded that the Defense Department cannot account for 25 percent of the funds it spends. A fourth! It was reported at a Senate hearing that $13 billion handed out to weapons contractors between 1985 and 1995 was "lost"—yes, gone, missing! Yet Washington is throwing even more of our tax dollars down this bottomless hole.

and get knowledge about it and experience with it." Tell me, Donnie, on the planet you come from, do they have oxygen there?

Battling terrorism is extra, too. The Pentagon wants a $10 billion annual slush fund, beyond the growth in its regular budget, to pay for its ongoing, unlimited, undefined campaign to catch all of the world's terrorists. It wants $7 billion more in new spending for a spiffy new counterterrorism unit that would operate sort of like the old CIA gang that kept trying to kill Castro with exploding cigars and the like. That worked so well they thought, hey, let's try it again, it's only money.

Among their plans—I AM NOT MAKING THIS UP—is a scheme to

I CAN'T BELIEVE THEY ATE THE WHOLE THING!

You might remember a thing called the "Peace Dividend." It was all the rage toward the end of the reign of Bush I (gosh, has it been a decade already?).

With the fall of the Berlin Wall and the implosion of the Soviet's "Evil Empire," the political air in the early '90s was thick with heady talk of what to do with all those billions of suddenly freed-up Cold War dollars. Citizen groups, members of Congress, presidential candidates, editorialists, business leaders, and others were in on the excitement, and the ideas ranged from building a national high-speed rail system to paying down the national debt.

So where did the Peace Dividend go? The Pentagon ate it. Then it began eating the budgets of domestic programs. Back then, the Pentagon budget was about $270 billion a year, and the idea was to convert up to $100 billion of that to needs here at home. Instead, today's Pentagon budget is $400 billion and bloating fast.

Why did Washington go from downsizing the war machine to supersizing it? Because the hoggish military contractors rose up and bellowed: **Get your pinko peacenik hands off *our* money!**

Well, it wasn't their money, it was yours and mine. But you and I don't make huge campaign contributions to those who divvie up the federal spending . . . and the contractors definitely do:

Top War Industry Contributions to Congressional and Presidential Campaigns 1992–2002 (ten-year totals)

Corporation	Amount	% to Democrats	% to Republicans
Lockheed Martin	$10,049,997	45	55
General Dynamics	$ 5,066,513	45	55
Northrop Grumman	$ 4,403,964	42	58
Raytheon	$ 3,889,165	48	52
Textron, Inc	$ 3,473,827	44	56
United Technologies	$ 3,264,059	48	52
Boeing	$ 2,591,306	46	54
TRW	$ 2,426,011	29	71
SAIC	$ 1,956,347	36	64

Source: Center for Responsive Politics www.opensecrets.org

"tag" key terrorists with special chemicals so they can be tracked by lasers anywhere on earth. Perhaps you're thinking, "But wait, if they can get to the terrorists to 'tag' them, why wouldn't they just . . . ?" Please, don't waste you breath. Tragically, these people were born without any commonsense genes. Besides, it's only money!

Psssssst. I have a secret to tell you. Pull the shades and sit down. The war machine costs you and me a lot more money than they want us to know about. A *whole lot* more. The White House, Pentagon, and Congress play a game that's much trickier than "Where's Waldo?"—hiding billions of war dollars inside other agencies:

- The War Resister's League calculates that half of NASA's budget and half of the Federal Emergency Management Agency's budget goes to reconnaissance and other military functions.
- More than a third of our foreign aid spending (so maligned by right-wingers as social welfare) goes straight into military and police operations abroad—the two largest recipients of foreign aid, Israel and Egypt, get three-fourths of theirs for military purposes.

- The stupid drug war, a waste of $19 billion a year, increasingly is being converted into a military operation abroad, especially in South America, where it's used to prop up the economic elites in struggles against rebels (in Colombia, for example, Bush has directed that our "drug war" dollars be used by the military to protect an Occidental Petroleum Co. pipeline that moves oil from the country's poverty-stricken interior to the coast for shipment to the U.S.).
- We pay tens of billions a year for past militarism, both in terms of former soldiers (military retirement pay, veterans hospitals, etc.) and in terms of interest paid on the national debt, more than half of which comes from past military buildups. (Thanks, Gipper, we needed that!)
- The Department of Energy's budget supplies billions to pay for the military's nuclear weapons stockpile and for the nuclear waste that comes from the military's nuke weapons factories.

THIS IS SICK

All those sophisticated, razzle-dazzle, video game weapons that we're shown on TV during any of today's remote-control wars are swell, but it's still the grunts who've got to do the dirty and deadly ground work. Yet the Bushites and Congress are leaving these essential troops "cash-poor and ill-equipped," according to disgusted senior army officers.

How ill-equipped? GET THIS: *The GIs who went cave to cave in Afghanistan in 2002 trying to root out al Qaeda forces were forced to buy their own gloves, cushioned socks, cargo belts, flashlights, padded rucksack straps, and other equipment!* The Pentagon eats more than a billion bucks of our money *a day*, but it doesn't supply the flashlights the grunts need to peek into killer caves?

The New York Times notes that last year's $690 million *cost overrun* on developing the unnecessary F-22 fighter jet would have paid for brand-new boots, fatigues, helmets, weapons, ammo, flak vests, night vision goggles, chem-bio protective suits, and other necessaries for the entire infantry, and then some.

That's not all of it. Now we have "The Thing"—Bush's $38 billion-a-year Homeland Security Department. Plus, the CIA, which is a $13 billion military operation, and the $4 billion FBI budget, which has been ratcheted away from fighting crime in our communities to a militaristic operation that spies on us in an often ridiculous, might-be, looks-like, who-knows effort to ferret out terrorists in our midst (it's not a good time to be dark-skinned and Muslim in America). And let's not even talk about "security" spending by state and local governments, airports, and other newly militarized budgets.

The Bushites literally wrapped their 2003 federal budget in the flag—the front and back covers of this document are wrapped by a slick, four-color photo of a rippling star-spangled banner. Inside, they offer a simple, budgeting-for-dummies pie chart that they labeled: "How Will the Federal Government Spend Your Tax Dollar in 2003?" Golly, the military slice was only 17 cents, so nothing to worry about there.

Except—*GASP!*—they were lying. Add in the hidden militarism, and take out some of the Enron-style accounting deception from the pie chart—and the total slice of Bush's budget allocated to military purposes is not 17 cents, but 56 cents out of every tax dollar . . . and growing.

Feeding the beast of empire can exhaust a county, but the Bushites are happy to do it. Why? Three reasons. First, they want empire. It's their thing, their mark on history. Second, the bulk of this spending goes to fatten their political cronies—Boeing, Lockheed Martin, Raytheon, GE, Oracle, and all the other warfare hogs that are dependent on military largesse. The military budget is a massive wealth transfer program from ordinary taxpayers to major corporations, and it has proven easy over the years to wrap this transfer in the red, white, and blue and have a portion of the American people burst out in a rousing chorus of the national anthem and applaud their own mugging.

Shortly after September 11, when Bush added $30 billion to the Pentagon budget and gave another $20 billion to Homeland Security, the eyes of these military contractors lit up like a fat man who'd just seen the Federal Express truck pull up with a full load of Twinkies. As one exulted: "I think it's real good news. This is probably going to be the first year of some very substantial investments in new technologies to create the new weapons systems to fight terrorism."

Among those grabbing with gusto was Boeing, which rushed to the front of the line for an extra-special gimmie that wasn't even new technology. Boeing deployed more than eighty lobbyists to win an appropriations amendment in December 2001 that *required* the air force to lease (not buy) one hundred of Boeing's wide-body commercial jets to be used as refueling tankers. Here's the math on Boeing's plunder: $20 million a year per jet × a 10-year lease on each jet × 100 jets = $20 billion.

Here's the stinker in the math: Twenty billion bucks to lease the jets is about four times what it would have cost the air force to buy them. Also, it will cost us taxpayers $3 billion more to convert the commercial planes to tankers. And in ten years the planes have to be reconverted to commercial use (yet another $3 billion) and returned to Boeing. All in the name of fighting terrorists.

Third, allocation of trillions of dollars over the foreseeable future to arm the empire means there's no money left for those rotten, weepy-eyed liberals to be frittering away on health care, Social Security, Head Start programs, and stuff. Need to spend $10 billion in the next decade just to bring America's existing school buildings up to code? Love to, pal, but no can do. Have another bake sale, and, here, hand out some of our "Leave No Child Behind" bumper stickers.

Here's a Republican president the Bushites should heed:

"GREED" DOESN'T SAY IT

Last year, I ran a name-the-scoundrel contest in my monthly newsletter, *The Hightower Lowdown*. Noting that we lacked adequate words to describe the perfidy of corporations that use Old Glory to disguise their looting, I invited readers to submit new words to fit the crime. The winners were:

Grabbiteurs
Profiteerists
Vulture Capitalists
Corporados
Corporats
Terrortunists
Pillage Idiots
Sleaze Whiz

This world in arms is not spending money alone. It is spending the sweat of its laborers, the genius of its scientists, the hopes of its children. . . .

This is not a way of life at all in any true sense. Under the cloud of war, it is humanity hanging on a cross of iron.

—DWIGHT EISENHOWER, 1953

LOCKING DOWN AMERICA

Clues that our national leaders have gone all slippery on the American people's inalienable right to liberty:

- John Ashcroft, perhaps our country's first certifiably cuckoo attorney general, threw up a blue screen last year to cover the twelve-foot-tall Art Deco statue called "The Spirit of Justice," which had reigned proudly over the Justice Department's Great Hall since the 1930s.
- The government's new computer database for screening airline passengers not only includes a secret "watch list" of U.S. citizens, but it also automatically pulls out passengers when the computer decides it does not have *enough* information on them.
- John Poindexter, the convicted Iran-Contra liar who's so autocratic he'd make a Nazi wince, was brought into the Pentagon by Bush to head an outlandish *1984*-ish agency to monitor every scrap of information on every American in every database. This omnibus prying-eye program was ominously labeled Total Information Awareness (official slogan: "Knowledge Is Power"), and it was so ugly that even Republican leaders in Congress gagged at the sight of it and effectively shut it down.

Just a month before his swearing-in, George W repeatedly said in talks before various groups, "If this were a dictatorship, it would be a lot easier—just so long as I'm the dictator." It was one of George's little jokes, but his handlers finally got him to quit using the line because, well, it was tacky, not funny, unpresidential—and not everyone was taking it as a joke.

If we'd only known! Three years later, the jokester and his cabinet cohorts have imposed a fundamental and systemic change in how America functions, undermining our historic and hard-won liberties with an autocratic, secretive, and invasive government, amassing an unprecedented concentration of power in the hands of the executive branch and federal police authorities. Thanks to their new rules, laws, and decrees, Big Brother is no longer a paranoid's nightmare, but is alive and very much on the prowl:

Were you at the rally?
Did you write a letter about the Florida vote tally?
Was that you at the mosque?
Have you ever criticized John Ashcroft?

Don't speak out, don't try to defy
Never question authority
Here's the reason why
BIG BROTHER IS WATCHING FROM ON HIGH!

HE'S

Reading your medical records
Scrutinizing your credit card bills
Searching your home or business without telling you
Patrolling your Internet use
Wiretapping your phone
Spying on you in your house of worship
Examining your travel records
Inspecting your bookstore purchases
Snooping on your library records
Monitoring your political activities

And these people claim to be the conservatives!

Perhaps you're the trusting type who would say to me, My dear Hightower, these are not measures to fear, but merely prudent steps that Messrs. Bush, Ashcroft, and other gentlemen of the watch have put in place to secure our peace, and our peace of mind, in the face of a changed world in which ugly, uncouth religious fanatics from beyond our shores threaten to destroy us and our way of life every second of every day—a small price to pay, I say, to preserve freedom in America.

Help me out, here. I know I'm not the brightest penny in the pile, but that last line, which the Bushites often use, confuses me. How do you have freedom without freedoms?

While I'm confessing confusion, let me add another perplexing point: It was not a lack of police and snooping powers that allowed the terrorists to steal airplanes and crash them into our buildings. Ample authority already existed for the FBI, CIA, INS, NSA, DIA, and other acronyms of expensive ineptitude to stop the hijackers—our "protectors" simply did a poor job with what they had. Why give dangerous, liberty-busting new authority to these same bumbling gendarmes?

> "It is times like this when the political system produces some of the craziest results and some of the biggest mistakes."
>
> —Rep. David Obey

Bush, Ashcroft, Ridge—the "Axis of Angst"—were not allowing any such questioning, however, as they eagerly reached for more tools of snoopervision and imprisonment to jack up the autocratic powers of their government.

Their first shot was a load of uglies packaged under a new law, clumsily titled the **U**niting and **S**trengthening **A**merica by **P**roviding **A**ppropriate **T**ools **R**equired to **I**ntercept and **O**bstruct **T**errorism Act. Yes: USA PATRIOT. The founding patriots would puke at such a perversion of the term by officials proposing to implement the very kind of imperious police powers that true patriots had rebelled against. Let's hear about it from Samuel Adams (the rebel, not the beer—though he was a brewer):

If ever a time should come, when vain and aspiring men shall possess the highest seats in Government, our country will stand in need of its experienced patriots to prevent its ruin.

They don't come vainer or more aspiring than John Ashcroft. The PATRIOT Act was his baby. It's a skunky spawn of 342 pages, giving federal agents broad new powers to spy, enter, intercept, tap, search, seize, detain, incarcerate, and prosecute— mostly on executive whim.

> *"I believe there's something out there watching over us. Unfortunately, it's the government."*
>
> —Woody Allen

While Jefferson, Madison, Old Ben, the original George W, and the rest of the revolutionary thinkers pondered at great length on the freedom-creating provisions of law that they crafted for us, the PATRIOT Act's undoing of their genius was slapdash and very rush-rush. In fact, Ashcroft demanded that his destructive bill be passed within three days!

It took a bit longer, but he got practically all of the new authoritarian powers he sought, with barely a peep of protest from Congress. Tom Daschle, the Senate Democratic leader, even tried to ram it through whole, without allowing amendments. When the Republican-led House Judiciary Committee showed a little spunk by adding a few protections for civil liberties, the White House got the House leadership to snatch the bill from committee and rewrite it in the dead of night to remove the provisions.

Of course, this was sold as an emergency response to a horrible attack on Americans by foreign terrorists, but here's a little bombshell that they didn't mention then or since: **The liberty-snatching provisions of the PATRIOT Act are not restricted to terrorists or foreigners. Most provisions specifically apply to U.S. citizens and are specifically available for police authorities to use in any and all federal investigations.**

Want to play the PATRIOT game? They play rough:

- The government is given expanded authority to run "sneak and peek" searches without notifying the person being searched, including investigations of American citizens in cases having nothing to do with terrorism.

- Police agents are now permitted to investigate you without showing probable cause, simply by designating their investigation as being for "intelligence purposes."
- Federal agents are given shortcuts around court review of their requests for wiretapping our phones and entering anyone's computer. Instead of a "request," which had required agents to show some reason for snooping, the new law allows agents merely to "certify" that the intrusion is relevant to an ongoing investigation. The judge *must* issue the order, even if the certification appears to be nonsense.
- The FBI is empowered to force libraries and bookstores to cough up lists of the books we have borrowed or bought.

Here's another fun part of the law: You might be a terrorist, too! It defines domestic terrorism as acts that "appear to be intended to influence the policy of a government by intimidation or coercion." Hello, peace protesters! Calling all abortion activists, on either side! Yoo-hoo, you union strikers and marchers! Attention, you demonstrators against the WTO, genetic pollution of our food, toxic waste dumps, or any other policies! Any people using anything remotely connected to direct action can be swept up in this catchall. Loose definitions are the playthings of would-be tyrants.

As if the PATRIOT Act wasn't punishment enough, the Bushites now have sprung PATRIOT Act II on us, which essentially amounts to Ashcroft on Viagra. It's such an atrociously un-American clampdown on our liberties that the Justice Department kept denying even to Congress that they were contemplating any sequel to PATRIOT Act I, much less secretly drafting one. It was not until the Center for Public Integrity obtained a leaked draft of this monster and put it on its website (www.publicintegrity.org) that Ashcroft's office had to quit lying and fess up to its plans for a PAT II. Among the horrors it proposed: authorizing secret arrests for the first time in U.S. history; taking American citizenship away from people who belong to or even support disfavored groups; giving more power to government agents to search our homes and personal records—from the prescription drugs we take to the books we check out of the library.

On top of their knee-jerk proclivity for autocracy, the Bushites added a big dollop of stupidity. They responded to September 11 by squealing: *I know what we'll do! We'll create a fat new bureaucracy. No, a Super-Bureaucracy, with two dozen existing agencies forced into it like some awful sausage made of gizzards, tripe, glands, and other bits of offal. It'll have everything from immigration agents to animal health inspectors, more armed federal agents than ever put in one organizational chart. Yes, let's jam it with 170,000 employees (whom we'll summarily strip of their union rights because . . . well, hell, just because we can—what a great country this is!). We'll give it $38 billion a year to play with, and how about a stout fascist-sounding name just to jangle the liberals: HOMELAND SE-CURITY. Yes, that'll do nicely, And we'll put Tom Ridge in charge, because we don't know what else to do with him (and we do owe Tom for making him stand up and announce those lunatic color-coded terrorist alerts—"Is it Red today, Tom?" "No, I'd say it's more of a Mauve." How ridiculous is that for an ex-governor to be doing?*

There. Feel safer? Sheesh! This horrendous hunk of bureaucratic junk isn't going to deter terrorists—170,000 employees, for example, and not a single one assigned to an Office of Stopping Guys with Box-cutters. Even Ridge admits that it'll take two to four years to get all the Homeland parts organized so the agency can function. Will al Qaeda be nice and wait?

Years ago, Jim Boren created the tongue-in-cheek National Association of Professional Bureaucrats. He issued three eternal guidelines for practitioners of the bureaucratic art: (1) When in charge, ponder. (2) When in trouble, delegate. (3) When in doubt, mumble. I would add a fourth: When flustered, reorganize. After September 11, Washington was totally flustered by the question of "What to do?" So they reorganized the government into the HSD.

In all fairness, though, the Homeland agency has its fans. One group, for example, loves it: corporate polluters. For many years, these poor, beleaguered spillers and spoilers have been bugged by the Freedom of Information Act and the right-to-know laws, which, drat it, require

BRING ME THE HEAD OF JOSE PADILLA

In some cases, Ashcroft has simply gone insane, including his bizarre performance over the 2002 arrest of Jose Padilla, a U.S. citizen who the AG claimed was a "significant" and "dangerous" terrorist tied to bin Laden's al Qaeda network.

Ashcroft, who was in Moscow at the time of the arrest, rushed to a local television studio to do a live satellite feed to all U.S. networks. He breathlessly declared to an astonished nation: "We have disrupted an unfolding terrorist plot to attack the United States by exploding a radioactive dirty bomb."

The weird announcement was made weirder yet by bad lighting in the Russian studio, which gave John what *The New York Times* described as "an eerie, Armageddon-like red glow.

Weirdest of all is the fact that it was all hokum. Two months after Ashcroft's alarm, the FBI had to concede that Padilla is just a Chicago street thug, a "small fish" with no ties to al Qaeda and no involvement in a dirty bomb plot. Yet Bush declared Padilla to be an enemy combatant and removed him from civilian jail to a military compound.

He is still being held there incommunicado, without charges, without any evidence having been presented, with no access to a lawyer, and with no plans to bring him to trial. Bush officials argue that he can be held until the government declares an end to its war on terrorism. Padilla should live so long

them to disclose some of their internal corporate information to the good-for-nothing public—information like how much of what toxic gunk the corporation is disgorging into the local water supply.

HSD to the rescue! As the Homeland law was being written, corporate lobbyists suddenly got patriotic, warning that terrorists could benefit by knowing such "critical infrastructure" information as what chemicals a plant is using or producing. Therefore, a provision was slipped into the law prohibiting all agencies of government from releasing any such information that a corporation gives to HSD. Cute. Now any corporate lawyer who can spell L-O-O-P-H-O-L-E has an out from public disclosure—anything the corporation wants to hide can be sent to HSD and safely tucked out of sight.

Bonus Gift: This HSD tuck-away also means that "critical infrastructure" information about a corporation's pollution, explosions, and other unpleasantness can't be dislodged for use in civil lawsuits that workers, neighbors, environmentalists, governments, or anyone else brings against the corporation. So why go to the expense of preventing pollution and safety problems when you can just hide them in HSD?

The lockdown of our democratic liberties, powers, and tools is ongoing, not only embedded in new laws, but also in the steady drip-drip-drip of executive directives, rulings, revisions, and other pronouncements:

- In a directive planned before September 11, Ashcroft notified all federal agencies in 2001 that they should reject all requests for documents under the Freedom of Information Act if there was even the slightest legal basis for doing so, promising that the Justice Department would defend them in court.
- Ashcroft issued new guidelines allowing the FBI to infiltrate churches and political organizations, and spy on U.S. citizens of any faith or political leaning even if there was no evidence of any criminal activity within the church or group.
- The CIA was "unleashed" to assassinate people, just like terrorists do.
- Ashcroft authorized detention camps for U.S. citizens who are declared by a Justice Department committee to be "enemy combatants," stripping these citizens of their constitutional right to an attorney and asserting that U.S. courts have no jurisdiction over these cases.
- Rumsfeld is considering a Pentagon proposal to abandon the Posse Comitatus Act, which prohibits the use of the military for domestic law enforcement.
- The Nuclear Regulatory Commission ruled that there could be no discussion

Now you're really scaring us, Tom

"Creating a new Department of Homeland Security is not the end of our reform efforts. It is the beginning."

—Tom Ridge

in a nuclear plant's licensing hearing about the facility's structural safety or vulnerability to a terrorist attack, because it might "unduly alarm the public."

- HSD was exempted from the whistleblower law, and Ridge was empowered to veto any audit or investigation by the agency's inspector general.
- Rumsfeld ruled that the Pentagon would no longer tell the public about the results of its Star Wars missile-defense tests, which have been embarrassing failures.

In a 2002 editorial cartoon for the *Milwaukee Journal Sentinel,* Gary Markstein drew a woman and a man walking down the street, casually chatting about the day's headline. The woman asks: "Why is it that ordinary citizens can be investigated, detained, interrogated, tried and punished secretly by the government with no legal protections?" The man responds: "So the terrorists won't erode our rights and freedoms."

With the zeal of all autocrats throughout history, the Bushites are using the fear of terrorism to make seismic changes in our nation's foundation of freedom—changes that We the People largely have not been told about, much less approved of. It's the nefarious beauty of their vague and limitless war on terrorism that they can hide so much from the press, Congress, and the people just by pointing excitedly to evildoers, shouting down voices of dissent with cries of "patriotism," and bulling their way forward with assertions that everything they do is necessary to protect our freedom!

How long will this go on? The Pentagon has devised a thirty-year war plan. Rumsfeld has said fifty years. Cheney has said for all of our lifetimes. After all, it works for them, so why would they ever choose to end it? It'll only end when you and I say "Enough," rising up to stop them from militarizing our society and trampling our liberties in pursuit of their empire. As a bumper sticker I've seen puts it: "Ignore your rights, and they'll simply go away." If our rights go away, so does America.

BE QUIET

Naturally, the Powers That Be prefer that we not be discussing any of this. More troubling, however, is that even some so-called progressive leaders of national groups have urged that we salute the president, fall in line, don't rock the boat, hunker down, swallow our dissent . . . be quiet.

Be Quiet? HOLY THOMAS PAINE! Since when do freedom-loving Americans cower in quietude? If you don't speak out when it matters, when would it ever matter for you to speak out?

Be Quiet? Notice that the corporate lobbyists aren't being quiet. In fact, they're being quite noisy, shouting "United We Stand" as a distraction while they unscrew the Capitol dome and reach in with their industrial-sized scoops to loot our country, grabbing subsidies, favors, and special breaks that they never could have gotten without wrapping their shameful avarice in the flag.

Be Quiet? We have no right to be quiet. Too many democracy fighters before us have fought, bled, and died to make it possible for us to speak out, dissent, protest, organize, and agitate in order to right our foundering ship of state. If we stay quiet, Bush and his autocratic, plutocratic pals win, and democracy, fairness, and justice lose.

Be Quiet? Silence is acquiescence. Worse, it amounts to a surrendering of our democratic vitality. After all, even a dead fish can go with the flow.

CHAPTER 5

The Wobblycrats

The Democratic Party of the nation ain't dead, though it has been givin' a lifelike imitation of a corpse for several years.

—GEORGE WASHINGTON PLUNKITT, Tammany Hall boss, 1905

In the 1950s, after my aunt Eula's husband, Ernest, died unexpectedly, she went to work as a waitress at a café in Maude, Texas, just outside of Texarkana. The café fronted U.S. 67, which then was the major highway to Dallas, linking several small East Texas towns to the larger world.

One day out of the blue, though, Eula took off. Flew the coop! It seems that a Mr. Green had entered the Maude Café and walked right into Eula's heart. He was a traveling salesman and apparently cut quite a dashing figure. That's about all we ever learned about him—I don't to this day, for example, know his first name.

But we do know that Eula was swept off her feet, spent a couple of days romancing with Mr. Green in Maude, then lit out for the West with him. Our first notice was a joyous postcard that landed in our mailbox all the way from Wyoming. Eula and Mr. Green had been to the Cheyenne Days Rodeo and Wild West Show out there, and what a time it was! They were off to Oregon next, said the card, full of Eula's giddiness.

But it was not to last. Somehow the whirlwind affair spun itself out—something about Mr. Green mistakenly thinking that maybe Eula had received a stash of money when Ernest died. So we got a mournful telephone call late one night from someplace in Oregon, and my folks sent some bus money up to her so we could bring Eula home.

While it didn't end happily with Mr. Green, it did for Eula. Back with her loved ones, she soon recovered and went on to enjoy a full life, living to be ninety. In fact, the thing I remember most about her is the lifelong cheerful spirit, optimism, and wonderful, soft laugh she had.

I think of Eula's fling when I look at my Democratic Party these days. It's run off with Mr. Green!

Green, as in the color of big political money. It has abandoned its loved ones, who yearn to have the party of Jefferson, FDR, Truman, JFK, and LBJ come home, back to the grass roots where us working folks, retirees, consumers, small farmers, independent businesses, young people, poverty families, and more need a champion. If we sent it bus money, would the Democratic Party come home?

Probably not, at least not right away. It has locked itself inside Washington, so infatuated with Mr. Green that it's doing unspeakable things there—not only dancing to the tune of Wall Street and the global corporate powers, but even sleeping with the Bushites!

The sad truth is that none of George W's agenda would be hanging around our necks without the complicity and often the direct support of national Democratic leaders. They've ditched the Red Wing work boot bunch and thrown in with the wing-tip crowd, going all wobbly on the whole concept of why America needs a Democratic Party.

Watch out, here come the Wobblycrats! The $1.3 trillion that Bush scooped right off the top of our public treasury and dumped on the rich would not have passed without the votes of twelve Wobblycrat senators. The vote for Ashcroft's liberty-sucking PATRIOT Act was 96 to 1 in the Senate (thank you, Sen. Russ Feingold), 337 to 79 in the House—overwhelmingly and almost unquestioningly backed by Wobblycrats. Rigging tax loopholes and loosening accounting rules for corporations was a specialty of the Wobbly Clinton Administration, with enthusiastic backing by the party's money-soaked congressional leaders. NAFTA and the WTO—twin sledgehammers giving global corporations the power to crush the strength of workers and environmentalists around the world—were rammed through Congress by Bill Clinton with Wobblycrat votes. The Homeland Security blob that further suffocates American freedom was passed 90 to 9 in the Senate, which was under Wobblycrat control at the time.

It's not just a legislative failure, though, it's a failure of spirit and purpose. The Democratic Party *exists* to be on the other side of these issues.

BASOPHOBICS

Perhaps it's not their fault. Perhaps the party leaders are suffering from an actual, clinical, and sometimes chronic condition called "basophobia." This occurs in physically sound people who won't even try to stand up, because they have an irrational but intense fear of falling down.

Oh my, but we don't have the votes to stand up to all the Republicans— Bush controls the whole government, oh my, oh my! wail the leaders of this once-proud party. But Bush didn't have the votes either on November 7, 2000, yet he took the presidency anyway. He didn't have the Senate in '01 and '02 either, but he rammed his agenda through anyway. Leadership—and winning—is about more than votes in Congress. It's about getting right in the face of BushCheney&Co. and not getting out; it's about standing with the peace movement, fair trade movement, human rights movement, civil liberties movement, and other grassroots people, giving them voice and unity against Bush's vainglorious reach for empire; it's about going to the people and waving the bloody shirt of the workers and of whole communities stabbed in the heart by Bush and his corporate Kleptocrats; it's about raising issues and hope and hell so the people can see that someone is on their side and willing to lead the fight for them.

Oh my, oh my, but George is so strong, he's got the war going for him— just read the polls—we can't stand up to that! You can read the polls . . . or your can *lead* the polls. If the Democratic Party would get in the debate, frame the people's issues with boldness and clarity, and get the hell out of Washington, fanning out across America week after week to talk directly with people rather than meekly waiting in line to get on *Meet the Press,* the poll numbers would change quickly and dramatically in favor of Democrats.

OH, SAY, CAN YOU SEE?

On election morning 2002, I opened the front section of *The New York Times* and immediately got a bad feeling. On page A3 was an eye-catching and ominous ad from Tiffany & Co. for a jeweled brooch in the form of a waving American flag. In tasteful type just below the ruby, diamond, and sapphire rendering of the red, white, and blue was this message: "Vote! The privilege is precious."

It was the perfect pitch to rally the privileged to the polls for their president—a fellow who, after all, had provided a generous tax cut that makes trifles like this $8,000 brooch so easily affordable for those at the top. The ad said to me that the comfortable set was feeling its oats and would be turning out in droves to support their precious W. And why wouldn't they turn out? Their flag-bearer had been energetically crisscrossing the country, proudly holding the wealth banner aloft, promising to make the tax cut permanent, and saying in no uncertain terms: I'm on your side, I'll deliver for you.

But where was the flag of the once mightily progressive Democratic Party? For most Americans, it was nowhere to be seen. It's hard to rally to a flag that's not waving.

Oh my, oh my, but didn't you watch Bush's sweep of last year's congressional elections? He's got all that money, he's got Karl "Achtung!" Rove running the GOP juggernaut, he's now won a mandate! Oh my! How can we beat that? OK, let's calm down here and take a reality sponge bath, if not an actual soak in the tub.

The Dismal Campaign

You know you had a rough election when one of '02's electoral bright spots for progressives was in the Oklahoma referendum to ban cockfighting—which we won with 56 percent of the tally! O progress. But it shows that issues do matter.

In the nationwide congressional races, however, progressive issues were stuffed in the closet, issues that might have roused the Democratic base—such as shifting payroll taxes to the rich, outlawing corporate greed, raising wages, getting health care for everyone, opening up college to working stiffs, etc. Instead, with a few notable and successful exceptions (Raul Grijalva in Tucson and Chris Van Hollen in Maryland, just to name two), the party's congressional candidates *ran away from* what could help them win:

- Enron, WorldCom, and all that barf-inducing corporate slime? *Uh, well, you see, we took their money, too, and let's not piss off those guys, 'cause we'll want more money, you know?*
- Bush's preposterous trillion-dollar tax gift to the wealthiest people on earth? *Oh, about that, uh, a lot of us voted for it, so . . .*
- George's Iraq Attack, putting the kids of working families and poor people on the line while the well-off families (including George's) get to watch it on Fox and CNN? *Well, now, we can't be unpatriotic! We voted for Bush on this one, so best just cheer the commander-in-chief and move on.*

What we had, then, was an election in which one side essentially chose not to contest the other. Here's the Democratic bumper sticker for its congressional candidates:

Hey-we-back-tax-cuts-for-the-rich-too-And-we-support-Bush's-war-and-also-his-Big-Honking-Homeland-Security-Department-Though-we're-not-quite-as-sure-about-it-all-as-the-Republicans-are-so-vote-for-us

It's hard for the donkeys to win the race if they're going to carry the elephants on their backs.

A textbook example of the party's patented formula for failure came in the Louisiana Senate race. In a state that has never elected a Republican senator, Democratic incumbent Mary Landrieu was a shoo-in. Daughter of a popular former mayor of New Orleans, she had name ID, the full power of incumbency, and three times as much money as her Republican opponent, who was an unknown, bumbling, right-wing novice and whose highest public position had been to serve one term as state elections commissioner.

Yet Landrieu boasted in her campaign ads that she had voted with Bush 74 percent of the time in the Senate—a more servile loyalty than many Republican senators gave! Mary went on national TV to say she had voted for Bush's tax package for the rich and wanted to return to the Senate so she could join him in making this special giveaway permanent. Imagine how excited this made the base of the Democratic voters in Louisiana—a state where nearly *half* of the population lives in households with *less than $15,000 a year in income*!

She was stunned when the poor and near poor simply took a pass on her election, forcing a runoff with the GOP nobody in Louisiana's free-for-all general election system. Explaining the poor turnout of the poor, a prominent black state senator said bluntly: "One Republican Party is enough. Two Republican parties is almost unconstitutional."

Landrieu also was losing her runoff race until she finally shifted to focusing on the issues of working people—and until, at 4 P.M. on the day of the runoff, Bill Clinton personally got on the phone to beg the black leadership in New Orleans to kick their get-out-the-vote machinery up to maximum. She won by only 39,814 votes statewide, saved by the very base she had scorned in her Senate service.

That night Senate Democratic leader Tom Daschle crowed that Landrieu's win "proves that the Democrats are alive and well." Take a cold shower, Tom. Her squeaker proves that Democrats better come home, or they're doomed to a hell of their own making.

CHOO-CHOO, CHA-BOOGIE

Q: What's the opposite of progress?
A: Congress.

In the last Congress, Democrats faced one of those whose-side-are-you-on, gut-check issues. It was over a vote on an arcane procedural rule called "Fast Track," which would let Bush bypass the normal legislative process and—literally—railroad more job-destroying, environment-whacking NAFTAs through Congress.

Like a boy eyeing a toy, George W loved the idea of Fast Track, not only because it would help his corporate patrons, but also because it would weaken democratic checks over his authoritarian whims.

But, surprise: When the vote was taken in the House, the forces of greed lost by a single vote. Hooray!

Never count out greed, though. In an unprecedented act of cheating (and that's saying something for Congress!), the White House got GOP leaders to refuse to gavel the vote closed. The clock had ticked to zero, the vote was tallied . . . but they held the vote open for *23 more minutes* while they surrounded a South Carolina Republican who'd voted against Fast Track and browbeat him until he switched to "yes."

To paraphrase Mo Udall, the difference between a cactus and Congress is that on a cactus, the pricks are on the outside.

But that one-vote switch shouldn't have mattered. Twenty-one Democrats had already voted with Bush.

Then the issue went to the Senate, where Democrats had a majority. But many of them also sided with the corporate powers, and majority leader Tom Daschle meekly negotiated a surrender in which Bush got his zippy Fast Track toy—and workers who'll lose their jobs because of Fast Tracked trade scams got a temporary health care extension. Corporations got the gold mine, and we got the shaft.

"I'm disappointed we couldn't do more," said the leader of the Democrats, "but I'm also appreciative of the fact that we've got to move on." Yeah, Tom, thanks for being there for us.

The Mandate

"GOP sweeps," trumpeted the headlines after last year's congressional elections, and the heavily moussed pundits of the airwaves were unanimous in hailing the brilliance of the Rove/Bush strategy. Now Bush can claim the mandate that eluded him in '00, marveled the pundits, practically in unison.

Mandate? Hold your tiny pony right there, George. The great majority of the people either didn't vote or voted against your autocratic, plutocratic regime. Curtis Gans of the Committee for the Study of the American Electorate reports that in the congressional races, where Bush claims his mandate, only about one-third of eligible voters could stomach casting a ballot. And 15 percent voted for Democrats, while 1.1 percent voted for candidates from Libertarian, Green, Working Families, Independent, or other parties.

So let's blow the foam off this beer. **The "Big Mandate" that the Bushites are claiming for themselves comes down to a puny 17 percent of the people.**

That's the Republican base, not a juggernaut. It's the same 17 percent that they won twenty years ago in the midterm elections during the Reagan infatuation, and it's nearly three points less than they got in the '94 midterms when Newt Gingrich surged to power.

Now, just as Newt did in his famous four-year flameout, the Bushites are pushing a corporatist and extremist agenda that is anti-working families, anti-poor people, anti-women, anti-environment, anti-liberty, and pretty damned much anti everyone who doesn't fit comfortably inside their 17 percent core group.

Also they've elected Tom DeLay to be their majority leader and their loudest voice in the House. This guy is Newt without the charm—not only is he a rabid right-winger and notorious corporate bagman, he's delusional. He has even declared that the Lord God Almighty is behind the GOP win and is using Tom himself as a godly instrument to promote "a biblical worldview" in American politics.

This is not a group determined to erect the welcoming Big Tent of political and economic inclusiveness.

But what are the Democrats going to do to break—dare we dream?—15 percent? The group now controlling the party apparatus calls itself the Democratic Leadership Council. It's corporate-funded, has a Republican-lite agenda, and practices political minimalism. Forget the party's base, is the DLC's message—instead appeal to a narrow strata of conservative-tilting soccer moms and office-park dads. The strategy is to appear not to be scruffy, working-family Democrats, but to dress up as the moderate wing of the Republican Party, hoping to siphon away two or three points from the GOP's 17 percent plurality. It's a loser strategy, as was forcefully demonstrated in the '02 elections, but it's also a cowardly one unworthy of a party that has been known in the past as The People's Party.

Putting the *Demos* Back in "Democrat"

In the mid-1970s, during Lloyd Bentsen's first term as U.S. senator, the Congressional Research Service got a query from the office of the multimillionaire Texas patrician: "What is a populist? Senator Bentsen thinks he might be one."

HA-HA! And I might be the king of France! Bentsen, while nominally a Democrat, was the political patron saint of bankers, insurance companies, and Wall Street investment houses—the opposite side of the well-secured gates from us populists. Unfortunately, the Democratic Party went with him, and in the years since, the party has seen its money rise and its voter turnout fall.

So excuse my impertinence here, but let me take a wild flier at something a tad different from the present Democratic strategy of collecting money from corporations and hurling it at television stations, hoping to seduce politically fickle soccer moms. What if Democrats went to the people? No, seriously! I mean really go to the people. You know, *in person.*

All of the people, is my thought, the snuffdippers as well as beansprout eaters. Wait—a voice is trying to reach me now. Yes, Eleanor . . . I hear you. (Shhhh, it's Eleanor Roosevelt.) Go where? Go where the Democratic voters are? Well, sure, why not! Democrats have tried winning over Republicans, so what's to lose by—think of the genius of this—appealing directly to: Democrats.

Specifically, what if the party reached out to the two-thirds of disenchanted to disgusted folks who aren't voting? Overwhelmingly, they're working stiffs and the poor (often both in the same person, thanks to today's wondrous economy—a twofer). That's 121 million people who are politically homeless. Add even 10 percent of them, and the Democrats start winning every race.

What does it take to win over such people, Hightower? You're going to think I've gone barmy beyond belief, but I'd suggest this appeal: self-interest. Just as Bush's base supporters respond warmly, even lovingly, to George's unabashed support of their interests, so might the Great Un-wanted begin to warm to politics if Democrats began to speak their lan-guage. Here's a short to-do list we could offer that would strengthen America by investing in the workaday majority:

1. A tax cut on working stiffs: Remove the cap (now at $85,000) on the grossly regressive payroll tax, reduce the percentage bite on people making less than that, and spread the burden up to include the bil-lionaires' club.
2. Health care for all, provided by a single-payer system.
3. Free education for everyone, preschool through higher ed, modeled after the enormously successful GI Bill.
4. Energy independence for America through a ten-year moon-shot project that'll put Americans to work building an oil-free future based on alternative technologies and systems.
5. Public financing of all elections, so we can get our government back from the greedheads.
6. [Add your favorite here.]

A six-pack is plenty. Stay focused.

Well, Hightower, I see you want to move the Democrats back to the wasteland of the left. No, stupid, the need is not to move left or right, but move out into America and get on the side of the majority of people who are alternately being ignored and stomped on by the economic and political elites of our country. As Paul Wellstone used to put it: "I'm in the democratic wing of the Democratic Party."

And when I say "move out," I mean literally and figuratively get out of Washington. At present, progressive groups and funders direct prob-ably 80 percent of their energy, talent, and money toward D.C., putting only 20 percent into the countryside. Yet our strength is not inside the Beltway but out here, where people are doing great things and wonder-ing why the Democratic Party isn't with them. Reverse that ratio and start focusing on building a grassroots organization across America, or-ganizing and mobilizing, block by block.

Politics can't be viewed as something that involves people only in the last thirty days of an election. Rather, to be a movement capable of governing, it has to be rooted in people's reality right where they live. In addition to a high-tech outreach, we have to get back to a high-touch politics that physically, emotionally, and soulfully connects with people's lives 365 days a year. Yes, talk issues. But communicate through potluck suppers, block parties, festivals, salons, and saloons.

Let's Put the Party Back in Politics. There's a bumper sticker.

Nothing's more fun than winning, and winning in politics requires getting more people (not more money) than the other side gets. To get people, there has to be a long-term strategy of listening to them, appealing to them, enlisting them, and trusting them. As the fighting populist Fred Harris puts it: "You can't have a mass movement without the masses."

II. AMERICA THE POSSIBLE
(The Good News)

CHAPTER 6

Even the Smallest Dog Can Lift Its Leg on the Tallest Building

It's never easy taking on power. Yet still we do it, again and again. It's intrinsic, central to who we are.

Wouldn't this be a good time for a sports metaphor, Hightower? Yes, I think it would. After all, sports at its best is an extension of our human aspirations and frailties—and of our general perseverance against mischievous gods, who always seem to enjoy throwing stuff at us just to see what we'll do, like kids messing with ants. But that's mixing metaphors, which the book gods frown on, so back to sports as a metaphor for challenging the powerful.

Maybe you've seen the movie *Bull Durham,* about the travails and triumphs of various characters involved in a minor league baseball team. In one scene, the team's veteran catcher, named Crash, is giving media-relations pointers to a kid named Nuke, who's a fireballing pitcher and a rising star:

CRASH: It's time you started working on your interviews.
NUKE: What do I gotta do?
CRASH: Learn your clichés. Study them. Know them. They're your friends.

So let's examine a trio of the hoariest clichés in sports:

"The Bigger They Are, the Harder They Fall"
Back in my football-playing days with the Denison High School Yellow Jackets, this was a favorite line of our coaches. They used it often, since

just about every team we played was bigger than us, not to mention quite a bit better. (How bad was our team? So bad that *I* was a defensive starter, even though I weighed only 115 pounds. "Scrappy" is how Coach Herman Bailey described me, which was code for: He's not any good, but he's stupid, so he just keeps throwing his scrawny body at 'em and every now and then one trips over him.) Still, there was that David v. Goliath thing that held out the possibility each week of our defying the gods and winning one. "Boys," the coach would bark at us in his pregame pump-up, "just remember: The bigger they are . . ."

What he didn't tell us, and undoubtedly didn't know, is that this cliché first came from the lips of Bob Fitzsimmons in 1902. He was a heavyweight boxer about to fight for the crown against the reigning champ, who outweighed Fitzsimmons by thirty-nine pounds. "The harder they fall" was a great line, but the big guy knocked Fitzsimmons out in the eighth round.

"Oh Well, You Can't Win 'Em All"

Another classic cliché used often by my coaches *after* our games, for obvious reasons. Still, this is the sporting spirit, and I daresay the human spirit, bucking ourselves up, dusting off, and, by golly, looking forward, not backward, ready to give it another go at the next chance. Again, my coaches would not have studied the line's origin, but this one is attributed to Cliff Curtis, a pitcher for the old Boston Braves. After a loss in 1911, Cliff said, "Oh well . . ." Attaboy, Cliff, that's the spirit. Still, it was Cliff's twenty-third *consecutive* loss.

"Let's Pull an Upset"

Now here's an upbeat cliché to end our set, for it shows that, hard as it is to challenge the odds, people must keep trying, for it's by trying that *we do win*. This term comes from a thoroughbred horse race in 1919. There was a famous and powerful horse named Man o' War—still considered one of the greatest champions ever. But in this race, Man o' War was bested by an unheralded horse named: Upset. Until then, the term applied only to being disturbed or to overturning something, like a vase. But this underdog of a horse gave "upset" a new meaning—and gave all of us strivers a rallying cry for doing the impossible.

REBELLION IS WHAT BUILT AMERICA

As I roam around the country speechifying at various events, invariably there's one person in the crowd who'll stand up during the Q & A period or come up to me after the talk and hit me with a comment that goes something like this: *Wwwwwwwwwhhhhhhiiiiiiiiiiiiiiiiiinnnnnnnnneeeeee.* Actually, the whine is slightly more specific, along the lines of:

> *What you're saying about fightin' to get our country back is fine and good, but I gotta tell ya that the people I know just wanta make money and go to Wal-Mart to buy junk and take their kids to McDonald's to eat junk, and they don't care, and I try to tell 'em about what corporations are doin' to us, but the dummies get all their information from the boob tube and talk radio, which the corporations control, like you were saying, and the polls show that Bush is still popular with people despite him screwin' 'em every day in every way, and meanwhile their side has all the money, the media, the politicians, the military, and how're we ever gonna beat that—sometimes I think it's hopeless, besides, I'm gettin' worn out and I'm not gettin' any younger, so when are we gonna win, and why aren't the people in the streets like we were back in the '60s—now that was a time, and maybe you don't remember what was goin' on back then, but lemme tell ya somethin'. . . .*

Whew! Sperm whales can't go that long without taking a breath! Nor do they go down so low or stay down as long as these pessimists do—nor spew so much froth when they surface. By the time an old wheezer like this runs out of breath, the crowd is fidgeting, the young folks are rolling their eyes, and some hisses are rising around the room like steam venting. My response usually is to interrupt gently about the time Ol' Wheezer is going to take a deep dive into the '60s, and say as politely, soothingly, and considerately as I can: GIVE ME A BREAK! COME ON, QUIT YOUR BELLY-ACHING, GUT IT UP, KEEP FIGHTING OR GET OUT OF THE WAY!

Here's the truth

"If there is no struggle, there is no progress.

"Those who profess to favor freedom, and yet deprecate agitation, are men who want crops without plowing up the ground. They want rain without thunder and lightning. . . .

"Power concedes nothing without a demand. It never did and it never will. . . . Men may not get all they pay for in this world, but they must certainly pay for all they get."

—Frederick Douglass

Of course it's hard to battle the bastards! So what's new? History—and certainly the history of our country—is the story of people struggling, always going uphill against the powerful to seek a little more democracy, a tad more justice, a slightly wider sliver of the economic pie. Old Mr. Power, The Man, The Machine—by whatever name, the establishment is not in the giveaway business. Striving for democracy is bone-wearying, agonizing, frustrating, cruel, bloody, and often deadly work. "You should never have your best trousers on when you go out to fight for freedom and truth." Henrik Ibsen said that, but he didn't mean by it that we should stay home and press our pants, rather that we should gird up accordingly and go forth into the fray.

Look at what we have in America, at the priceless opportunity that has been handed to you and me by those who've dared to make this struggle in past years. Very few people in today's world, and very, very few in history, have even had the *possibility* of trying to create an egalitarian society ruled by the common good. Those who came before us risked all of their property, their reputations, their freedom, and their lives to push the boundaries of democracy for us.

And you're telling me that *you're* tired or impatient that the promised land has not yet been reached? A little perspective, please:

• Daniel Shays, a Revolutionary War veteran, organized Shays' Rebellion in New England in 1780. A poor farmhand, he'd fought at Lexington, Bunker Hill, and Saratoga. He was wounded in action, but he never got paid for his service in the army, so finally he quit and went home, only to find himself in court for nonpayment of debts! It turns out that the blessings of America's newly won liberties were not meant to be extended to riffraff like Shays—they could fight, but they couldn't vote or run for office. So Shays gathered up a ragtag army of one thousand outcasts like him and led a rebellion against the merchant and landed classes of America's new "democracy." The farmers sought justice, but it was not to come in their lifetimes, for they were soon routed. Shays lost it all—his rebellion, his freedom, his livelihood—later dying in poverty. Yet his revolt helped advance the cause, awakening more people, including some of the founding elites, to the hypocrisy in their democracy, eventually leading to more rights and an extension of voting to citizens like Shays. Indeed, it was Shays' uprising and others like it at the time that prompted Jefferson to write to a friend: "I hold it that a little rebellion now and then is a good thing. . . . God forbid that we should ever be twenty years without such a rebellion."

- Elizabeth Cady Stanton, Lucretia Mott, Lucy Stone, Susan B. Anthony, Sojourner Truth, Sarah and Angelina Grimké, and others organized a movement in the 1840s to obtain voting rights for women. They were ridiculed, harassed, and defeated again and again. None of the founders lived to cast a single vote. But they advanced the cause, eventually won some seventy-five years later with the passage of the Nineteenth Amendment in 1920.

- Some names you should know, but probably don't, since school textbooks delicately avoid the common heroes of America's story, are: Big Bill Haywood, Clara Lemlich, A. Philip Randolph, Elizabeth Gurley Flynn ("The Rebel Girl"), and John L. Lewis. These are but a few who have been the fighters (literally, in many cases) for American labor, challenging brutal corporate power that uses everything from the national guard to hired thugs to break the skulls of labor leaders and break the back of the

GET THIS BOOK, READ IT, AND USE IT:

A People's History of the United States, by Howard Zinn

labor movement. Few of these lived to see the success they envisioned, yet all advanced the cause for economic justice that has now gone global.

- Native Americans not only had their lands stolen—beginning in the East and pushing across the upper Midwest, the South, the Southwest, the Plains, the Far West, and eventually everywhere—but also had their populations decimated in what was one of the longest, most horrific terrorist campaigns ever. As explained by one of the worst terrorists, General William T. Sherman, in 1867: "The more Indians we kill this year, the less will have to be killed in the next war." But still the Natives persevered, and they fight yet today to advance the cause of justice for a long-suffering people targeted for annihilation by a succession of presidents, congresses, and generals in the Land of the Free.

- The struggle for civil rights for African Americans didn't begin (or end) in the '60s. It started when the first slave was put on a boat to America, and it has moved steadily through slave rebellions, the abolitionists, the Civil War, the vicious terrorism of Jim Crow, the Klan, civil rights marches and murders, Bull Connor's dogs, Malcolm X, and on into today and tomorrow, each generation advancing the cause, step by hard step.

> "A child born to a black mother in a state like Mississippi . . . has the same rights as a white baby born to the wealthiest person in the United States. It's not true, but I challenge anyone to say it is not a goal worth working for."
>
> —Thurgood Marshall

Inhale a bit of our country's pungent, brawling, inspiring history of grassroots rebels, then tell me that battling the bastards today is too hard, too uphill, or takes too long. What are you doing that is more worthy of your efforts than trying to establish the moral principles of fairness, justice, and equality for all in our America?

Well, you say, *Hightower, I've got a family to care for.* Of course, and that's first. But stretch a little on what "care for" includes. Bettering their lives and yours is also about making a better America right in your own community. I'm not talking about quitting your day job and becoming a full-time Thomas Paine. But do what you can, where you can, and especially reach out to others to be a part of a group—or two or three groups, or better yet a coalition of groups, so our individual efforts are multiplied as we try, bit by bit, to take our country and our ideals back from the elites who have stolen them. Plus, I can tell you from experience: It's fun! In fact, joining with others in the ongoing, historic effort to realize the *great possibility* of America is just about as much fun as you can have with your clothes on.

GET WITH THE PEOPLE

Some thirty years ago, Lee Trevino became one of the first people of color to crack what had been a cozy, country club, white-bread world of professional golf. He went on to become one of the game's greats. After he first hit it big and pocketed a few winner's checks, he bought a fine home in one of Dallas's upscale, all-Anglo neighborhoods. Shortly after moving his family in, he was outdoors washing the windows of his house when a well-manicured, jewel-bedecked woman of means pulled her Lincoln to the curb, summoned Trevino over to her, and asked how much he charged to do windows. "Lady," he said, "the woman in this house lets me sleep with her."

You can imagine the window of that big Lincoln—*bzzzzzz*—going up as fast as could be in Trevino's face as that lady dropped the car into drive and screeched out of there.

Stereotypes can be tricky, including the one that the Powers That Be have drawn of We the People, telling us that we're essentially a conservative, Bush-happy bunch of consumer-minded drones content with the way things are going. This is, of course, a convenient picture for those in power, and it's repeated to us in the "news," in advertising, in politics, and in so many other ways that we begin to believe it as well—not about ourselves, but about other people.

In my travels, I regularly hear people say to me, "Well, *I'm* all for a national health system that'll serve everyone, but the public won't even consider the idea," or they'll say, "I *personally* favor doin' what needs to be done to clean up the air and water, but the majority of people don't want to do anything that gets in the way of growth."

(READERS' WARNING: I'm going to have to use some technical jargon here. Sorry. Skip ahead if you're allergic.) The Public Opinion Survey Industry has a phrase that applies to the aforementioned widespread perception that people of the progressive persuasion are in a tiny minority on the big questions of public policy. Their technical phrase is: "Liar, Liar, Pants on Fire!"

In fact, the members of the public (aka the Great Unwashed, the Hoi Polloi, the Hillbillies, the Flyover People, the Rabble, the Cudchewers, or simply "Them") are quite progressive, both in their hearts and on specific issues. The Bush agenda? It's bushwa (an actual word meaning "rubbishy nonsense") to most of the folks.

While it doesn't get much media coverage, and while the politicos of both parties ignore it, polling data consistently find that people largely are with us—and not with Bush. I'm not referring here to some single poll taken among the twenty-seven card-carrying members of the Order of Left-Handed Socialist Cabbies in the Borough of the Bronx, but to the steady flow of conventional polls taken over the last several years—polls from CNN/*USA Today,* Pew Center Survey, Gallup, Fox News, NBC/*Wall Street Journal,* CBS/*New York Times,* ABC/*Washington Post,* and other peers of the Official Society for Keeping the Lid on the Kingdom (OSK-LOK). Samples? Sure:

Budget Priorities

Bush says this is a no-brainer (and who would know better about that?), that the first thing people want in the way of spending priorities is tax cuts, tax cuts, tax cuts—so he's just doing the people's will with his multitrillionous-dollar assault on the public treasury.

Maybe he's doing the will of the people who give large chunks of campaign cash to him, but it's not the will of The People:

- 67 percent would prefer to have more spending on such needs as education and health care than to have Bush's latest tax cut (ABC/*Washington Post*).

- By a two-to-one margin, the public thinks that Bush's tax plan will benefit the wealthy, not all Americans (NBC/*Wall Street Journal*).
- If there's to be a tax cut, 58 percent think it should be targeted to middle-income and low-income folks, while 40 percent think taxes should be cut equally for all income brackets—I'm not great at math, but I think that leaves only 2 percent thinking it's a good idea to target tax cuts for the rich, as Bush is doing (Pew Research Center).
- Instead of federal funds being given away as tax cuts, 74 percent prefer that the money be used to stabilize Social Security (Fox News).

Speaking of Social Security, should this trust fund's surplus be spent for domestic programs, including tax cuts, as George is doing? Good God Almighty, NO! shout 79 percent of the people—and 78 percent of *Republicans* say the same thing (CBS News). What about using the surplus for "national defense and homeland security"? asks a wrapped-in-the-flag poll: Nyet, uh-uh, no, go away, say 77 percent of the public (CNN/*USA Today*).

Health Care

The insurance giants and HMOs convinced the media that the people rejected the very idea of a national health plan back in '94, when Bill and Hillary botched their feeble effort to pass a plan. So don't even think about it, is today's conventional wisdom—and, sure enough, the media and politicos don't, instead fussing around the margins of the health care mess; the current "debate" is over how many of the elderly poor should get a prescription drug program.

Meanwhile—*Hellooooo*—41 million of us have no health coverage at all, and most of us who supposedly are covered pay a ransom to the insurance greedheads for a policy that doesn't cover anything ending in "itis" and that requires us to see a doctor who lives in the woods, takes appointments only when there's a full moon, and demands upfront payment in gold bullion. Of course, the media and the politicos have full Cadillac coverage (paid by us taxpayers in the case of Congress and the White House) so, hey, where's the problem? While the elites have their heads up their own butts, ordinary people continue to want a government program to assure good health care for all:

- 64 percent say it's the federal government's *responsibility* to make sure all Americans are covered (Gallup).
- More than half say government should create a plan to cover everyone *even if it requires a tax increase* (*Washington Post*/Kaiser Family Foundation).
- 89 percent say that our Medicare program should provide prescription drugs for all seniors, and 81 percent say this should be done even if it requires them to pay more taxes (ABC News).
- 81 percent say patients ought to be able to sue their HMOs for mistreatment (Kaiser Family Foundation).

Public Education

George W, right-wing activists, the privatization profiteers, and much of the media have pretty much said: To hell with the public schools, let's create a private system using tax dollars. But while the people have been saying for years that public schools are generally a mess (though they usually give good marks to the schools their own children attend), they by no means want to abandon the public system:

- 98 percent (!) say they favor continuing the government guarantee of a free public education (Democratic Leadership Council).
- 71 percent say educational improvements should focus on reforming the existing public school system rather than finding an alternative to it, and 75 percent favor improving public schools over providing vouchers for private schools (Gallup).
- 73 percent say there is *too little* education spending—only 7 percent say too much (Gallup).
- 70 percent are willing to pay more in taxes if the money went to education, and 84 percent would pay more taxes if the money went specifically to raising teacher salaries, reducing class size, fixing rundown schools, improving security, and putting more computers in classrooms (NBC/*Wall Street Journal*).

Environment

The Bushites have never seen a spot too sacred to drill for oil, a tree that they wouldn't turn to sawdust, a wetland they wouldn't suck dry, a . . .

well, you get the point. For this gang, Green is about money. Period. Let's hope oil is not discovered under the White House, or you'll see derricks on the South Lawn. (Impossible, you say, too tacky for anyone to do? Check out the state capitol grounds in Oklahoma City sometime— oil rigs with corporate logos on them, merrily pumping away!) If aesthetics are an issue they can just take out the elevator in the Washington Monument and put the drill in there.

Again, BushCo is on the wrong side of public opinion:

- Six out of 10 Americans say the U.S. government is doing too little to protect the environment from corporate plunderers—only 10 percent say it's doing too much, which presumably is the pro-plunder vote that Bush is playing to (Gallup).
- Two-thirds say that environmental protections should be the priority, even at the risk of curbing economic growth (Gallup), though 68 percent reject the idea that the environment and growth have to be at odds (Wirthlin Worldwide).
- 67 percent feel *strongly* that our country should do whatever it takes to protect the environment, with only 5 percent feeling strongly that we've gone too far (Pew Research Center).

Trade Deals

In the abstract, we Americans have long approved of the liberal notion of "free trade" among countries. But few of us live in a place called Abstract, and we've since learned the hard way (lost jobs, lost farms, shuttered factories, deserted communities) that the old liberal notion of free trade has been corporatized, turning the "free" into a verb, meaning to free the traders to impose their ethic of greed on all the peoples of the world.

Yet, Clinton, Bush, and leaders of both parties in Congress continue to hang more trade deals around our necks, against the oft-polled will of us folks back home who pay the price for "free" trade:

- 64 percent say global trade pulls down, rather than pushes up, U.S. wages (Market Strategies/Committee for Free Trade).

- Two-thirds say large corporations are the ones that benefit from the trade deals, while about the same percent say workers are hurt by them (Peter Hart).

> **The official attitude**
>
> *"I can't believe that we are going to let a majority of the people decide what is best for this state."*
>
> —Louisiana Rep. John Travis

- 72 percent say the White House and Congress give too little consideration to working Americans when making global trade policy (University of Maryland).
- 73 percent believe that worker rights and environmental issues should be made a central part of all trade agreements (Wirthlin Worldwide).
- Even larger majorities want certain specific issues made central to trade deals: the right to form unions (78 percent), minimum wage based on a country's poverty line (81 percent), freedom to strike/protest (92 percent), prohibition of child labor (93 percent), protection for workplace health (94 percent) (Peter Hart).

A VEIL OF IGNORANCE

I'm a big fan of the funny pages, and one comic strip that I like a lot these days is called "Pearls Before Swine," which features a rat and a pig, plus a supporting cast of a zebra, a goat, and other anthropomorphic animals. In one strip, the rat, who is considered the smart one, and the pig, considered dumb, are sitting together. Rat asks, "If you could have a conversation with one person, living or dead, who would it be?" Pig answers, "The living one." Then he adds, "You must really think I'm stupid."

Maybe I'm stupid (no need to shout a chorus of agreement, here—it's just a figure of speech, a writer's artifice), but there's one dead guy I wish I could talk with: John Rawls. He died last year at age eighty-two. He was a political philosopher, and some scholars rank him in importance right up there with John Locke, John Stuart Mill, and Immanuel Kant.

I didn't know of him until his death, but as I read of his work and ideas, I realized my entire political life is based on an instinctive belief in theories that he developed and articulated. My belief, unburdened by any academic study, is that we can trust the regular folks of our country—and trust them *with* our country.

Quite a few political types—on the left as well as on the right—disagree strongly, saying that you don't want the bubbas making any big decisions. Of course there are some ugly people out there, but my experience has been that, given half a chance and good information, even the bubbas (and, I daresay, *especially* the bubbas) will do the right thing most every time, choosing what's best for the common good.

It's not that I believe in the Fairy Godmother of Saintly Altruism, but I believe that the self-interest of most people generally coincides with the common good. Hence the depth of support for the public schools, public libraries, and other things public, even in a time when nearly all the cultural forces are pushing privatization.

Example: In Colorado Springs, a place where the leading industry is the manufacture and distribution of right-wing ideology (How right wing is it? The town removed all left-turn lanes. *Ba-da boom*), environmentalists and neighborhood activists put a proposal before the city council a few years ago to expand trails, open space, and parks. A socialist plot, screamed some of the council members, we don't need government building more parks!

But to the surprise of the ideologues, the people of the Springs did want the government doing just that.

Marshall Johnson, a friend of mine who heads the central labor council there, showed up to testify in favor.

"What are you doing here?" demanded baffled council members. "This is not a labor issue, and why are you siding with these socialistically warped environmentalists?"

"Because my members don't have condos in Aspen and Vail for weekend getaways like you do. We're the people who need the parks and trails and baseball fields for our kids. This is where we vacation," Marshall said.

They got their park expansion.

I think this fits into John Rawls's theoretical construct, though he certainly had a more refined thought process. He was famous for an experiment that he often ran with students and other groups. The members of the group were asked to construct a hypothetical society, choosing the ethical principles that would guide the relations of all members of the society. As self-interested, rational people, they were to decide what principles of behavior would best serve their own interest.

Want to play? Hey, you might think, why not a kingdom in which I'm royalty and we royals rule? Or maybe a Bush-style, laissez-faire empire in which there are no regulations, so I can do anything I'm big enough to do to advance my personal interest.

But here's where Rawls tosses in a startling and sobering qualification to the exercise: "The Veil of Ignorance," he called it. As you go about designing the guiding principles for your new society—*you are not allowed to know anything about who you'll be in that society.* Whoa— now we're having some fun! You don't know your race, your parents' economic class, whether you're old or young, a Christian or Muslim or Jew or Buddhist or atheist, whether you've got a disability, whether you live in a slum or a penthouse.

What do you choose? What principles would you want to have governing your world? What Rawls found over and over is that under this Veil of Ignorance, self-interested rational people go for principles of the deepest and broadest egalitarianism to ensure that the least well-off person is treated justly, since they might be that person.

I believe that this core of justice is within all of us, and that it's yearning to come out, to become the guiding principle of our society. Sure, people seek their own gain, striving to get ahead (or not fall back too far). But that's not the sum of the American soul, nor the center of it. César Chávez, who knew something about heart and built an important movement on it, said, "*The love for justice that is in us is not only the best part of our being, but it is also the most true to our nature.*"

Surprise!

"*But suppose God is black. What if we go to Heaven and we, all our lives, have treated the Negro as inferior, and God is there, and we look up and He is not white? What then is our response?*"

—Robert F. Kennedy

We don't always act on this deeper part, and rare is the political leader who even acknowledges that it's there, much less attempts to tap into its phenomenal potential. But I sense that in the midst of today's grab-what-you-can culture—the most materialistic and self-aggrandizing on earth—people are drowning and are eager to reach for something more meaningful, more satisfying, more engaging, more *spiritual* in their secular life than, say, tax cuts, war, and the opening of yet another Starbucks.

THE AMERICA THAT *CAN* BE

What a burden we twenty-first-century Americans shoulder. In a time of great possibilities for our country, a time when the world cries out *not* for our military and corporate might, but for the moral example of our people's commitment to justice and equality—our "leaders" in Washington, on Wall Street, in the media, and elsewhere are mostly a bunch of ten-gallon hats hiding half-pint heads.

If they are the best we can do as leaders, then give me Clay Henry. He's the mayor of Lajitas, Texas, a delightful burg down on the Mexican border in the Big Bend country, where cacti greatly outnumber the people and the people like it that way, so please don't move to Lajitas, especially if you're another rich person from Houston or Hollywood seeking the Wild West experience, thank you very much.

Locals here have what we Texans call "an attitude," and more power to them. Mayor Henry is the perfect representative of their attitude. He's a goat. Literally. In fact, he's Mayor Clay Henry III, the third goat named Henry duly chosen in a succession of democratic elections to serve as Hizzonor of Lajitas (and the Bushes think they're building a political dynasty!).

Unlike George W, who to this day tries to be coy about his "drinking period," Mayor Henry is up front about his enjoyment of serious beer-swigging. One of the bigger tourist attractions in Lajitas, in fact, is to buy a long-neck bottle of beer at the trading post, give it to Clay Henry, and right in front of your very own eyes he'll tip the bottle all the way up and drain it quicker than you can say, "Chug-a-lug, Mr. Mayor."

As popular as he is, though, the mayor suffered a terrible injustice last year. We're talking far worse than mere political insult. (Flashback: Mayor Richard Daley, the old boss of Chicago, once described an attack his enemies had made on him: "They have vilified me, they have crucified me, yes they have even criticized me." Now back to our story in progress.) We're talking injury. Mayor Henry is not the only one who gets tanked in Lajitas, and one Sunday, a small group of malcontents got so juiced up that one of them decided there was nothing better to do than—O cruel fate!—castrate Clay Henry.

As you might imagine, this was a five-alarm catastrophe in Lajitas, a town that truly loves its mayor and was furious to find him in a mess of blood and in danger of death. The vet was summoned to rush down from Alpine, a good eighty miles away. The constable, county attorney, and district attorney were on the case pronto, and the culprits were soon nabbed. They were promptly charged with animal cruelty—though the lawyers tried hard to hit them with the much more severe charge of assault on a public official, but that law explicitly refers to "persons" (yet another distressing example of goat discrimination in our society).

It ended OK for Clay Henry. Reports from Lajitas are that he survived the ordeal, is back to swigging beers for tourists, and is doing fine, albeit a little lighter in the groin region.

At least Mayor Henry offers entertainment value to the people, and he clearly did have some testicles to surrender. Can as much be said for our society's leadership? Here's my question:

Where's the gumption to call forth the greatness of the people of this country?

We were attacked on September 11. At the very least, we deserved some honesty about what was going on in the world that could cause this. Instead we got bellicose clichés of bravado, like boys playing war games— we're going to "smoke 'em out," said the president, though he didn't, instead diverting to "regime change" in Iraq.

All that Bush has called forth are soldiers, asking them to be shot at and for many to be killed. Is that all there is? Is that the only way that regular Americans can count—as war fodder? Is that the only response the United States of America can make at a time when the world is looking for a show of our true mettle, of our values? What about the other 99.95 percent of us who are not in the military? Remember what Bush urged us to contribute shortly after the attacks:

- Go shopping
- Hug your children

And five months later, presumably after he'd had time to reflect on the public's role in a time of crisis and world alarm, he offered this inspiring challenge:

> *"You know, I'm asked all the time, 'How can I fight against terror? And what can I do, what can I as a citizen do to defend America?' Well, one thing you can do is not purchase illegal drugs."*

Gosh, yes. Buying a couple of bags of cocaine was right at the top of my to-do list, but when George issued the call for America, I chose not to make the purchase. Take that, Osama!

What an insult to us.

It would be somewhat comforting if the leadership of the opposition party would offer an alternative to Bush's Big Four of soldiering, shopping, hugging, and abstaining. But no. Indeed, the Democrats' best-known figure, Bill Clinton, chastised his party after the 2002 elections for not being militant enough about supporting Bush's war and Homeland Security clampdown. He asserted that Americans are "scared" and seek the comfort of powerful leaders: "They'd rather have someone strong and wrong than weak and right."

Thank you, Bill. Now go away. (Can't he get anyone to play golf with him?)

We the People are *not* scared (except for a gnawing fear that our leaders are wobblier than Jell-O and maybe not as smart). Americans are a gutsy, roll-up-our-sleeves, can-do people, eager to do something worthy of this moment in history. What might that be? Here's one idea.

Energy Independence for America

Let's shoot for the moon. What could be more patriotic, more productive, more unifying—and more of a useful model for the rest of the world—than to make our country totally self-sufficient in renewable energy sources within a decade? Not only would we become independent of the "*oili*garchies" of Saudi Arabia, Kuwait, Iraq, and elsewhere, but we'd also not need a drop of oil from such worldwide corporate kingdoms as ExxonMobil, BP/Amoco, Royal Dutch Shell, and Chevron/Texaco.

Unshackling America from oil wells and oil wars would be akin to the moon-shot effort that Kennedy and Johnson launched in the '60s, intently focusing our people's energies and efforts on building something positive for this generation and future ones. But energy independence would be even better than the man-on-the-moon program, for we only got to watch that on television. This time, ordinary folks in every community would be enlisted, employed, and excited by it, made central to the achievement of this common national goal.

> ### TAKING THE PULSE
>
> **Q:** What percentage of the American people would support an energy security plan based on more solar power, higher fuel-efficiency standards, and fuel-cell technology?
> **A:** 88 percent (with 63 percent expressing strong support).
>
> —Greenberg, Quinlan poll, 2001

Ready to go, America? Here are some of the steps we could take toward Energy Independence Day 2014:

- Enlisting our very best scientists in a crash program of collaboration, as was done in the Manhattan Project in the 1940s. But instead of making a horrific bomb, as those folks were asked to do, this collaboration would ask scientists to resolve any remaining technological impediments to the mass use of fuel cells, biomass, solar, wind, geothermal, and other abundant, clean, and cheap energy sources. Lock them in a room, and don't let them out until they make the advances needed.

This would be a heroic team effort to retool our energy economy and regain our energy sovereignty.

- Issuing an open challenge to our entire nation of tinkerers, backyard inventors, mechanics, web-heads, and puzzle solvers to bring their downhome ingenuity to the task of energy freedom, offering rewards and incentives for breakthroughs that advance our national goal.

- Building a high-speed, energy-efficient, twenty-first-century train system to crisscross the nation, linking all major cities with fast, reliable service. This would be a huge undertaking and a proud national achievement, comparable to putting a man on the moon—only we'd all get to ride on this rocket. It would also give our economy a stupendous ride, rehiring the machinists, electricians, steelworkers, laborers, and so many other union workers who Boeing, GM, ExxonMobil, and their ilk claim are no longer needed in the USA. Once built, America's rail system would provide good jobs and careers for generations to come.

- Launching a ten-year door-to-door "America Works" project to retrofit every home and building across our land, hiring and training legions of skilled workers to weatherize, plug holes, insulate, and do the construction needed to save the energy each of us pays for each month, but loses. George W's home in Crawford, Texas, and Dick Cheney's home in the V.P.'s mansion have already been retrofitted to

A DANGEROUS ADDICTION

When OPEC forced America into gasoline lines in the '70s, officials cried "Never again," promising diversification and an end to dependency on foreign crude.

We were getting 40 percent of our oil from OPEC back then. Today, we are 60 percent dependent on OPEC.

Tomorrow? Bush said late last year, "We must have an energy policy that diversifies away from dependency," but he's provided quite the opposite. His Energy Department now says that by 2020 we'll be even more dependent on OPEC oil.

great effect, stopping energy waste and slashing costs. So if it works for them, why not our homes, too? Such simple steps of commonsense conservation are proven solutions that can cut America's electricity use in half and cut consumers' utility bills by a total of $17 billion a month! Doing this job will put hundreds of thousands of our people to work, putting badly needed paychecks into the grassroots economy and instantly lifting our nation from recession to recovery.

• Getting smart about such power-suckers as cars, trucks, appliances, and lightbulbs, offering zero-interest loans, cash rebates, trade-ins, and outright gifts of energy-saving versions of these products as incentives for consumers to make the switch and advance U.S. independence. We're not talking here about living in the dark or scrunching everybody into putt-putting Yugos, but of sleek, fast, comfortable, cool products that already are on the market, work better than today's inefficient models, cost less to operate, and are affordable. More innovation and refinement of such cars and appliances is under way, and manufacturers (often small businesses) can be called forward in a patriotic, publicly supported drive to speed their development. Mass production would drastically lower the price of the products, and producing them will create a new, made-in-America manufacturing boom.

Yes, but what about the jobs of oil workers if we make such a dra-

OIL WARS

Our vehicles burn nearly two-thirds of the oil consumed in the U.S., averaging no better than twenty miles to the gallon. Goosing that average up to merely thirty-three miles per gallon would completely eliminate the need to import any oil from the Persian Gulf. That's all—a simple increase in fuel efficiency of thirteen miles per gallon.

We've had our second war in a decade in the Persian Gulf to protect the oiligarchies. Will we put our kids into a third because we lack the gumption to put them into 33-mpg cars?

matic conversion? We're talking about Green *Growth* here, creating hundreds of thousands of good, new energy jobs at good wages—union jobs with a future and middle-class promise. America still has to have energy, so it's a *shift* of jobs, not an elimination. This deliberate transition in jobs must be made central to the moon-shot plan, with all displaced workers given priority in filling new energy positions. Instead of Bush's phony stimulus package of trickle-down giveaways, this energy independence project would provide a true, percolate-up stimulus for America.

It's only one idea, but one is a big number in the Land of Zeroes, and it certainly competes well with "Go Shopping" and "Buy Duct Tape." On the practical front, a national campaign for energy independence gives us an exit from the endless highway of oil wars, it puts jobs and a clean planet on the same side, and it provides a positive alternative to scolding people for their fossil-fuel use.

Equally important, however, is the spiritual front. Such a campaign can revive people's sense of belonging, sense of really being united in a historic effort for the common good. Fifty, a hundred, two hundred years from now, future generations won't look back on this moment in history and judge us on whether the most powerful nation on earth was able to kill Osama bin Laden and kick Saddam Hussein's butt, but on whether we Americans had the vision and courage to make a positive out of something horrible, finally freeing the world from a stupid addiction to the products of a grasping, self-serving oil industry that gouges us, pollutes the planet, ruins our health, corrupts our governments, and puts us into wars.

We can wait on some leader to come make this happen, but you might as well wait for your cat to bring you the morning paper and serve you breakfast in bed. Not good odds. It's up to us. Always has been. We have to put the ideas forward and put the politics in play. It's heavy lifting, but that's sometimes what democracy requires.

A fine San Antonio writer, Jan Jarboe Russell, recently told a story about our mutual friend Maury Maverick Jr.

Maury, who died this year at eighty-two, was as crusty a fighter for fairness as ever lived. When it came to liberties and the downtrodden, he was a brawler on the side of justice. To some degree, he was born to fight, hailing from the famous, iconoclastic, and determinedly progressive Texas family that gave the word "maverick" to our language. But Maury never rested on the family laurels—he was the real thing, a *practicing* progressive all his rich life.

Jan notes that she was having a dog of a morning a few years ago, in such a funk she couldn't get out of bed. At 8:30 the phone rang and it was Maury. Jan proceeded to whine . . . but Maury cut her off cold. In his bulldog voice, he barked, "Stop bellyaching. I know things are tough, but I want you to get up off your ass and go do something brave for your country."

She did. And so should we.

CHAPTER 7

Legacy

What do you want your tombstone to say? Some of the good lines are already taken:

Here lies	Here lies a man
Johnny Yeast	Named Zeke
Pardon Me	Second fastest draw
For Not Rising	In Cripple Creek

Owen Moore	Hi!
Gone away	Stay High
Owin' more	Bye
Than he could pay	[Tombstone with an etching of a marijuana plant on it.]

Not that I'm preoccupied with *el muerte,* but even as a fairly young fellow I'd sometimes think about what I call "deathbed regret"—coming to the end of life, reflecting back over my years, and thinking: "Is that all there was? Why didn't I do more?" I'll occasionally see an obituary in the newspaper these days and get worried anew about that deathbed-regret problem. Here are some actual obit headlines, summing up people's lives, that I came across in the past year or so, causing me to cringe:

• *Invented Corporate Voice Mail.* He's the one! I hate those things. You have to wait through twenty-six options before you finally get to: ". . . or, if you want to speak to a real person, press twenty-seven," which you do, then a recorded voice says, "Thank you for calling. Goodbye." Thanks a lot, fella. I'll never stop forgetting you!

- *Innovator in Late-Night TV Ads.* Oh, dandy. Spent his life making those blaring 120-second ads for D-Con rat poison, Hair Wiz, *101 Great Moments in Music,* and other stuff pitched to bleary-eyed, late-night TV viewers. "If they are tired," said this guy of his target market, "their subconscious will accept without their consciousness fighting it." There's marketing ethics for you. R.I.P.
- *Master of Hostile Takeover.* A life well lived, I'm sure. Let me quote the obit: "[He] controlled public companies as diverse as Arby's . . . and Sharon Steel. He mismanaged many of these companies into bankruptcy, but enriched himself as they foundered. Even as shareholders suffered, he was one of America's highest paid executives for years." Thanks for your service, sir.

Well, we've all got to make a living (dammit). And since I've managed to go most of my adult life without having what you would consider a real job (getting paid even as little as I do for essentially running my mouth would be condemned as sloth by many a culture), who am I to judge?

WHAT'S POSSIBLE

But what will the Big Tombstone say about the America we live in today? What you and I do with our private lives and the chances we get is one thing. But there's a bigger accounting to be made of what we as an American people do with the incredible treasure we've been given, which is nothing less than the freedom and the wherewithal to advance the democratic potential of this great country. Consider some possibilities:

> *What if* a carpenter, factory worker, nurse, shopkeeper, student, clerk, or anyone else of modest means had the same chance as a millionaire to get to Congress?
> *What if* the work ethic actually was rewarded, so that, say, farmworkers and night-shift cleaning women get premium

wages and special treatment in exchange for the extraordinarily hard work they do for our society?

What if our rivers and lakes were clean—so clean that our
kids could swim in them anytime and we could fish in them
with no health worries? What value would this add to the
quality of life for people in Boston, St. Louis, Chicago, Pittsburgh, Washington, Austin, Dallas, St. Paul, Albuquerque,
Little Rock, New Orleans, and so many other population
centers with rivers running through them?

What if every child had a computer with regular upgrades
to it, for free, so "no child left behind" was more than a crass
political slogan?

What if trade deals couldn't be passed unless workers,
small farmers, environmentalists, community leaders, in-
digenous people, and all others directly affected by the deal
were sitting at the table negotiating as full partners with the
corporate and government elites pushing the deals?

What if there were affordable housing, health care, college
education, child care, transportation, and dignified retirement for everyone?

What if [add your possibility here]:

_____

_____

_____

(Send to: info@jimhightower.com)

You might say, sure Hightower, and what if pigs fly? Well, that'd be a
beautiful thing to see (Oh, my, Elvira, look at the wingspread on that
spotted Yorkshire!), but that's up to the gods, not us. Yet it is within our
grasp to have the kind of country we want, complete with all the fairness, justice, and egalitarianism we dare imagine—if We the People put
our minds, our collective energy, and our democratic spirit to the goal.

Not only should we, but we must, for we're in another of those "When
in the course of human events" moments that Jefferson wrote about in
1776. The Bushites, the Wobblycrats, and especially the corporate Kleptocrats are stealing our America. Jefferson wrote about this, too: "Unless

the mass maintains sufficient control over those entrusted with the powers of their government, these will be perverted to their own oppression, and to the perpetuation of wealth and power. . . ." You go, Tom.

Unfortunately, we're there. You know that stenciled message on the right-hand mirror of your car: "Objects are closer than they appear"? Don't look now but the corporate SUV is not just tailgating us, it's running us over. We don't control the powers of government—corporate lobbyists and campaign contributors do, and we're reaping the oppression and perpetuation that flows from our loss of power.

If this is to be America, it is essential that we grassroots folks assert ourselves again in a little rebellion, which is what America is all about. Just as the Sons of Liberty, abolitionists, suffragists, populists, unionists, civil rights activists, and other democracy fighters stood up and shouldered both the burden and the risk of challenging entrenched, antidemocratic forces, now it's our time.

It's not merely the power of Bush that has to be confronted—he's the carrier, not the disease. Rather, it's the power of global corporate greed that we're up against. This power has not only entrenched itself, but is tunneling into every aspect of our lives and culture. You see it anywhere you go:

- It's in your schools with its lesson plans and "teaching" materials.
- It's in your retirement plan, transforming the company pensions you were promised into fund-it-yourself, 401(k) prayer beads.
- It's in the universities, buying scientists, diverting the public science agenda to its own, and dictating scientific results for its profit goals.
- It's in public services, privatizing our mail delivery, water supplies, and anything else that lets it profit on the taxpayer's dollar, while curtailing service.
- It's in your health records, banks, credit card accounts, government records, and any other private place where it can mine your personal data for its own profit.
- It's on our public airwaves, squeezing out small competitors and controlling what gets covered as "news" and how it gets covered.
- It's in your financial future, constantly scheming for new ways to cut your income and benefits, or simply replace you altogether, whether you're a factory worker or a high-tech manager in the "new economy."

• It's in the backrooms of your city hall, legislature, and White House (no matter who's the temporary resident), writing the rules that we have to live with.

GREAT MOMENTS IN CORPORATE ATTITUDE

"We seem to be at a point now where the word 'sprawl' has been totally demonized."

—Clayton Traylor, National Association of Homebuilders

"Thank you for dialing in this holiday weekend. I hope you and your family are enjoying your time together. I have some extremely urgent and sad news to share with you today. . . . Your employment ends immediately."

—John Brinko, CEO of Consolidated Freightways, on a recorded hotline that seventeen thousand employees were told to call on Labor Day 2002

"We paid $3 billion for these television stations. We decide what the news is. The news is what we tell you it is."

—David Boylan of Fox affiliate WTVT in Tampa

"As of tomorrow, employees will only be able to access the building using individual security cards. Pictures will be taken next Wednesday and employees will receive their cards in two weeks."

—Microsoft

"The free television that we've all enjoyed for so many years is based on watching these commercials. There's no Santa Claus. If you don't watch the commercials, someone's going to have to pay for television, and it's going to be you."

—Jamie Kellner, CEO of Turner Broadcasting, chastising viewers who use their clickers and DVRs to bypass the ads

"Lucent Technologies is endeavorily determined to promote constant attention on current procedures of transacting business focusing on innovative ways to better, if not supercede, the expectations of quality."

—Company memo, circulated nationally

"You have to look at them like I do, as your mortal enemy. I wish they were dead. I wish their children would starve to death. I wish they would lose their houses."

—Herbert Lanese, president of McDonnell Douglas, telling union negotiators that their union brothers and sisters over at Lockheed Martin should be treated as vicious competitors (Herb later tried to claim that he didn't say this, but he admitted that he had ordered the transcripts destroyed)

- It's in our elections, at all levels, soiling them with its campaign cash and controlling what issues get discussed.
- It's in your air, water, and food with its contaminants, which means it's in you, your babies, everyone else, and every other creature on earth (as well as beyond, now that its contaminants have reached into space).
- It's in your name, flying your flag as it shamelessly exploits child, sweatshop, and prison labor around the world; denies lifesaving AIDS medicines in poor countries that can't pay the inflated price; and sides with military thugs to repress democratic struggles of people in various countries while profiting from the expropriation of their natural resources.

Can we defeat a force that is this powerful and pervasive? Are you kidding me—we're Americans! Plus, we've got the kids!

It doesn't get much coverage, but young people are on the move in our country, teed off about and zeroed in on the very corporate imperiousness that permeates our world. From getting child labor out of soccer balls to creating their own media, from battling the WTO to rejecting the campus recruiters of polluting corporations, from beating back the prison industry to standing up for peace—we have an activist, progressive, and focused generation of young folks, from elementary schools through college and beyond, who're in the lead in the burgeoning, joyous, grassroots fight to reclaim our democracy from the Kleptocrats.

There's a bumper sticker that says: "It's Forbidden to Catch On." That's the problem with these kids: They've been taught American

CHARLOTTE'S WEB

In April of 2002, when she was twelve, Charlotte Aldebron wrote this essay for a competition in her sixth-grade English class in Presque Isle, Maine:

What the American Flag Stands For

The American flag stands for the fact that cloth can be very important. It is against the law to let the flag touch the ground or to leave the flag flying when the weather is bad. The flag is to be treated with respect. You can tell just how important this cloth is because when you compare it to people, it gets much better treatment. Nobody cares if a homeless person touches the ground. A homeless person can lie all over the ground all night long without anyone picking him up, folding him neatly and sheltering him from the rain.

School children have to pledge loyalty to this piece of cloth every morning. No one has to pledge justice and equality and human decency. No one has to promise that people will get a fair wage, or enough food to eat, or affordable medicine, or clean water, or air free of harmful chemicals. But we all have to promise to love a rectangle of red, white, and blue cloth. Betsy Ross would be quite surprised to see how successful her creation has become. But Thomas Jefferson would be disappointed to see how little of the flag's real meaning remains.

Did Charlotte win the competition? Not exactly. Her teacher called her "unpatriotic." But she won the bigger prize, which was her self-respect and the respect of so many others who learned about the essay when her mom, Jillian, sent it to the www. commondreams.org website, drawing fifty thousand hits in the first week.

At a time when all of officialdom was pumping knee-jerk patriotism, Charlotte touched a nerve (and gave some nerve) to people throughout the world, drawing thank-yous from every state as well as places as far away as Slovenia, Japan, and Brazil. She heard from lawyers, military officers, grandmothers, teenagers, homeless people, and so many others, creating a web of support. She read it last year as part of a speech she gave at a Mother's Day rally in Bath, Maine. As her mom told me, "The most remarkable thing about Charlotte's essay is the response it has elicited. There is clearly a large reservoir of public dissatisfaction with the direction that our government is leading us—regardless of what the pollsters say—and it runs across political, educational, and socioeconomic spectra."

Charlotte is but one example of the phenomenal strength that we can draw on from young folks today. It is strength from within, the one place we can trust. It reminds me of something from our strongest president ever, Abe Lincoln, who said he wanted to conduct his difficult presidency in such a way that when he was done, even if he had lost every other friend he had on earth,

"I shall at least have one friend left, and that friend shall be down inside me."

ideals and—uh-oh—they took them to heart! Then they took a look at the world around them and realized there's a corporate reality stomping on every one of our ideals. They caught on.

This is also a generation that's had adult conversations at the kitchen table from an early age on, and was encouraged to speak up. So they are. They're daring to say, "The emperor has no clothes." Of course, the emperor's courtiers in the media and in both political parties continue to comment on the splendid quality of the corporate raiments, and they have either ignored, clucked at, pooh-poohed, or mocked the young who make such outrageous assertions of royal nakedness.

One thing that couldn't be ignored, however—so therefore has been ridiculed and condemned by the faithful courtiers—is the impressive presence of tens of thousands of young people going into the streets of Seattle, Quebec, Washington, D.C., and elsewhere around the globe.

What has drawn the kids in these mass protests is the usually sedate gatherings of government heavies and corporate honchos for meetings of previously invisible organs of the emperor's empire—the WTO, IMF, World Bank, FTAA, and the like. These are astonishingly elitist get-togethers, usually at posh spots where the invited parties sip cosmopolitans at corporate-sponsored receptions, come out to make pompous statements to a sycophantic media about the glories of globalization, then withdraw behind closed doors to make decisions that bankrupt farms in Iowa and Veracruz, Mexico, shut down union-wage factories in South Carolina in order to open slave-wage factories in China, and open the natural resources of rain forests to corporate plunder. Then they break for lunch.

Thanks to the kids, though, we peasants have now discovered these global, secretive, antidemocratic, rule-making outfits that essentially exist to impose the corporate agenda on even the most remote village, without the villagers getting so much as a postcard notifying them that, say, Big Behemoth Inc. will henceforth be allowed to to suck up their local water supply and sell it to private golf clubs in Palm Springs.

The kids learned that such things were going on behind closed doors and asked, with the innocence of youth: Why? Because . . . well . . . uh . . . you see . . . it's . . . well, it's just the way things work. But it's not right and not fair, said the kids. What can we do? Write your congressperson, they were told, for that's the American system in action. They did. Congressmen Festerhead responded with his form letter G-67(j)-kids, which extolled the magical merits of globalization, then thanked the youngsters for having participated in the democratic process. *Hmmmmmm,* said the kids amongst themselves, so that's how it works.

That's when they remembered their history classes—about the Declaration of Independence, the First Amendment, the Boston Tea Party, and all that stuff about standing up for democracy. So they decided not just to read history, but to practice it—"Let's go knock on the door of the WTO," someone said on the Internet, and thousands of them streamed from throughout this country, Canada, Mexico, Europe, Asia, and elsewhere to the WTO's 1999 meeting in Seattle.

I was there. Susan DeMarco and I broadcast our radio show for five days from protest central, the First United Methodist Church in downtown Seattle. I can tell you that the heavies and honchos were absolutely stunned to be discovered. The protesters effectively shut down the WTO meeting, and the elites were afraid to leave their luxury hotels. (TIDBIT INVOLVING A SMALL BUT SWEET DEGREE OF POETIC JUSTICE: The hotels soon ran out of food, and—Oh, the horror—the big shots were reduced to kneeling in front of the minibars in their rooms, scarfing up every scrap of cheese, chips, peanuts, and pretzels they could scrounge.)

Suddenly, what would have been a small, boring news item about the WTO meeting became a major international story about a citizens' revolt. Naturally, the corporate media rushed to the defense of the emperor, giving this huge protest the most biased coverage I've ever seen. By deliberately and repeatedly focusing on about forty vandals out of the fifty thousand protesters, they trivialized the stunning significance of an open rebellion against global corporate rule.

What Seattle really gave us was a glowing new textbook example of democracy at its best. When the American people are locked out, as we literally are by the WTO, we

---

SHHHH. THE PRIME MINISTER IS SPEAKING

At a barricaded, thirty-four-nation trade meeting in Quebec in 2001, Prime Minister Jean Chrétien was the host bigwig, and he was aghast that his exclusive meeting of the global elite had drawn thousands of commoners to assemble and speak out in protest.

"This type of behavior is contrary to all democratic principles."

crash the party. That's what happened in Boston in 1773, when Sam Adams and his Sons of Liberty illegally boarded the *Dartmouth,* the *Beaver,* and the *Eleanor* and destroyed the property of the British East India Trading Company. Their Boston Tea Party rallied the colonies' rebels to the democratic cause.

The kids provided the passion and democratic idealism for the Seattle Tea Party. They drummed their rhythmic and raucous plastic buckets, surged up and down the streets with their giant puppets, coordinated on the run through laptop computers that they'd duct-taped to themselves, and went right in the face of battalions of riot-geared police who were firing rubber bullets, splitting heads with long clubs, and filling the air with cloudbursts of tear gas.

Why would they do this? What is it these kids want? are the perplexed questions that media anchors, pundits, and analysts keep asking from behind their glass broadcast booths, looking down on the protesters in Seattle, Quebec, and elsewhere. After all, cluck the commentators, shaking their coifed heads in purse-lipped disapproval of the democratic spectacle, *there are so many different groups out there—unions, save-the-turtles people, gays and lesbians, farmers, anti-sweatshop agitators, women's-righters, churchies, food activists—what can they possibly have in common? The message is too muddled. I don't get it. I think I'm going to need another Valium.*

The message isn't muddled at all. The message is that we've caught on to all of the corporate intrusions into our lives, liberties, and pursuit of happiness. Yes, the participants are diverse, which is the beauty of it! This movement is not one color, not one gender, not one age, not one issue, not even one nation. What is it we want? **Democracy!** We want everyone, no matter what the issue, to have a voice that counts. We want people to rule, not corporations.

> *"What the people want is simple. They want an America as good as its promise."*
>
> —Barbara Jordan

The protests against the WTO and other global corporate entities waned for a while after September 11 as people necessarily turned to the urgent protest against Bush's invasion of Iraq and his military reach for empire, but the fervor against global corporate greed has not waned one bit—indeed, it has deepened and spread. It was this global democratic movement that fueled and informed the phenomenal peace movement that sprang up around the world against Bush's war. Much of the war protest has had a corporate focus—demonstrating at the offices of the Pentagon contractors (such as Halliburton), Fox TV's warmongering studios, and the facilities of Coca-Cola and other brand names that have come to symbolize the arrogance of corporate domination.

This grassroots rebellion will continue to spread and deepen as more and more of us catch on, realizing that we're being had by the Kleptocrats. This is *who we are* as Americans, born in rebellion and striving yet for the promise of democracy. As we keep relearning, there is nothing ordained about democracy, even here. We have to keep scrapping. William Jennings Bryan said it right:

> **"Destiny is not a matter of chance, it is a matter of choice; it is not a thing to be waited for, it is a thing to be achieved."**

III. AMERICA THE BEAUTIFUL

(The Best News of All)

CHAPTER 8

A Progressive Optimist
in the Age of Bushwa

There's something about being a Texan that makes you think all things are possible. Maybe it's because we've gone through so many tornadoes, several level-five hurricanes, some seven-year droughts, plagues of locusts, a long succession of goofy governors, seventy-nine sessions of the Texas legislature, and the public humiliation of having Phil Gramm represent us in the U.S. Senate—yet we're still standing!

How optimistic are we Texans? The U.S. government did a little-known study during the past five years, installing black boxes in hundreds of pickup trucks. The idea was to get data on truck crashes, like they do when airplanes go down. They found that in forty-nine of the fifty states, the last words of drivers in the majority of crashes were: "Oh, shit!" But the researchers were surprised to find that in the vast majority of pickup crashes in Texas, the last words were: "Hey, y'all hold my beer and watch this!"

Even in the dark swirl of national and global politics, with BushCo in charge and the corporate Kleptocrats on a bull goose rampage, *I think that this is a great time to be alive and a progressive in America.* You might think that's loopier than riding the double Tilt-A-Whirl at the state fair, but there it is, and I'll tell you why: You.

The ordinary folks of this century are extraordinary. Forget George W, forget Tom DeLay, forget the Wobblycrats, forget the Enroners and high-tech hustlers, forget the stupid *Nightly News* and stupider blather of Fox, forget Big Money politics, forget the boneheads of Washington and the greedheads of Wall Street, forget the Powers That Be—and look instead at what's going on with the *Powers That Ought to Be*, the workaday people of grassroots America.

This is where the establishment media and politicians rarely look, but it's where the phenomenal strength of our country is, where our hope is. And it's certainly where I draw my inspiration, ideas, and optimism from.

For the last decade or so, I've done a great deal of speaking around America, going down the road not only to all the major cities, but also to such places as Albuquerque, Allentown, Asheville, Bangor, Bloomington, Buffalo, Charlotte, College Station, Colorado Springs, Corvallis, Duluth, Durango, Hartford, Huntington, La Farge, Little Rock, Missoula, Newport, Oklahoma City, Peoria, Rock Island, St. Petersburg, San Mateo, State College, Toms River, Tulsa, Tucson, and Wenatchee. This has allowed me to be in touch with just regular people—in meetings, in cafés and bars, at their festivals and games, on campuses, in churches and union halls, in their neighborhoods . . . and, especially sitting around their kitchen tables.

More good has been launched by more people from kitchen tables than from any other platform in the land. I suspect this is because the kitchen is an unpretentious, relaxed place where folks can get together, share a bite, have a cup or glass of something, get to talking, get honest with each other—then, when it comes time to begin drawing up plans, they can spread out their papers (or flip open laptops) right there on that sturdy table. Many a kitchen has become the "official world headquarters" for many a grassroots rebellion.

I've been privileged to be at some of these tables and hear people talk about some oozing toxic waste dump on their side of town or about trying to make ends meet in today's glorified, corporatized, globalized, downsized world economy. But the stories mostly are not of their woes, but of their local organizing efforts around this issue or that, trying to do what they can to create a society that embodies their hardy egalitarian values and that treats families like theirs as more than disposable job cogs, consumer units, a dumping place, and war fodder.

At this point, you might be thinking: *Hightower, why don't we see what Woodrow Wilson Guthrie had to say about this kitchen-table spirit?* Good idea! Woody G. was a fellow who spent a lot of time in his day going down the road as what he called "a ramblin' man" and "a little one-cylinder guitar picker." As he rambled, he met hardworking folks who, like him, were feeling "stranded and disbanded, busted, disgusted," and he wrote their stories into songs that tell of the beautiful strength and tenacious spirit of the American people.

Even in the darkness of Hooverism, the Dust Bowl, Pinkerton thugs, the Depression, and soup lines, Woody found that people weren't sitting around moping, but were organizing and making plans about how *"this old world could be fixed so's it would be twice as level and half as steep and take the knocks out of it, and grind the values, and tighten the rods, and take up the bearings, and put a boot in the casing—and make the whole trip a little bit smoother, and a little bit more like a trip instead of a trap."*

That common, let's-fix-it spirit created the New Deal, Social Security, labor rights, the weekend (forty-hour workweeks), public parks, farm security and conservation, public art, consumer rights, the Fair Deal, the GI Bill, rural electrification, affordable housing—a better world for more people. None of this was handed down by politicians and the elites; it all came from the ground up, from the people themselves.

Today's Powers don't realize it, but it's coming again. All across America, in just about every zip code, I've found people, groups, and coalitions lighting little prairie fires of rebellion that are burning brighter and brighter, showing the way out of the darkness. Meet a few of them in the stories that follow, connect with them, and best of all join with them. This is how we take control over everything from the food on our tables to the con artists of globalization. It's how we take our country back.

CHAPTER 9

Public Spirit

And now, back to the Sports Desk, where our insightful analysts are always on top of their game:

> *"The Utah Jazz know where their butt is breaded."*
>
> —Basketball announcer Quinn Buckner

> *"Each game is unique, and this one is no different."*
>
> —BBC's John Sleightholme

> *"Statistically, when the Hawks score more than a hundred points and the defense holds the other team to less than a hundred, they almost always win."*
>
> —Atlanta Hawks announcer

Meanwhile, down on the field, let's hear what the players themselves have to say:

> *"We're going to turn this thing around 360 degrees."*
>
> —Basketballer Jason Kidd upon joining a new team

> *"We have only one person to blame, and that's each other."*
>
> —NHL player Barry Beck

"He treats us like men. He lets us wear earrings."

  —College footballer Torrin Polk, commenting on his coach

And what's a sports report without a comment from the coach?

"There are some teams who will try to circumcise the rules."

  —Coach Bill Cowher of the Pittsburgh Steelers

Ouch!

But these inanities from the world of sports* are nothing compared with a big one that is often hurled at me by right-wing talk-show pontificators: *"Don't give me that guff about the public needing health care, Hightower, or better public schools or whatever. Don't need any of it—it's just more big government gettin' in our way. All I want the government to do is give me plenty of police and military to protect me from the public, and I'll take care of everything else for myself. That's the American way, bub."*

What a breath of hot air, huh? Interesting that these hidebound "self-made" foghorns are using the *public* airwaves to make their point about going it alone in life. Also, unless they can levitate as well as they bloviate, they most likely drive on the *public* roads and highways. I would guess that quite a few of them went to *public* schools and universities. They probably deposit money in *publicly* protected accounts, shower in water provided through *public* pipes and purification systems, count on the *public* fire departments and EMS to respond to their emergencies, gladly accept the annual *public* subsidy of their home mortgages (including vacation homes), fly out of *publicly* built airports under the well-trained guidance of *public* air traffic controllers, enjoy the *public* splendor of our national parks and seashores, take medicines developed by *public* research, eat at restaurants that meet *public* health standards,

---

*A tip of the hat to Richard Lederer, a diligent collector of all sorts of verbal gems like these, publishing them regularly in the delightful and useful rag *Funny Times* (www.funnytimes.com).

and . . . well, enough from me, here's space for you to make your own additions to the very long list of "Public Services and Subsidies Used Every Day by Boneheads Who Rant That They Are Lone Strangers and Rugged Individualists Who Don't Need Nothing from the Public": ____

_____

_____

Yes, the pioneering spirit built our country, but the pioneering was mostly done by families and groups, not by lone individuals. We're a country of settlers—the *Mayflower*, wagon trains, Ellis Island, and all

GOING IT "ALONE"

Especially charming are the gabillionaires who brag that they are self-made, claiming that they acquired their fortunes through "hard work." (I always want to ask them: "Oh, whose?")

Last year, the Portland *Oregonian* ran a fun item about Steve Fossett, the super-rich ego who kept putting *public* rescue squads in great danger fishing him out of various oceans in his failed quests to be the first human to circumnavigate the globe in a hot air balloon . . . alone. (He finally made it in 2002.)

"Yup, it was just him," wrote *The Oregonian*. "Just Steve . . . and his Project Manager, a Chief Meteorologist, an Assistant Meteorologist, a Launch Master, a Systems Director, a Chief of Capsule Construction, a Mission Control Director, an Air Traffic Control Coordinator, an Assistant Air Traffic Control Coordinator, a Media Coordinator, a Website Team, and a Radio Actualities Team."

For real go-it-alone gutsiness, *The Oregonian* prefers (as do I) "Lawn Chair Larry" from Los Angeles. In 1982, Larry Walters strapped forty-two helium-filled weather balloons to his Sears lawn chair and, with nothing more than a few sandwiches, some beer, and a pellet gun (to shoot out the balloons), went up to sixteen thousand feet. ALONE.

Come on, Steve, let's see you match *that*.

the rest. People came seeking opportunity, for sure (except, of course, for that little unpleasantness with slavery, which would be the opposite of opportunity). But people came also—came especially—in search of *community*.

And wherever they landed or moved, they immediately set about building the commons—a town well, a storehouse, a school, a council, a meetinghouse, a central park or gathering place, a community bill-board, and other public needs, including, often, a public alehouse.

In the latter category falls the story of Spoetzl Brewery in the little Texas town of Shiner. Drop off I-10 about halfway between Houston and San Antonio, take State Highway 95 south for nineteen miles, and nestled there in the rolling farmland of South-Central Texas is the white-brick brewery that is a living testament to German-Czech sturdi-ness and sense of community. One of the first things done by the lead-ers of the new town, settled by farmers from the old country at the turn of the twentieth century, was to form a beer-making cooperative, called the Shiner Brewery Association.

Unfortunately for them, they were much more adept at drinking beer than at making it. Faced with a choice between bad beer and no beer, they did what any group of serious beer drinkers would do: in-vented a third choice. The leaders met, pondered, pooled their re-sources, and sent out a search party to find an honest-to-God German brewmaster willing to relocate to Shiner. They found their man in Kos-mos Spoetzl, for whom the brewery was renamed in 1915, and the Shiner brand not only survives today but is the unofficial state beer of Texas—and, I can attest, good stuff, too.

Yet the leaders of both major parties, quickstepping to the shuck and jive tune of their campaign donors, keep pushing in the opposite direc-tion from this concept of shared public assets. It's a scream to watch George W pop out every seventeen seconds or so with yet another pub-lic program that he says should be privatized for our benefit. Like some talking bobblehead, he's constantly in motion, demanding that the "pri-vate sector" (a code phrase that politicians use, meaning "my cronies") be allowed to take over Social Security, Medicare, Medicaid, the military (for example, much of Bush's war in Colombia is under the direction of a private contractor, Dynacorp), the postal service, the weather service,

NASA (much of it is already in the clutches of Boeing, Lockheed Martin, and other profit-seeking giants), park rangers, and even the air controllers. (Oh yeah, that's just what I want to see—some guy in an ill-fitting Wackenhut uniform with two hours of training, a low-wage paycheck, and a sullen attitude bringing in my plane: "*Thump-thump* . . . Hello? Is this thing on?")

Meanwhile, far away from Washington, the public remains deeply committed to the concept of . . . well, public. The common good, community need, the whole, the general welfare, the commons—by whatever name, poll after poll shows that this notion of "we're all in this together" is a value that truly is of value to the American people. The embodiments of this shared value—public parks, schools, hospitals, swimming pools, transportation, etc.—are things that the majority of us want more of and better of, particularly wanting more of our tax dollars going into these services that give back to us, making our lives better and putting a little more unity in "community."

LIBRARIES: CHECK THIS OUT

What is it about budget-whackers at all levels—city, state, national—that prompts them to go after some of the smartest, most useful things that government provides, like libraries? Are they naturally stupid, or are they taking steroids to soar to such heights?

Governors across the country, for example, face serious budget squeezes, yet they continue to pour vats of taxpayer dollars into various corporate subsidies and boondoggles while swiping the paltry percentage of state money that goes to keep libraries open. Mayors and city councils add to the problem by subtracting big sums from their library funding. So branches close, hours are slashed, children's pro-

IN THE GREAT DEPRESSION, NOT A SINGLE LIBRARY WAS FORCED TO CLOSE ITS DOORS. BANKS CLOSED—BUT NOT LIBRARIES.

grams are eliminated, staff is fired—despite the fact that the use of libraries is up and the demand for their services is greater than ever.

In New York City, for example, sixty-seven of the eighty-five branches have eliminated Saturday openings, thanks to a $16 million budget cut by the mayor, despite a 7 percent increase in library use. (Sorry, that's a lot of numbers in one sentence—here's what the numbers say: More people want to use the city's libraries, so officials are going to cut the library hours. I'm telling you, they're taking stupid pills.) In this city, 40 million people a year go through the library doors—more than the audience for all of New York's museums, concert halls, and professional sports teams combined.

There's proud news on the people front, however. You're rebelling again. Cincinnati planned to close five branch libraries this year . . . BIG public outcry . . . branches still open. Here in Austin, it was proposed to close each branch one weekday to save money. Total savings: $323,000. In a *2 billion* city budget. That's 0.01615 percent. People swarmed the hearing on the issue, and the branches did not close.

The Stevens County Rebellion

In addition to stupid politicians, anti-tax zealots are also prone to go after our libraries. Out in far northeast Washington state, there was a heck of a dustup last year over the Stevens County Rural Library District.

This district had only been created in 1996, designed specifically to meet the needs of the small-town and rural folks who live in this remote, poor, forested, and isolated corner of Washington, spanning some 2,400 square miles and reaching from the edge of Spokane all the way to the Canadian border. Nine libraries were scattered through the county, and the people flocked to them as if the libraries were dipping out free ice cream cones. Thousands in and around towns like Tumtum, Suncrest, Hunters, Onion Creek, Loon Lake, and Kettle Falls proudly took out library cards, checked out books, joined the children's summer reading program, used the computers, made use of the research service, had community meetings in the libraries, and generally made these places home.

When I say "libraries," we're not talking here about the marble classic of New York City or some of the fine Carnegie buildings around the country, but about utilitarian, plebeian facilities. One has washers and dryers in it so locals can do their laundry while browsing the shelves. Another one is in the Onion Creek General Store, operating on the honor system and consisting of a visiting librarian coming up the mountain with a load of requested books once a week. Another shares space with a state liquor store—"Books 'n Booze," they've nicknamed it. The one in Hunters operates two days a week out of the Grange building.

Modest as they are, after four years of operation, these homegrown libraries had become fixtures for the Stevens County community— which is why folks were stunned last year to learn that a group of anti-taxers had gone around and quietly collected enough signatures to try shutting down the entire rural library district by referendum.

The antis grumped about the taxes required to keep the system func-tioning. Dave Sitler, one of the instigators of the referendum, is a local landlord and Realtor: "With all the property I own, I'm probably paying up to $500 in taxes for the library." Awww, poor babykins. With "all the property" he owns, I'd guess $500 a year isn't pinching his bottom line all that hard. (Sitler turns out to be a member of the American Heritage Party, a right-wing bunch that favors elimination of all property taxes and rule by biblical law. One local farmer refers to the party as "Amer-ica's own version of the Taliban.")

The real motivation behind this library assault was not the taxes (which average only $38 a year per household), but the very idea of pub-lic service. Hank Radezkey, a rancher and staunch anti, groused that as a matter of principle he didn't think the library system was a good thing: "I don't depend on anyone else to educate me. If I want a book, I go buy it." I don't get the feeling he's ever bought a bunch of them.

Besides, snapped the antis, who needs libraries now that you've got the Internet, Blockbuster Video, cable TV, Barnes & Noble, and Ama-zon.com? Still carping about his $500, Dave Sitler said: "That's just $500 wasted on something we don't need."

We?

- "They say everybody is on the Internet, so we don't need a library," says Linda Arrell, who lives almost at the Canadian border. "Well, some of us don't have credit cards, and some of us don't have [electric] power."

- "I can't imagine what we'd do without the library," says Leland Reiche, who lives around Suncrest and has six kids. "They've got everything we need here. And if they don't, they'll get it for us."
- "The library is so important in this town," says Dianne Eppler, who runs an antiques store in Hunters. "When you start losing things like a library, you lose the things that make a community."
- "We're seeing a disconnect in our society. People don't understand that you need tax money to pay for the public good," says Regan Robinson, the director of the district libraries. "I'd like to see someone face the women I see every day with three kids and a stack of books and tell them they can't have a library anymore."
- "This is something that helps our whole community," says Terri Charbonneau, owner of the Onion Creek General Store, who points out that lots of folks in her area can't afford to buy from even discount booksellers. "It is special that they can come in here and get books."

November 7, 2002, rolled around and the vote was taken on the question of "Shall the Stevens County Rural Library District be dissolved?" NO! said 65 percent of the voters.

Walt Kloefkorn, a chicken farmer from Springdale and a trustee for the library district, says that the two-to-one victory is more important than just saving the libraries, though that's a big thing. More important, he says, is that the people squarely faced the basic question of whether the egalitarian ethic of the common good ought to prevail over the ethic of separatism, which boils down to "I got mine, you get yours." The separatists were richer and noisier, but they're a small minority. The best result of all, says Walt, is that "the people of the community came together and got to know each other better than before this fight," and he's thinking that they'll stay together and work on other issues of public need.

And that, bub, is the American way.

STANDING UP TO CORPORATIONS

In a time not so very long ago, America was a commercial giant. But today we seem to be a giant of commercials.

Is there any space or moment in our lives that has not become just another place or time for Schlock Inc. to demand that you buy more of its crap? ("And we can super-size that sack of crap, sir—for only a dollar more!")

Have you seen the little TVs that blare nonstop ads on gas pumps, at supermarket checkout counters, in elevators, and at bathroom urinals? (I've not seen the urinal screens yet, but I wonder, who advertises there? Maybe beer companies: "Hi, whatcha doin'?" Now there's an opener. "Well, now that you're about to hit empty, what say you tank up with a six-pack of. . . .")

> ### Child's play
>
> Advertising and promotional budgets aimed at children total nearly $12 billion a year. The average child sees more than 20,000 commercials a year—some as many as 40,000. Children as young as age three recognize brand logos.
>
> —American Academy of Pediatrics

When you pay to go to a movie, can you escape ads? No, about fifteen minutes' worth of them yammer at you before your movie runs (I truly hate these and scribble a list on a napkin to make sure I don't buy from any outfit messing up my movie moment). Go to a beach and not only are ads all around you, but now they're imprinting them in the sand itself, using special sand rollers.

Crass commercialism isn't all that new in America—indeed, the orgy of Christmas gift-giving got started just after the Civil War when merchants such as Macy's were looking for ways to unload end-of-the-year inventory and began decorating their windows with Christmas promos. And Ol' St. Nick himself wasn't the jolly fat fellow we know today until the 1930s, when Coca-Cola drew this image of him and promoted the rosy-cheeked, red-suited one in ads to pump up its winter sales, depicting him not with a hot cup of cocoa, but with a frosty Coke, saying, "It's my gift for thirst." In 1930, along came Rudolph the Red-nosed Reindeer—invented by an advertising copywriter for Montgomery Ward.

EVERYTHING GOES!

Cash-strapped cities have been selling off the "naming rights" to our public property for some time—letting some Gross And Gigantic Corporation (GAGCorp) plaster its name on the walls of stadiums, museums, concert halls, and such as though the corporations own them rather than Tommie Taxpayer.

Now this commercialization of the commons has been expanded to police cars and other "billboarding opportunities," but the peak has been an effort by Mayor Michael Bloomberg of New York to hold a naming rights flea market. Last year, he proposed allowing corporations to put their names and logos on city parks, pools, rec centers, senior centers, homeless shelters, and even social service programs. Then he proposed *selling* the Brooklyn Bridge and, what the hell, offered to throw in the Manhattan and Queensboro bridges in a package deal.

Luckily, public ridicule has held off Bloomberg's audacious auction gavel so far, but these guys won't quit—and there are plenty of corporate bidders who'd feel no embarrassment about slapping their logo on, say, Disney Central Park, or Marriott Gracie Mansion, or TeamNike City Council.

To keep up with these kinds of betrayals of the public trust (perhaps in your city, too), and to learn how to fight them, contact Commercial Alert. Also, join this watchdog's effort to enact a "Parents' Bill of Rights" to let parents control corporate access to their children:

www.commercialalert.org
503-235-8012

It's been downhill since then, as commercials and commercialism have become ubiquitous, cacophonous, intrusive, and overbearing. Major corporate advertisers assert their "right" to assault us anywhere and everywhere, even attempting to redefine the American people's identity. No longer are we treated as citizens, or even as broad-shouldered workers—but as slump-shouldered shoppers. Are you depressed? *Go shopping.* Is there a war? *Go shopping.* Do you love someone? *Go shopping.* Do you love someone a lot? *Go shopping a lot.* Is it Labor Day, Memorial Day, Martin Luther King Jr's. birthday, or any of those other "Monday" holidays? *Go shopping.* Is the economy crashing? *Go shopping.* Are consumer debt and bankruptcies at an all-time high? *Go shopping.* Did some rooster somewhere crow at sunrise this morning? *Go shopping.*

They've given our nation a bold new slogan as we surge into the twenty-first-century: "America—We Buy Stuff!"

The only problem that the crass commercializers have is that you blankety-blanks keep messing it up for them. Yeah, *you*—you brats and pushy parents who have been winning local fights from Nashville to Seattle to throw "Channel One" out of the schools, stunting this corporate effort to turn classrooms into captive audiences for ads; and *you*—you prissy citizens of New York City who forced Microsoft to come out and clean off the sidewalks and trash cans that it had splattered with ads for one of its products without bothering with such niceties as asking anyone's permission to litter the public walkways; and *you*—you aging flower children in San Francisco who persuaded the wimpy board of supervisors to return the name of Candlestick Park to (we hate this) Candlestick Park instead of reselling the name to 3Com or some other corporation with a nondescript and stupid name; and *you*—you creeps in Boston who are so stuck in yesterday that you killed the governor's effort to sell the names of four of the city's main subway stations to corporations—hey, the "Hooters Back Bay Subway Station" would've added a little pizzazz to the town; and *you*—you weenies in Texas and California and elsewhere who've banned the sale of junk food and soda in your elementary and middle schools—are you not aware that Twinkies and Mountain Dew are a perfectly balanced combo of sugars and fats, plus being loaded with Vitamin Q?

Despite the establishment's best efforts to reduce us to consumer cogs in the perpetual work-buy-work-die merry-go-round, we people of the USA have a deeper, more spiritual sense of ourselves, our families . . . and our communities.

About here some of you might be mumbling to yourself, or even saying out loud: *Hightower, now you've rowed your little boat right onto the shoals of wishful thinking. Don't you know that average people in this country are so slow that their lips move when they read stop signs, don't you know that we're such suckers that we've bought a jillion of those Big Mouth Billy Bass thingies advertised on late-night TV (a singing fish you hang on your wall, for chrissake), don't you know that people are such sheep that they'll flock—baaaaaaaa—to McDonald's and Starbucks and Gomer Pyle's Fried Pigknuckles without any thought about local identity or a community's soul?*

Well, I know that that's the image the Powers That Be have of us and constantly seek to reinforce. (A QUICK ASIDE: Dick Armey, the ex-Republican leader and well-known mental giant, made a fine contribution to this denigration of We the People when he offered this keen insight last year: "Liberals are, in my estimation, just not bright people. They don't think deeply, they don't comprehend, they don't understand a partial derivative." Ohhh, that *is* deep, Dick. Of course those who do fully understand a partial derivative have names like Ken Lay and Andy Fastow of Enron infamy. We'll get back to you, Dick, when we need another of your laser-sharp sociological observations. Until then, stay under your log. NOW BACK TO THE NARRATIVE.)

The Powers That Be would have you believe that average Americans are well below average, shallow, and don't give a damn about anything but their next Big Mac, so it's useless to try to talk to them, much less organize them to battle the McWorld that is America's happy future. Revolt is futile . . . go with the flow . . . enjoy . . . go shopping.

I find a very different America, filled with rebellious, ingenious people who care a lot about the corporatization of everything around them and are not meekly submitting. The national media conglomerates (which routinely put every local bad-news story on the air and hype it to hell and back: "Horror in a West Virginia Town," "A Brutal Death in a Los Angeles Neighborhood," "People in British Village Watch Gruesome Murder") ignore the remarkable, *everyday* stories of people standing up so beautifully in their neighborhoods and towns—probably where you live, too.

Would you like to tell us about it, Hightower?

Yes, thank you, I would. Last year, for example, on a single trip up to Washington state, I came across four beauties. I've already related one of them to you—the Stevens County victory—and I'll tell you about another one involving Fair Trade Apples later in the book. Here are the other two.

The Seven Day War for the Soul of Chelan

This was less of an organized campaign than a case of spontaneous civic combustion exploding in the face of both the city council and a very large fast-food conglomerate famous for thrusting its garish yellow arches into every neighborhood and town on the globe . . . except for Chelan.

It's been my joy to visit this small resort city on the edge of Stormy Mountain, not far from the Grand Coulee Dam. When I say "resort," put away your image of posh getaways, dazzling casinos, or the plastic Disney imitations of reality. Chelan *is* reality—a beautiful location on Lake Chelan with several low-rise hotels that cater to tens of thousands of working-class folks who flock here with their families each year, enjoying the water sports, games, restaurants, scenery, and laid-back fun of one of the great little spots on our earth. It's a chain-free town—no chain hotels, restaurants, or other franchise intrusions here.

A favorite place for locals and tourists alike is Lakeview Drive-in, a superb burger joint that's right out of *American Graffiti*. Situated smack in the center of things on a jut of parkland overlooking the lake, this drive-in is a jewel. The city owns the land and building, and for forty-five years the place has been leased to locals, most recently the Michael Mack family, which has been turning out classic drive-in grub and shakes for twenty years.

Then came August 15, 2002. At a Chelan council meeting, it was revealed that the city was in the final stages of secret negotiations to oust Mom and Pop from the Lakeview and turn the primo location over to: McDonald's. Won't this be great, thought the majority of council members—not only will we get credit for bringing the golden arches to town, but taxpayers will love us, too, since McDonald's came in here waving money, offering to sign a twenty-year lease at $36,500 a year—way above the 20K the Mack family has been paying.

"Is the council stupid, or just nuts?" was one of the first and gentlest of the letters, emails, and phone calls that deluged city hall and the media. A *Seattle Times* columnist ran a piece about the council's deal with the devil, and he got emails from former Chelan visitors from as far away as Russia—all screeching at the absurdity of giving up something good and genuine for something that's just another plastic copy of the franchised mediocrity found everywhere.

Locals, too, were appalled, finding it unfathomable that their elected officials would even think of selling out a local family—selling out Chelan's soul!—for a measly $16,500 a year in corporate lucre. Surely some big cloud of loco-dust had entered the council chambers and momentarily turned them into yelping, mouth-foaming lunatics.

Whatever, the council clearly swallowed a bottle of Old Civic castor oil, for at their next meeting, only one week later, they were miraculously cured of McDonald's-itis, voting 7–0 to terminate negotiations and return to the Mack family.

Guerrilla Art

The beauty of the American people's deeply ingrained public spirit is that it doesn't focus solely on publicly *owned* spaces. The thing that matters is community and the public good, and the spirit often asserts itself in the most unexpected places and in the most delightful ways.

It raised its pretty head in Seattle, in a hard-hit neighborhood that had long been notorious for drug dealing and street crime. The "event" took place on a stark street in mid-August 2002 at about 1 A.M. It would've gone unrecorded except that Marcus Brown, a college student, was up late working on a paper in his apartment across the street. He said he heard what sounded like heavy construction, so he went to the window. There was a group of a dozen men and women—twenty- and thirty-somethings. They wielded blowtorches, bolts, heavy sheet metal, and tools. He called out to them, asking what was up . . . but no response, nobody would talk to him. They moved efficiently and professionally, building a metal structure on the sidewalk.

What quickly emerged was a sturdy but stylishly modern table. A flower vase was bolted to the top and four metal-and-wood seats were built around the table and linked to it with heavy chains. One of the seats was a metal replica of a suitcase, which opened to reveal an electronic board game and a set of vintage playing cards. The artists were thoughtful enough to provide batteries for the game.

They then took a picture of themselves around their artistic game table, put a big bouquet of fresh flowers in the vase, and—*ppffft*—they were gone.

The table was built outside of a coffee shop, Café Stellina, opened by a couple only four months earlier. The owner of the building said of the surprise gift, "I take it as an artist's investment in the neighborhood to support this place for people to gather."

Café owner Teri Esensten was more ecstatic: "It's incredible," she enthused, calling it a "big sweet kiss." She says the people of the neighborhood, who've not seen a lot of beauty or philanthropy in these rough city blocks, have been gathering around the table at all hours, even when the café is closed—and keeping the vase filled with flowers.

Such acts are not at all uncommon. For example, a few blocks from my home, there's a small traffic median on a side street. It was a barren and forlorn patch of dirt and weeds, a triangle of maybe twenty feet on each side. No one paid it any mind—it was functional. Until a couple of years ago when it suddenly flowered—blossoming into an island of native perennials.

Had the city come out to do this? No. Was it the work of garden clubs? No. Who did it?

We still don't know. We know that it's the hands-on contribution of an older woman who lives somewhere nearby, for she's been seen digging, planting, watering, and nurturing this spot of public beauty. A few do know her name, but she wants absolutely no acknowledgment, so they rightfully keep her secret. Some have offered a bit of money to offset the water bill and upkeep, but she won't hear of it. It's her contribution.

I can point to dozens of these kinds of public gifts in Austin alone, and I know you can find them where you live, too.

I contrast them to what I call the "conspicuous philanthropists"—corporations and rich people, such as Michael Dell (Dell Computer) in my town and Bill Gates and Paul Allen (Microsoft) in Washington state. They have uncountable wealth, but they only dab bits of it out here and there with great ceremony and press conferences, getting their names chiseled into the building and their pictures on the front pages while taking care behind the scenes to make sure that their accounting departments get them a full tax deduction for their philanthropy.

The guerrilla sidewalk artists of Seattle didn't leave a card, much less cut their names in the metal table. Austin's lady gardener of the traffic triangle would be so offended she'd faint if anyone suggested that she seek a tax deduction for the summer water bills she runs up keeping that little spot beautiful for all of us who pass it.

This is the true spirit of America, the *public* spirit that the rest of the world rarely glimpses—and that we're rarely shown by our own media and political powers. This is the spirit we must highlight, tap into . . . and build our democratic future on.

CHAPTER 10

Wal-Mart:
How to Play Beat the Devil

When going out to rumble with the forces of greed and arrogance in our country, it's always good to go with a long-term strategy, for the first foray is rarely the victorious one. We have to learn as we go, have patience, and share what we learn with each other. As Willie Nelson told me:

> **"The early bird might get the worm, but remember, it's the second mouse that gets the cheese."**

Another lesson worth learning is to have fun. Fun is not against the rules. Yes, it's serious work to try taking your country back from Kleptocrats, but it's not a mopey task, and a little laughter is good for morale, good for the soul, good for the cause . . . good for its own sake.

I think of my friend Ed Garvey when I think of having fun in the midst of confronting the horrors of corporate pillaging. Ed's a first-rate lawyer and political scrapper who's taken on all kinds of stupefying avarice in his career, from the NFL owners association to Perrier, the global water plunderers. He's a committed and proven believer in the Four Principles of an Enlightened Democracy: Fairness, Justice, Equality . . . and a Good Time for All!

This guy *enjoys* the fight. If you can't laugh at yourself, at the odds stacked against you, and even laugh right in the face of the devil, then you don't belong in one of Ed's periodic runs at various bastions of power and privilege.

I once rode his corporate jet. In 1998, Garvey was the Democratic nominee for governor of Wisconsin, making an impossible uphill run against the longtime incumbent, Tommy Thompson (now in George W's cabinet). Tommy's a sour grouse of a guy, but he had enough lobbyists' money to build the Great Wall of Cash around himself. Still, Ed and his running mate, Barbara Lawton, ran a spirited race, and they asked me to do a stretch of stumping with them, so I boarded the "jet."

Thompson had use of corporate planes. Ed did not. Not to be outclassed, however, the Garvey-Lawton campaign was loaned an old RV to traverse back and forth across Wisconsin, and they proudly attached a sign proclaiming it: ED'S CORPORATE JET.

When I say "old," I mean decrepit—held together by chewing gum, baling wire, and campaign bumper stickers. But they kept it running, and it was perfectly functional—except for the heater.

Did I mention that it gets chilly in Wisconsin during the winter months, which include all of those months with an "r" in the name? The heater had two speeds: full blast and dead cold. For a while, they tried alternating—run the heater 'til it got too hot to breathe, then cut it off.

But "off" was not good if the RV was moving (and when campaigning, moving is important), for the vehicle was not exactly, shall we say, tight. Wisconsin's icy winds howled right through the abundance of cracks in our jet's body. So on to Plan B, which was that old reliable: duct tape. They slapped so many silver strips on the walls and seams of that RV that it looked like a duct tape factory had exploded.

Still, though, the icy fingers of winter found their way in, so, Plan C: blankets. At a roadside convenience store where the group had stopped for coffee, a stack of blue flannel blankets was spied, on sale for something like five bucks each. That did the trick. Everyone wrapped themselves in the blankets and stayed toasty warm on the rest of the ride to the campaign's next stop.

Once the jet finally arrived, there was a good crowd of supporters waiting at the café. Ed and Barbara rose, stripped away their blankets, and prepared to step outside to greet the voters—only to discover that their suits were now covered solid in blue blanket fuzz. So Plan D was implemented: They pulled off strips of duct tape from the RV's walls and used the sticky side to pluck away the blue fuzz. Then they stepped out as though nothing weird had happened.

This is the kind of on-the-run pluckiness that I've found in all grass-roots campaigns that matter. Ed and Barbara didn't win this particular race, but they came much closer than anyone figured they could, they lifted folks' spirits, and they inspired a lot of young people to believe that it's worth it to be in this common fight for democracy for the long haul. Last year, Barbara was elected lieutenant governor of Wisconsin, and Ed continues to be one of the best lawyers that exist for America's underdogs.

You don't win every fight, but the cause is advanced, people learn about the issues and develop their democratic skills, and the fight moves on to the next level.

TAKING ON THE BIG ONE

About all you need to know about the avaricious nature of big corporations was demonstrated in 2002 when the Anaheim Angels won the World Series. This was one of those goat-to-gloat sports stories that really rally the fans—the Angels had been around for forty-three years, winning exactly nothing, and in 2002 they were not expected to finish better than fourth in their five-team division.

But with a bunch of young no-name players who were enthusiastic and talented, the Angels made it to the play-offs, thumped the mighty New York Yankees, bumped off the powerful Oakland A's, then bested Barry Bonds and the San Francisco Giants in a down-to-the-wire, seven-game series, becoming the improbable champs of baseball.

The long-suffering fans were ready to celebrate their Angels, whom they'd supported with their ticket money for all of those losing years. As is usually done, the team's owner—Disney Inc.—arranged a parade and rally so the fans could cheer the players. The event was staged on a parking lot inside Disneyland. Great!

Not so great, however, was that Disney executives decided to charge all the fans, including the kids, *an admission fee* to get into Disneyland for the "free" parade and rally! Disney honchos later said there could have been "logistical problems" if the fans had been allowed to get in for free.

These are people who know everything about price and nothing about value.

The Beast of Bentonville

The apex of avarice and arrogance has been achieved by ol' Sam Walton's little chain operation out of Bentonville, Arkansas. Ironically, Mr. Sam tried to instill a small-town retailing ethic of treat-the-people-right as he built his Wal-Mart chain. But Sam's dead . . . and his spirit is even deader at Wal-Mart.

Among the cold-eyed executives who now rule this retailing empire, the only thing left of the small-town ethic is rank pretense. They spend half a billion bucks a year on carefully crafted, poll-tested ads to convey the image of aw-shucks-we're-just-folks-from-Arkansas, a friendly group of neighborly storekeepers and hyper-friendly "greeters" trying to bring good prices to you and yours.

Most everyone knows Wal-Mart by that image—yet few of the people who see the ads or shop there have any awareness of how big, powerful, ruthless, and predatory this global corporation has become, deliberately stomping on its workers, the towns and neighborhoods it enters, the local businesses it goes after, and its own suppliers. One who knows the company up close and personally is Bill McDonough, a leader of the United Food and Commercial Workers, who calls Wal-Mart "this devouring beast of a corporation."

Let's measure this sucker:

- Wal-Mart is now the largest corporation on earth, having passed both General Motors and ExxonMobil for the top slot. It'll rake in nearly $250 billion in revenue in 2003—more than the entire GDP of Ireland and Israel combined (on *one day* late in 2002 it had $1.4 billion in revenue—more than the GDP of thirty-six nations).
- It has some 4,400 stores worldwide (3,600 in the U.S.), including its SuperCenters and Sam's Clubs and its new, quaintly named Neighborhood Markets.
- It has surpassed GM as the world's largest employer, with 1.3 million workers—about one of every 120 workers in our country, and one of

every twenty retail workers (more employees than the U.S. Army has soldiers).

- Not only is it the biggest corporation and biggest retailer, it also has become the biggest seller of groceries, surpassing Kroger after having launched its supermarket operation only ten years ago.
- It's the biggest seller of jewelry, photo processing, dog food, vitamins—and now it's moving into banking, gasoline, used cars, travel, flower delivery, Internet access . . . and who knows what all.

Well, so what, Hightower, like it or not, we live in a world of gigantism these days—didn't you know that the smallest coffee you can buy at Starbucks is a "Tall" and that your choices at 7-Eleven are the Big Gulp, Super Big Gulp, or Extremely Big Gulp? You've got your regular beers and your Tall Boys, but you don't see any "Small Boy" beer, do you? Besides, Wal-Mart delivers low prices, so who gives a damn how big it is?

Glad you mentioned that price thing. On their stores' walls, in their ads, on their trucks, and probably on the toilet paper in the executive washrooms, Wal-Mart emblazons its slogan: "Always Low Prices." More than a mantra, "low, low prices" is Wal-Mart's modus operandi. So one might ask: *How do they produce those low prices?*

Do they simply take less in profits? Surely you jest. Wal-Mart sucks up nearly $7 billion a year in profits, more than any other retailer on the planet—taking twice as much as the next fifteen retailers combined.

Do they keep a tight rein on the pay packages of top executives? Get serious. The CEO alone hauled off $11.5 million in personal pay last year.

Do the top owners (Sam Walton's widow and children) hold down their take in keeping with his small-town, don't-put-on-airs ethic? Now you're getting delusional. *Of the ten richest people in the world, five are Waltons, with a total of $100 billion in personal wealth—more than Bill Gates.*

And, as you can clearly see from the omnipresent sprawl of its stores wherever you live, Wal-Mart spends a fortune on buildings and trucks and equipment, including a computer network that is rivaled only by the Pentagon's. So where do they make their cuts? Who pays for those "Always Low Prices"?

Meet the Associates

This corporation doesn't have workers or employees, it has "associates," and not since Walt Disney's old animated cartoon of the Seven Dwarfs singing "Heigh-ho, heigh-ho, it's off to work we go" have you seen such a happy work group. For public consumption, that is.

Every shift at Wal-Mart begins with a mandatory pep rally, where all the associates are expected to demonstrate their unbridled enthusiasm for the job, the company, free enterprise, the Waltons, and probably the Seven Dwarfs cartoon. In 2002, Bill Moyers sent reporter Steven Greenhouse into a store in Rogers, Arkansas, where he exposed the hokum of these "rallies" by simply turning the camera on one and letting PBS viewers see it for what it is. It was 6 A.M., and the rally was conducted by the store manager under the watchful eye of a Wal-Mart vice president, sent to make sure the spin was right.

The scene began in the "associates area," a back room where the workers stash their purses and whatnot prior to their shift.

Vice President: "This is our heart right here. It talks about respect for the individual, and that's what we always go back to." Uh-huh. Nice opening spiel.

Store Manager: "Good morning, associates. Please come over to menswear for the morning meeting." And over they traipsed. (Was it just me, or did they seem especially perky for the cameras?)

Store Manager: "Good morning, everybody."

FEEL THE POWER

In a *Dilbert* comic strip, the pointy-haired boss comes up to two employees and hands each of them a button. He says: "Every employee will wear a button that says 'I'm empowered.'"

One of the stunned employees stammers, "I don't want to." But the boss, oblivious to the irony, says, "You have to."

As the two employees walk off with their "I'm empowered" buttons dutifully pinned to their shirts, the second one says, "That was everything you need to know about life in one package."

Associates: "Good morning, Matt!" (No, it wasn't just me, they *were* especially perky.)

Store Manager: "Well, great day in sales yesterday. It was a fantastic day. Great job, thank you, Debbie."

Call me the class cutup, but what do you think headquarters would've done to Matt if he'd said for the cameras, "Jeez, you people really stunk up the place yesterday! The fruit stand down the road made more sales than you did. I'm thinking of replacing you all with a herd of goats." I'd have *paid* to see the perky faces of the associates after that. But no one got off script.

Store Manager: "Who's number one?"

Associates: "The customer, always!"

Walt would have puked.

Behind this manufactured cheerfulness is the fact that the average Wal-Mart employee makes $15,000 a year for full-time work. Most are denied even this poverty income, for they're held to part-time work. While the company brags that 70 percent of its workers are full-time, it defines "full-time" as twenty-eight hours a week, meaning that these employees gross under $11,000 a year.

Health-care benefits? Only if you've been there two years, then the plan hits you with such huge premiums and high deductibles that few can afford it—only 38 percent of Wal-Marters are covered.

Thinking union? Get outta here, you Bolshevik! "Wal-Mart is opposed to unionization," reads a company guidebook for supervisors. "You, as a manager, are expected to support the company's position and you may be asked to be a campaigner for your company. This may mean walking a tightrope between legitimate campaigning and improper conduct."

This company is rabidly anti-union. John Lehman, a former Wal-Mart manager, notes that a confidential document titled "Manager's Tool Box to Remaining Union Free" is given to every manager, and it includes a toll-free hotline direct to HQ in Bentonville, where "labor relations" teams (a corporate *nom de guerre* for "union busters") stand ready to board a company jet and be deployed to any spot where there's so much as a whisper of organizing talk among the associates.

Lehman told PBS that the jet whisks in and guys in ties spill out, "and they interview all the managers, they interview the associates. They start talking antiunion, 'We don't need a union.' They start showing videos. They start going through personnel files looking for dirt on any associate that is a union supporter, so that they can get 'em out legitimately."

The company goes to any length to crush even the smallest outcropping of union sentiment. Eleven meat cutters who worked at a Super-Center in Jacksonville, Texas, learned this in February 2000. These derring-do employees were sick of being pressed to work harder and longer for the same low pay. "We signed [union] cards, and all hell broke loose," says Sidney Smith, one of the Jacksonville meat cutters who established the first ever Wal-Mart union in the U.S. Sidney was making $15,000 a year.

They voted to join the United Food and Commercial Workers. And a week and a half later, Wal-Mart announced that it was closing its meat-cutting departments in all its stores and would henceforth buy its meat prepackaged from companies using nothing but nonunion labor.

No wonder, then, that turnover in the stores is above 50 percent a year, with many having to replace 100 percent of its employees each year, and some reaching as high as 300 percent turnover! The Bentonville overseers care not, however, since there's a ready supply of cheap labor across the land, and since high turnover means that few workers reach the two-year point when they would qualify for the company's miserly health care plan.

Spreading the Empire

Wally World, as the company is called by its irreverent associates in their off-camera moments, is a colossus, having amassed more power and wealth than any other single company since ol' John D. Rockefeller's Standard Oil Corporation a century ago.

Wal-Mart got to the top the old-fashioned way—by roughing people up. The corporate ethos of the Bentonville headquarters, which runs a more regimented chain of command than the Pentagon, dictates three guiding principles for all of its managers: Extract the very last penny possible from human toil, squeeze the last dime from every supplier, and don't let anyone stop you from carrying out the expansionist agenda we hand you.

BANANA REPUBLIC

Although the Jacksonville Eleven had their butcher jobs eliminated, Wal-Mart couldn't legally fire them for supporting a union, so they kept them on doing other work . . . for a while. Sidney Smith says that managers soon began picking on them: "They found little faults that they never, ever dreamed of before," he told PBS in an interview.

On Labor Day(!) 2000, Sidney was called into the manager's office and confronted by his supervisor, assistant manager, store manager, and "a representative from Bentonville" . . . and fired on the spot.

Why? [Cue the *Dragnet* theme]—*Dum de dum-dum:* **Stealing a banana.** *Dum de dum-dum dummmm.*

Now, cue the Three Stooges. The brass leaned into Sidney and accused him of theft of company property, specifically in the form of a half-eaten banana. It seems that he had bought a box of over-ripe bananas from the produce section for 50 cents. But . . . BUT, Mr. Smith . . . you ate one of those bananas *before* you ponied up the cash, didn't you, Mr. Smith? . . . DIDN'T YOU? CONFESS!

Actually, countered Sidney, he'd eaten only half of the banana, and besides, he had the fifty cents at the ready to pay for the box. Not good enough, snarled the brass. As Smith tells it, they said: "'Well, we gonna have to terminate you anyway, for stealing.' And that's how they got rid of Sidney Smith, just like that." On Labor Day. Nice.

Asked later about the slapstick absurdity of this, Mr. Cole Peterson, the executive vice president of Wal-Mart's "People Division" (again I'm making none of this up, including these titles), told PBS, and I quote: *"Ah, the termination for, ah, grazing, is a, a well-understood and well-accepted policy within the retail area."*

Find this priceless exchange at **www.pbs.org/now/transcript/ transcript_walmart.html.**

It would be dangerous enough if its power was wielded only through its own far-flung empire, but Wal-Mart now sets the standard for all retailing and much of manufacturing. For example, it's on a messianic mission to impose its own unremitting, exploitive, low-wage, no-union dictate on the entire business world.

It has, and it uses, the swat of its shelf space to enforce its will. Wal-Mart sells from a tenth to a fourth of all of the products made by such giants as Kraft, Kimberly-Clark, Heinz, Fruit-of-the-Loom, Clorox, Revlon, RJR Tobacco, Gillette, Rubbermaid, Procter & Gamble, Hasbro, Dial, and Rayovac. It has even more power over smaller companies, especially start-ups wanting to get onto Wal-Mart shelves.

Its marketing clout is so enormous that 450 manufacturers have opened offices in Bentonville, with another 800 planning to open offices there—all ready to jump as high as they can when the big dude shouts, "Froggie!" You want clout? There are two daily nonstop flights from New York City's LaGuardia Airport to Bentonville (population 19,730), or "Vendorville" as it's become known.

More than 65,000 companies supply the retailer with the stuff on its shelves, and it constantly hammers each of them about cutting their production costs deeper and deeper in order to offer cheaper wholesale prices to Wal-Mart. It even requires some suppliers to open their books so Bentonville executives can red-pencil what CEO Lee Scott terms "unnecessary costs."

Of course, among the unnecessaries to him are the use of decently paid labor and the need to produce anything in the US of A.

WAL-MART GOES COMMUNIST!

While cynically running ads featuring the flag and proclaiming "We Buy American," the vast majority of the products sold at Wal-Mart are made in cheap-labor hellholes, especially China.

It is the largest importer of Chinese-made products in the world, buying $10 billion worth of merchandise from several thousand Chinese factories each year. In 2001, it even moved its worldwide purchasing headquarters to China.

"Follow our lead overseas" is the insistent message. Wal-Mart is un-abashed about pointing its finger in the direction of China or other low-wage places to scavenge for abysmally low production costs. It doesn't even have to say "Move to China," for its purchasing executives demand such an impossible low-ball price from suppliers that they can meet it only if they follow Wal-Mart's cheap-labor example.

With its dominance over its own 1.3 million low-wage "associates" (expected to number 2.1 million in the next five years) and over its 65,000 suppliers, plus its alliances with ruthless labor abusers abroad, this one company is not merely the pacesetter for all corporations, it is now the world's most powerful private force for lowering labor stan-dards and stifling the middle-class aspirations of workers everywhere.

Using its sheer size, market clout, and massive advertising budget, the company also is squeezing out competitors and forcing its remain-ing rivals to adopt its price-is-everything approach. Even such big boys as Toys "R" Us and Kroger are daunted by the company's brutish power, saying that they feel compelled to slash wages and benefits and to search the globe for sweatshop suppliers in order to compete in the downward race to match Wal-Mart's prices.

"You have to mimic their operations," a big supermarket competitor said sadly, "and you get reduced to the lowest common denominators."

BEAT THE DEVIL

There are at least three pieces of advice worth heeding in life:

> *Never* ride a bull drunk.
> *Never* drive 100 mph through a Southern town with the sheriff's drunken sixteen-year-old daughter on your lap.
> *Never* ring the devil's doorbell unless you're prepared for him to answer.

That last one applies to anyone daring to stand up to the Benton-ville Bullies, for they maintain a diabolical force of legal sharpies, lobbyists, accounting slicks, union busters, predatory pricers, development schemers, and other operatives whose sole reason for being on the payroll is to make sure that Wal-Mart gets its way, always.

So who would dare confront such an awesome array, such a corporate superpower—the largest profit-seeking force in the world, possessing an unlimited budget for battle, as well as what amounts to economic weapons of mass destruction and a maniacal willingness to use them?

We the People would, that's who!

The national media establishment has mostly averted its eyes from the story, and the politicians who pocket Wal-Mart's campaign cash don't even want to hear about it, but thousands of us regular Janes and Joes in hundreds of places all across our country are part of a rising and remarkably successful grassroots rebellion against the bullying beast.

Whose Town Is It?

Does Wal-Mart—and other big-box stores like Home Depot, or formula chains like Starbucks—have any inherent right to storm into your neighborhood or town, destroying the local identity, engaging in predatory pricing to force out local competitors, busting the middle-class pay scale, sprawling its garish stores and traffic over any sense of community scale, rigging secret backroom deals with politicians and developers—and generally occupying your community while it extracts cash from your local economy and hauls it off to corporate headquarters?

No.

You have the rights. You're still the sovereign in this country, not corporations. It's your town, not theirs.

That's what Kathleen Lewis decided when she learned in 2001 that her community of Glendale, Arizona, was about to be Wal-Marted. It was a typical Wal-Mart sneak attack. A local developer in Glendale, a middle-class suburb of Phoenix, had earlier announced its intention to build a "neighborhood shopping plaza," promising that it would be a "visual oasis" of shops and restaurants. Sure, OK, said the city council, and few folks paid any attention, until . . . KABLAM! With the deal sealed, the developer finally dropped the bomb: The anchor "shop" in the development was to be Wal-Mart.

Not a mere store, either, but a SuperCenter. I don't know if you've ever been to one of these things, but they are to big what Enron was to naughty. Big doesn't say it—this one was to be 220,000 square feet. That's more than four football fields under one roof. Plus parking lots. Plus the roar of delivery trucks and a constant snarl of traffic, with thirty-six thousand cars a day added to the neighborhood. Plus those orangish Day-Glo lights that add such a charming touch of urban ambiance. Plus the fact that this was to be a twenty-four-hour, seven-days-a-week operation.

Kathleen Lewis considers herself conservative, a Republican even, and certainly a supporter of free enterprise. But this wasn't free enterprise—it was corporate bullying by an enormous outfit that feels free to sledgehammer its way into any community—without even asking locals what they think. "One thing I know," says Kathleen, "is the difference between right and wrong. And this was wrong."

She made some calls and talked to neighbors, finding that she was not alone in her outrage that some faraway pencil pushers would be so arrogant and mendacious as to decide unilaterally to remake this Arizona community in the Wal-Mart image. Around their kitchen tables, Kathleen and other mad-as-hellers, who had not previously considered themselves to be rebels, organized The Glendale Rebellion. Kathleen's local shop, the Headlines Styling & Barbering Service, became the headquarters for their new group, The Glendale Citizens for Responsible Development.

Like a rhinoceros flicking at a gnat with its tail, Bentonville paid no mind to the group until—whoa! What is this?—the city council withdrew its zoning approval for the project, citing the obvious fact that it had been lied to. All the way from Arizona, you could hear the corporate jet revving up in Arkansas.

"Unfair!" screeched Wal-Mart operatives. And, in a remarkably obtuse bit of irony, the autocratic behemoth demanded something it had already denied the people: democracy. It called for a citywide referendum on the project, hired a lobbyist to direct its campaign, and proceeded to dump hundreds of thousands of dollars into slick ads, a special five-minute video mailed to twenty thousand homes, and other campaign tactics, including mudslinging denigration of the opponents.

Against this show of corporate firepower, the Glendale group had only $8,600 to spend, but it mustered a wealth of people power and democratic determination. Local 99 of the United Food and Commercial Workers joined the fray, going door-to-door, engaging thousands of families in front-porch conversations about this wage-busting corporation. Local businesses got involved against the Arkansas predator, knowing of Wal-Mart's ruthless practice of selling beneath its own costs in order to drive out local competitors.

Even the *Arizona Republic*—a paper owned by Dan Quayle's family—stood against the corporate intrusion, noting that "we pay a price in civic capital" when a Wal-Mart muscles its way in over independent business, adding that "a workforce of part-time employees hardly builds the wealth necessary to allow families to get ahead."

Wal-Mart kept reaching into its bottomless bag of money and political tricks to pull out a victory. For example, to confuse the issue, it got the ballot question worded so that voters wanting to say "no" to the project had to vote "yes"—Orwell meets Kafka. It ran ads and distributed fliers in this conservative town warning that "Big Labor" bosses and goons were picking on poor little Wally and trying to dictate to the people of Glendale—apparently unaware that quite a few of the town's people *are* union members who have extended family, friends, and solid roots there (more than could be said of the Bentonville bunch).

As election day approached, Wal-Mart got goosey about its chances and rushed to court to demand a postponement. Yes, a postponement of an election that it had set. But the court nixed the ploy, the election was held, the turnout was twice what it usually is . . . and Wal-Mart was stunned that the tally wasn't even close—Glendale voted 60–40 against being Wal-Marted.

More stunning was that this was *the tenth time in three years* that local coalitions had come together in various Arizona cities and stopped new Wal-Mart stores. Arizona!

Nothing all that unique about Arizona, either, for people coast to coast have been standing up to Wal-Mart projects . . . and winning. Here are a few of the community victories in just the past couple of years: Belfast (ME), Chestertown (MD), Dallas, DeLand (FL), Denver, Dubuque, Henderson (KY), Inglewood (CA), Manor (PA), Martinez (CA), McKinney (TX), New Orleans, Old Saybrook (CT), Sandfly (GA), Santa Fe, Spring Valley (TX), Reedley (CA), Taos, and Westerville (OH).

VICTORIOUS SECRET

Wal-Mart is the leader, but it's not the only giant that's feeling the jolt of citizen rejection. Home Depot, Ikea, Barnes & Noble, Stop & Shop, Lowe's, and other supersized stores have been defeated as well.

Al Norman's terrific organization, Sprawl-Busters, works with citizen groups and communities nationwide and in Canada to battle these corporate invaders. A strategist, planner, speaker, writer, debater, and burr under the saddle of the giants, Norman is known as the guru of the anti–Wal-Mart movement. Here's his latest list of "Victorious Secrets" that the media isn't telling us about—170 towns and cities that have beaten a big-box store at least once:

Chandler, AZ	Silverhorse, CO	Evergreen Park, IL
Douglas, AZ	Woodland Park, CO	Lake in the Hills, IL
Flagstaff, AZ	Canton, CT	Mokena, IL
Gilbert, AZ	Colchester, CT	Plainfield, IL
Glendale, AZ	New Milford, CT	Wheaton, IL
Mesa, AZ	Old Saybrook, CT	New Albany, IN
Phoenix, AZ	Orange, CT	Lawerence, KS
Scottsdale, AZ	Plainville, CT	Manhattan, KS
Tucson, AZ	Tolland, CT	Overland Park, KS
Auburn, CA	Rohoboth, DE	Witchita, KS
Eureka, CA	Bonita Springs, FL	Fort Wright, KY
Grass Valley, CA	Clermont, FL	Henderson, KY
North Auburn, CA	Hallandale, FL	Barnstable, MA
Reedly, CA	Lake Forest, FL	Billerica, MA
San Francisco, CA	Naples, FL	Boxboro, MA
San Juan Capistrano, CA	St. Petersburg, FL	Braintree, MA
Santa Maria, CA	Temple Terrace, FL	Dartmouth, MA
Santa Rosa, CA	Athens, GA	Easthampton, MA
Simi Valley, CA	Atlanta, GA	Greenfield, MA
Yucaipa, CA	Savannah, GA	Lee, MA
Fort Collins, CO	Hawaii Kai, HI	Northboro, MA
Jefferson County, CO	Mason City, IA	Plymouth, MA
Longmont, CO	Hailey, ID	Reading, MA

Saugus, MA	Reno, NV	Clemson, SC
Somerset, MA	Aurora, NY	Arlington, TX
Westford, MA	Buffalo, NY	Cooleyville, TX
Yarmouth, MA	Cazenovia, NY	Dallas, TX
Accokeek, MD	East Aurora, NY	Fort Worth, TX
Chestertown, MD	Hornell, NY	Houston, TX
Easton, MD	Hyde Park, NY	Kennendale, TX
Gaithersburg, MD	Ithaca, NY	McKinney, TX
Hagerstown, MD	Lake Placid, NY	Murphy, TX
Kent Island, MD	Leeds, NY	Richardson, TX
Paradise, MD	New Paltz, NY	Layton, UT
Bangor, ME	New Rochelle, NY	Taylorsville, UT
Belfast, ME	North Greenbush, NY	Accomac, VA
Ellsworth, ME	Saranac Lake, NY	Roanoke, VA
Rockland, ME	Beavercreek, OH	Warenton, VA
Wells, ME	Broadview Heights, OH	Williamsburg, VA
Bedford, MI	Burnsville, OH	St. Albans, VT
Fenton, MI	Highland Heights, OH	St. Johnsbury, VT
Olivette, MO	Lorain, OH	Williston, VT
Springfield, MO	North Olmstead, OH	Gig Harbor, WA
St. Louis, MO	Ottawa, OH	Port Townsend, WA
Warsaw, MO	Strongsville, OH	Brookfield, WI
Asheville, NC	Westerville, OH	Menomonce Falls, WI
Durham, NC	Westlake, OH	Racine, WI
Hickory, NC	Yellow Springs, OH	Waukesha, WI
Lincoln, NE	Warren, OR	Morgantown, WV
Claremont, NH	Lower Gwynmed, PA	Park Royal, BC
Peterborough, NH	Milford, PA	Surrey, BC
Deptford, NJ	Mount Joy, PA	Miramichi, NB
Englewood, NJ	Warrick, PA	Brampton, ONT
Hamilton, NJ	West Hempfield, PA	Guelph, ONT
Manalapan, NJ	Barranquitas, PR	Oakville, ONT
Albuquerque, NM	Utado, PR	Waterloo, ONT
Tijeras, NM	Middletown, RI	

www.sprawl-busters.com 413-772-6289

Localism

I hail from a small-business family—my daddy and momma ran both a wholesale magazine operation and the Main Street News in Denison, Texas. And to paraphrase George W, I also know about small-business people, because "I are one"—my Saddle-Burr Productions is a small (bordering on tiny) enterprise that develops my books, radio work, newsletter, columns, speaking engagements, and whatever other trouble I can stir up with pen and mouth.

So, in the spirit of full consumer disclosure, I'm biased for local, independent, unique, smallish business. I like the spirit of places like Twin Oaks Hardware, which was located just a few blocks from my home in Austin. Donna and Harry DeFoy ran it for years until they retired last year, declaring on a big banner, MOM & POP ARE POOPED. You could get a gizmo for any gadget there, get anything fixed, and get a load of B.S. from Harry on any topic. It was wonderful.

You might also get crossways with the DeFoys' bassett hound. Not because he'd snap at you or anything like that, but because the portly old fellow spent much of his day snoozing, sprawled across one aisle or another, and you could trip over him if you weren't watching. Naturally, they nicknamed him "Speedbump." That one dog provided more genuine ambiance than you'll ever find in a Home Depot.

But there are a host of unbiased reasons for saying that we ought not let the giant chains remake our local economies. One is price. I don't mean the price tag on the products, but the exorbitant price we pay for Wal-Mart's "low price" model. Such companies are predators, hitting neighborhoods and towns like a neutron bomb, leaving buildings standing, but sucking out all of the economic and democratic vitality.

Wal-Mart concedes that when it comes to town, it's out to eliminate competitors. Any store it opens can crush our local groceries, pharmacies, hardware stores, clothiers, and other retailers, not by being more efficient (and damned sure not with super service), but by slashing its prices below what it pays for the products—a tactic known as (WARNING: TECHNICAL TERM APPROACHING) "predatory pricing."

I hear your mind whirring. With my supersensory perception, I can

GET HELP

The Institute for Local Self-Reliance, based in Minneapolis, is a creative group of thinkers and doers who help people figure out how to develop their homegrown economies without becoming dependent on the big-box operators.

Stacy Mitchell, one of the institute's researchers, is author of *The Home Town Advantage: How to Defend Your Main Street Against Chain Stores and Why It Matters.* She notes that decisions about the makeup of our local economy "should be made by the people who feel the impact of those decisions. That's the essence of democracy." Mitchell says that when local business is dominated by absentee owners, "decisions that affect our communities—whether to close a bookstore in a distressed neighborhood, protect a watershed, stock a controversial book, pay a living wage, or contribute to a local cause—are made in distant boardrooms where the values and needs of the local community carry little or no weight. In the case of locally owned business, those decisions are made locally by people who live in the community and who are going to feel the impacts.

"Small, local businesses also keep dollars in the local economy. If you shop at a local store or support a local farmer, those dollars in turn tend to be spent with other locally owned businesses, and so they help support a network of community-based enterprises."

The institute tracks grassroots efforts to revitalize local economies, and it advises communities nationwide on solutions for strengthening homegrown business.

www.ilsr.org

hear you thinking, *What're you talking about, Hightower? Even Wal-Mart can't sell below cost and stay in business.* No trick to it. Wal-Mart has 4,400 stores. It can lose money at the one in your area 'til the cows come home and not hurt its companywide bottom line one bit. But your local stores don't have a global network of stores to subsidize them, so Wal-Mart can just sit on top of them with a losing hand . . . and still win.

This isn't competition—it's mugging. And when it's over, when the local competitors are bled to death, this Wal-Mart store's prices rise. Then, the dollars you spend there are used to subsidize another mugging down the road.

I'm hearing you again. You're saying, *Give me a for-instance on this predatory pricing thing, or I won't believe that those nice friendly country people from Arkansas would do such a thing.* Right you are. Check out Wal-Mart's gas pumps, now in the parking lots of seven hundred of its stores and soon to spring up like dandelions all across Wal-Martland . . . assuming its lobbyists can change the laws.

The company is selling gasoline at prices below what it pays to get it into the pumps. Eddie, or Felipe, or Maybelle, or Khanh, or Royce, or whoever's selling the gas down the road can't do that—they don't have the deep pockets to match a losing price.

How do I know Wal-Mart is doing this? Because several states have laws against it, and rather than comply, Wal-Mart is openly trying to repeal the laws, essentially claiming a right to kill its competitors by predatory pricing. Caught selling below cost in Florida, where it's illegal, Wal-Mart launched a lobbying and petition drive to make it legal. Likewise in Oklahoma, Wal-Mart was caught and has run to federal court, claiming a constitutional right to kill competition.

In Wisconsin, the legislature was quietly moving to do Wal-Mart's bidding on this, slipping a provision into the budget bill in 2001. But then the media reported a poll commissioned by the state's independent gas station operators. It showed that seven out of ten Wisconsin consumers opposed letting the giants sell below cost, knowing that this would kill competition and leave them at the tender mercies of, say, Wal-Mart. The provision was taken out of the budget bill.

Well, I hear you saying, *at least Wal-Mart is a job creator for our communities.* Sorry, no. By crushing local businesses, this giant *eliminates* three decent jobs for every two poorly paid, part-time, high-turnover Wal-Mart jobettes that it creates. It's an extractor of community wealth, not a creator. It doesn't buy locally. It doesn't bank locally. It doesn't advertise locally.

In Kirksville, Missouri, a Wal-Mart SuperCenter opened a few years ago. In short order, four clothing stores, four grocery stores, a stationery

KEEP AUSTIN WEIRD

I live in a great city, made great by all of its iconoclastic, maverick, funky, artsy, rascally, political, laid-back, agitating, rocking, fun people. I know that some of those adjectives seem contradictory, but it's all here—often in the same person, which is what helps make Austin weird. The neighborhood I live in has a slogan: "We're All Here Because We're Not All There."

In the last couple of years, though, the official unofficial city-wide slogan (causing the Chamber of Commerce suits to grind their teeth, for they're promoting a proper corporate image) has become: "Keep Austin Weird." It's on people's bumpers, on our T-shirts, mugs, websites, and wherever else we can plaster it, for it's our rallying cry for the ongoing battle for the soul of the city. Are we to be just another splotch of CorporateWorld—or something different, special, interesting . . . Austiny?

In the past year this battle came to focus on a vacant block at 6th and Lamar. Whole Foods Market, which began in Austin as a funky health food store and has now sprawled across the country as a huge chain, is developing this block to serve as its headquarters store and offices. This would be no problem, except that Whole Foods execs chose to add an out-of-state retail partner to its block: Borders, the book and records chain out of Michigan.

Alright, we're not purists here. Austin already has two Borders superstores, six Barnes & Noble Superstores, Tower Records, and the rest of the full corporate set. And, aside from the perverse symbolism of our homegrown Whole Foods hitching up so whorishly with a big-box operator, this would not have been such a stunner and rallying point for us advocates of Austin weirdness except for two things.

First, Whole Foods was trying to bring Borders to a spot right across the street from two Austin originals: BookPeople and Waterloo Records. These independent businesses are not merely great stores (among the finest in all of America) but they are also a cultural, economic, and spiritual lifeline linking local musicians, writers, and artists to a city full of people who are readers and music lovers. Why slam them, threaten their existence, and insult everything that Austin stands for by putting a predator in their own front yard?

BookPeople is the finest book-signing venue in the city for all authors who either are from here or travel to Austin on their book tours. It ranks with Tattered Cover in Denver, Politics & Prose in D.C., Ruminator in the Twin Cities, Powell's in Portland, Elliot Bay Book Company in Seattle, Cody's in Berkeley, Inkwood in Tampa, Midnight Special in Santa Monica, Boulder Books, and all the other wonderful independent stores that are shrines to readers. BookPeople has a phenomenal stock, and it holds readings every day (including, I'm proud to disclose, several appearances by *moi*)—it's a jewel.

And across Lamar from BookPeople is Waterloo Records—an Austin icon, considered one of the best music stores in the country, that really is a community center for our city's wonderful music world. This store nurtures local musicians—holding CD-release parties at least a couple of times a week, prominently featuring Austin artists, taking their CDs on consignment, and being an advocate for them. Asleep at the Wheel, W. C. Clarke, Omar & the Howlers, Marcia Ball, Ruben Ramos, The Mighty Bells of Joy, Willie Nelson, Michelle Shocked, Joe Ely, Toni Price, Floyd Domino, Angela Strehli, Jimmie Dale Gilmore, Nanci Griffith—plus dozens of talented folks you've not heard of yet, but will—have gotten a boost from Waterloo.

Foisting the deep-pocket Borders empire on these two was insult enough, but here comes the injury part: The developer of the property mooched a $2.1 million subsidy from the city officials to do this dirty deed, picking our pockets to destroy two local businesses that represent the very best of Austin! Holy Adam Smith!

Austin's laid-back, but we were not about to roll over for this one. BookPeople and Waterloo don't just have customers, they have supporters, and they rallied the cause.

BookPeople's head guy, Steve Bercu, says, "It's un-American to be against competition," so he doesn't sweat going head-to-head with the boxes, since he's been doing that for years. But he does have a teensy problem with his tax dollars, and those of his customers, being siphoned across the street to build his competitor. Steve's quirky like that.

So are most Austinites. A new group called Liveable City came together in 2002 to promote homegrown enterprise. It commissioned an independent economic analysis that found:

- The two local businesses each return more than three times as much economic value back to the community as the chain retailer would:
  −Borders: $800,000
  −BookPeople: $2.8 million
  −Waterloo: $4.1 million
- The proposed Borders will result in a net loss to our local economy, for it would be expected to take as much as $3 million a year from the sales of BookPeople and Waterloo, diverting much of that money to its Michigan headquarters.
- Borders would employ far fewer people in Austin and at lower wages.
- The independent stores spend their accounting, advertising, and other budgets here; Borders houses its service functions in Michigan.
- Borders would offer little support for local talent—while Waterloo, for example, produces $600,000 a year for local musicians who sell their CDs there, Borders only sells CDs of those Austin artists who are on major national labels.

In April 2003 weird won over corporate as Borders announced its withdrawal from the project. The chain made no mention of the community upheaval, but it didn't have to—even a giant can feel the ground moving out from under it.

store, a fabric store, and a lawn-and-garden center were gone. And with their demise, the *Kirksville Daily Express* has lost major ad revenue and is struggling. Townspeople now go to Wal-Mart, or have to leave town to shop. The SuperCenter sits there on the edge of Kirksville like a demonic tombstone sucking up local money and channeling it to Bentonville, where a portion of it can be used as capital for Wal-Mart's assault on the next Kirksville.

On the Job

Walter Reuther, the great (an overused term, but it applies to this fellow) labor and social leader, head of the United Auto Workers, was once being given a tour of an ultramodern auto plant by a top executive at Ford. The official stopped, pointed to several robots on the line, and said to Reuther, "How are you union people going to collect union dues from these guys?" Reuther shot back, "How are you going to get them to buy Fords?"

By dictating a new economy for low-wage workers, Wal-Mart and its corporate disciples are not merely cutting their wholesale prices, they're doing something far more radical and dangerous to America's social equilibrium: They are cutting themselves loose from America's two-century-old quest for an egalitarian society. Let me put it in real-life terms: *They are abandoning the notion that the middle class is essential to America.*

And since Wal-Mart is by far the biggest employer and is capable of compelling so many other major corporations to take the low-wage road, the upshot of their actions is that America itself is abandoning its middle-class pretensions and possibilities. Thanks to this shift, the fastest-growing class in America is the working poor. For decades, our country's social cohesion has been grounded in a broad agreement that full-time work will afford you a middle-class slice. The Wal-Mart model breaks that agreement—its own "associates" can't afford to buy a Ford on Wal-Mart pay.

WAL-MART'S CONTRIBUTIONS TO BUSH AND THE GOP, 2000 AND 2002: $2,159,330

How long do they think they can hold down so many hardworking people?

Already, the rebellion is simmering

within the belly of the beast. The company tries to hide it, and the media rarely probes (whatever happened to the idea of the "inquiring reporter," anyway?), but those happy little "associates" have been hauling Wal-Mart's corpulent hulk into court constantly. It's the most sued corporation in the country, facing more than five thousand actions per year (almost fourteen a day!), for it is an unrepentant, recidivist criminal, routinely violating practically all employee rights and all of America's labor laws. For example:

• The Equal Employment Opportunity Commission has had to file more suits against the Bentonville billionaire's club for cases of disability discrimination than against any other corporation. A top EEOC lawyer told *Business Week*, "I have never seen this kind of blatant disregard for the law." In Arizona, the company was caught in such shameful discrimination against the disabled that a judge not only assessed a $750,000 fine, but also required it to run commercials admitting it was guilty of disability bias.

• Sidney Smith and the Jacksonville Eleven aren't the only ones roughed up for trying to organize a union. The National Labor Relations Board (not exactly a fierce proponent of labor organizing) has issued more than forty formal complaints in twenty-five states in the past five years against Wal-Mart for using illegal tactics to deny its workers the right to have a union. The former top lawyer for the NLRB found that the company's tactics (illegal spying, threats, firings, etc.) were so widespread that he was considering issuing a rare national complaint naming Wal-Mart's top executives. But George W came into office, this lawyer was replaced, and the new Bushized NLRB has airily dismissed any action, declaring that "there is an insufficient basis to seek a nationwide order against Wal-Mart."

• The largest class-action suit in the country is under way on behalf of nearly 1 million women who've worked at Wal-Mart, charging massive sex discrimination in pay levels and promotions. Women make up 65 percent of the employees, but only 10 percent of store managers, and they fill only 33 percent of overall managerial positions (assistants, department supervisors, etc.), while Wal-Mart's major competitors have 56 percent women managers.

• The few women who have become store managers are paid an average of $16,400 a year less than the men. In Wally World, women quickly hit the glass ceiling and are then asked to Windex it. Cases abound of women who have had to train the men promoted above them.

Then there's an especially irksome practice that has really stirred up the rank and file. It's called "off the clock," which might sound like a TV game show, but it's a way for Wal-Mart to get overtime work out of its employees and—BONG! HERE COMES THE GAME—not pay them.

DEAD PEASANTS

Stopped by the cops for a traffic violation in the 1940s, New York City mob boss Lucky Luciano was asked to explain why the back-seat of his car was filled with guns and ammo:

"We just got back from hunting," said Lucky.
"What were you hunting?"
"Oh, peasants."
"Pheasants?"
"Yeah, that's right, pheasants."

Apparently, Wal-Mart has been taking lessons from Lucky, for it's been a leader among corporations engaged in an elaborate, money-grubbing scheme called Dead Peasants life insurance. Under some state laws, the corporation can take out up to $750,000 worth of life insurance on a single employee—without ever telling the employee.

The macabre aspect of this is that the policy is not for the worker, but for the corporation! When the worker dies, the insurance money goes to the corporation, while the family of the deceased doesn't get a dime or even know that such a policy existed.

When Douglas Sims died suddenly of a heart attack in 1998, for example, Wal-Mart quietly pocketed $64,000 from a Dead Peasant policy it had taken out on him. His widow, Jane, got nothing and knew nothing. When she later learned about it, she told a *Houston Chronicle* reporter: "I never dreamed they could profit from my husband's death."

(Am I the only one to notice that this scheme could make an employee worth more to the company dead than alive?)

The laws say the employees are supposed to give their consent, but it turns out that you can consent without knowing it, for it can be buried in the legalese of an employment form you sign—there's no requirement that the company actually tell you what you're signing.

Wal-Mart has taken out some 350,000 of these policies on employees, buying them from Hartford and AIG insurance companies. Its green-eyeshade accounting whizzes even jiggered the deal so Wal-Mart could get a tax deduction on the premiums. The company hires a firm to run sweeps of Social Security numbers—called "death runs"—every quarter to find out who has died, then it submits those names to the insurers . . . and collects.

A Wal-Mart spokesman told the *Chronicle:* "The company feels it acted properly and legally in doing this."

Some of the "peasants" have rebelled, however, filing lawsuits from Texas to Maine. Wal-Mart is fighting them in court, but because of the workers' suits and bad publicity, it says it has now stopped buying Dead Peasant policies.

Now we're having fun. When workers—I'm sorry, "associates"—finish their shifts, it's common for managers to tell them to go ahead and clock out, but assign them to do this or that before going home, taking an extra hour or two a day or more.

"I would work ten or fifteen hours a week off the clock," Liberty Morales told a reporter for Bill Moyers's *Now* show on PBS. She's a mother of three and worked for Wal-Mart in Texas. Instead of going home to her kids, she'd sometimes have to spend an extra few hours working at the store—unpaid. Why not just go home? She needed the paycheck, poor as it was: "And I knew that, if I were to leave, I would've—I wouldn't have a job when I got back."

Moyers's crew talked to forty-eight current and former Wal-Marters who confirmed that working off the clock was S.O.P. It's also flat illegal, a big no-no under both federal and state laws, because it's . . . what do you call it . . . oh yeah, *stealing,* theft of wages. I believe the Bible takes a firm position against stealing—one of the Ten Big Ones. I interject religion only because this particular corporation is a big Bible pounder, quite insistent that its stores embody good Christian values. But, I wonder, where would Jesus shop? (Rhetorical question—I don't think he did much shopping.)

Former managers confirm that they manipulated not only the clock, but also payroll records, and they say the practice is systemwide. You had to do it, they say, because of relentless pressure from the top to hold labor costs to an absolute minimum. There is an iron rule from Bentonville that managers must keep their store's payroll down, no matter what it takes. It's a matter of survival for managers: "If you miss your payroll two times, three times," says a seventeen-year veteran, "you may not have a job. You'll get demoted."

The stingy payroll imperative also means that stores don't have enough employees to get all the work done in regulation, so something has to give—and those lowest on the totem pole do the giving: *OK, Loretta, time to check out . . . then report back here to me.*

Even when employees think they are getting overtime pay, their paychecks later tell a different story. When managers prepare their weekly reports to Bentonville and see that they've gone over payroll, some simply doctor time cards, erasing some of the hours worked (and money earned) by associates. Dorothy English worked in the payroll department of a Louisiana store and says she's the one who did the altering on orders from management: "They will adjust those hours in that computer. It's the system. It's Wal-Mart's system that does this. People like me who went in there and did exactly what they told me to do."

John Lehman, a longtime store manager now retired, says: "I gave direction to do that, and I was following the direction that was given to me. This is the way that people, that store managers bring their payroll in. And all my friends were doing it, too. All my other store managers in the district."

In the Texas stores alone, this wage theft is figured to add up to $30 million a year—part of the corporate ethic that lets Wal-Mart brag: "Always Low Prices!"

Time to get a comment from headquarters, and who better than our friend Cole Peterson, the veep of the "People Division." He and another vice president, Carol Taylor, were asked by the PBS crew about this off-the-clock ugliness. After they pointed out that Wal-Mart has "clear policies" against such shady tactics, their response was classic corporate babble:

PETERSON: We know that there can be allegations, but we would say like any other organization, if there are violations of that policy, then we hold the managers accountable to that and will respond with disciplinary action. . . .

PBS: How often have managers been disciplined for having people work off the clock?

PETERSON: I'm not sure I can, I can respond to that. Carol, do you have a sense for that?

TAYLOR: I, I can tell you that my experience is that—I can't tell you exactly in my area, but, um, I can tell you that it has been, um, taken care of on any issues that's, that's been brought up to us.

Off-the-clock cases against Wal-Mart are pending in twenty-five states. It has already paid $400,000 to settle a case brought by associates in one New Mexico store, and about $50 million to settle a Colorado class-action suit brought by employees. An Oregon jury has recently found Wal-Mart guilty of forcing unpaid overtime work—including having locked associates in the building.

All of this from a corporation banking $250 billion a year and sending a steady torrent of cash into the coffers of "Simple Sam" Walton's five heirs, who already are billionaires.

CHAPTER 11

Taking Charge of Dinner

When the fifty surviving *Mayflower* settlers decided to have that first Thanksgiving feast in 1621, they sent an emissary asking Massasoit, leader of the local Wampanoag tribe, to join them, figuring that he and his brother would show up. So imagine their surprise when, on the appointed day, Massasoit and ninety Wampanoags arrived!

It's Massachusetts, 1621—you've got a village full of hungry Wampanoags, many with faces painted red and black, and you can't just ring up the deli for carryout. Plus, they've come for a three-day stay!

Not to worry, though, for Massasoit knew his manners. Writer George Plimpton, researching through letters and diaries of the time, reports that the natives provided much of the grub for the feast, and it would put today's standard spread of turkey and dressing in the shade:

> Five deer, innumerable wild turkeys (the Indian name for them, *furkee*, is remarkably similar), wild geese (undoubtedly the Canada goose) and duck (the Canvasback is conjectured). From the sea and nearby estuaries they produced eels, lobsters, clams (called "slams") and mussels (called "muskles").
>
> Almost no vegetables were served. In those times they were considered fit only for those who could get nothing else. . . . As for bread, there was a considerable variety of biscuits, hoe cakes, ash cakes. Some chronicles mention "popcorn balls," a confection made by Indians with maple syrup and corn. There may have been an Indian pudding made of cornmeal and molasses boiled in a bag. . . .

There would have been a considerable choice of fruits and nuts—gooseberries, cranberries, strawberries, plums, cherries, and a little ground nut known as the bogbean, which were consumed in such numbers by early settlers that very few are to be found today. . . .

The celebrants may have had a variety of small beer made from barley, and quite likely a native wine so newly made as to be somewhat "green" and thus probably spiked with brandy—what the Indians called "strong water"—from the settlement's stores.

What a cornucopia nature provided! We've come a long way, food-wise, from that feast nearly four hundred years ago—and not all of it has been positive, especially in the last fifty years or so. We now live in the period exultantly touted as the "agricultural revolution" by the tirelessly self-congratulatory cabal of chemical corporations, government agencies, and land-grant colleges that produced it—though it turns out to be less of a revolution than a *devolution.*

Until maybe ten or fifteen years ago, few Americans were paying much attention to food beyond its price, generally unaware of where it was coming from or what was being done to it, because . . . well, people were busy, food was food, and besides, we'd become a thoroughly urban nation, more in touch with McDonald's than Old MacDonald.

Ask city dwellers how many legs a chicken has, and they might say six, for that's how many come in a family bucket of KFC. Likewise, the big majority of lawmakers are from cities, and they've lost touch with and interest in all that "ag stuff." (There are stories of urban politicians deciding to run for state office and, when they venture out to the rural areas, trying to connect with the locals by saying something farmer-y, like: *Do you raise any Spams on your farm?* Or, *How's the escargot crop doing this year?*)

In recent years, however, there's been a food awakening with the rise of "good food" grocery stores, the popularity of chef shows on television, and the spread of quality restaurants in places where a "blackboard special" previously would've been the two-fer-one spaghetti nite at the Chow Down Café. But something else happened, too: People awakened to the startling realization that industrialized dinner had become a threat to us, from mad cow disease to pesticide residues to genetic splicing.

WHAT'S HAPPENED TO OUR DINNER?

Harry Truman said, "No man should be president who doesn't understand hogs." The problem with our recent presidents, however—including *los dos* Bushes and Bill Clinton—is that they understand hogs all too well. While they certainly don't know pig stuff about the four-legged varieties, today's presidents are expert on the care and feeding of those fat, two-legged oinkers who are the CEOs and lobbyists of global agribusiness corporations.

With an oink-oink here and a ton of campaign contributions there,

WHO'S IN THE KITCHEN
MAKING FOOD POLICY?

Top 10 Agribusiness Contributors to Congressional and Presidential Campaigns, 1992–2002

Company	Amount
Philip Morris	$16,325,765
RJR Nabisco	$ 7,442,333
Coca-Cola	$ 5,110,747
Archer Daniels Midland	$ 4,987,114
PepsiCo	$ 3,091,967
ConAgra	$ 2,744,023
Outback Steakhouse	$ 2,522,052
McDonald's	$ 2,043,274
Pilgrim's Pride	$ 1,669,155
Tyson	$ 1,290,396

Source: www.opensecrets.org

a handful of agribusiness giants are able to dictate America's food and farm policies in both Republican and Democratic administrations. This is why our present policies are so bassackward, discombobulated, Rube-Goldbergish . . . and stupid.

Policy is not written for farmers and consumers—the two groups whose well-being logically would be the rationale for having any policy at all—nor is it written for workers, conservation, small business, rural communities, good health, or even good food. Instead, it's written for the profit and global expansion of the corporate business elite—names like ADM, Cargill, McDonald's, Monsanto, Nestlé, Philip Morris, Tyson, Unilever, and Wal-Mart.

These powers have none of the dirt and grease of honest farm toil under their fingernails. They're well-manicured, soft-hands people who do their agricultural work in faraway executive suites, genetic engineering labs, banks, and the back rooms of governments. With the greased-palm complicity of our presidents and Congress Critters, they've industrialized, conglomeratized, and globalized food—a substance that by its very nature is agrarian, small-scale, and local. Here are some of the products of their perverse policy:

- Out of each dollar you spend on groceries, only 19 cents goes to the farmer, with corporate middlemen grabbing the rest.
- Thousands of good, efficient family farmers are being squeezed out of business each year by rising costs and falling commodity prices.
- As farm prices continue to fall, consumer prices keep going up, creating enormous, windfall profits for the conglomerate shippers, processors, and retailers in the middle.
- An $8 billion-a-year federal farm program delivers zero to 60 percent of farmers, while feeding million-dollar payments to giant corporate farms.
- Agribusiness dumps 8 billion pounds of pesticides on farmlands each year, with the result that 45 percent of America's groundwater is now dangerously contaminated with pesticide runoff, while farm families, farmworkers, and people living next to the fields suffer poisonings, cancers, birth defects, and death.
- A handful of corporations now monopolize each and every aspect of the food economy—from seeds to chemicals, grain shipping to

cotton trading, processing to retailing.

- Workers in fields, processing plants, and supermarkets are routinely paid poverty wages, exposed to serious injury and death, harassed, fired without cause, and denied the right to organize.

- Food itself, nature's own product, has become a clear and present danger as industrialized, quick-profit agriculture has produced feces contaminants, irradiation, infusion of sex hormones, genetic manipulation, a toxic stew of chemical residues and additives, and an epidemic overdose of fats and sugars.

- The typical food product at any supermarket has traveled more than 1,500 miles to get there, wasting tankfuls of energy, destroying both freshness and nutrition, and denying shelf space to local producers.

MR. POTATO HEAD

That potato you're serving tonight—is it a potato . . . or a pesticide?

Without so much as asking your permission or even informing you, Monsanto did a little transgenic engineering in its labs in the 1990s to create a bucolic sounding "New Leaf" potato, which contains a built-in toxin to kill pests as it grows. But the toxin is not merely in the plant's leaf, which an insect might devour, but in *every cell* of the plant, including in every bite of the spud itself.

In fact, this potato is registered with the EPA as a pesticide! McDonald's uses some in its french fries, as does Frito-Lay in some of its potato chips.

IT'S OUR FOOD, OUR FAMILIES, OUR FARMS, OUR COMMUNITIES, OUR ENVIRONMENT, OUR VALUES, OUR FUTURE

If you don't control what you're putting in your mouth and the mouths of your babies, you don't control much of anything in your life. The bad news is that, while we weren't noticing (and weren't being informed by either political party), the corporate powers grabbed control of dinner and have been messing with it in the most destructive ways.

But there's good news, too, and the good is beginning to outweigh the bad. While the profiteers and politicians are headed one way with our food system, We the People are headed in quite another direction.

Whether it's called "sustainability," "organic," "beyond organic," "pure food," or just plain common sense, there is a mass movement and growing coalition among consumers, farmers, workers, entrepreneurs, communities, conservationists, nutritionists, chefs, food activists, and others to take back control of America's food economy and culture.

Despite ongoing, Big Money assaults to kill this movement, I believe that it's unstoppable. After all, it is food we're talking about, not widgets, gizmos, or just some other consumer "product." Food is essence—it embodies life, health, nature, motherhood, family, ethnicity, childhood, culture, art, beauty, religion, skill, pride, ego, comfort, sex, friendship, community, pleasure, joy, fun . . . our general well-being. Corporations that mess with food mess with us.

The first big rebellion against the corporate messers has come in the marketplace, where there has been surging consumer demand for organic food. What began in the late '60s as a fringe market selling out of funky health food stores and the rickety VW buses of ex-hippies is now mainstream. Sales are topping $10 billion in 2003 and are growing 20 percent annually as even conventional supermarkets rush to stock their shelves with these goods. In addition, our top export markets—especially Europe, Japan, and Latin America—are even more insistent on organic production. If you look at the polling data or talk to folks anywhere, you'll find that the vast majority of people want wholesome, nonindustrialized food, period.

Two more factors: Producing organically is economically viable for struggling farmers, and it's environmentally essential, so this is the future. The question is no longer whether "organic" will become the major force in the food economy—but rather what it means to say "organic" . . . and who will control it.

While the big boys can't kill the movement, they are working mightily to co-opt it, primarily by trying to have "organic" defined strictly in terms of minimal production standards. In 2002, the U.S. Department of Agriculture promulgated its new green and white "USDA Organic" label—an official seal of approval that assures us shoppers that foods with that label have been produced without the toxic chemicals, artificial fertilizers, antibiotics, growth hormones, GMOs, irradiation, and other brutish techniques of agribusiness.

Getting this label was no small battle. The food giants vehemently opposed any such certification at first, and when the public beat them in that fight, their lobbyists snuck around back and got the Clinton Administration to include genetic modification, irradiation, and even the use of toxic sludge as approved "organic" methods in the first draft of the labeling rules. However, the people roared back. *En masse.* The USDA got more protests against this perversion than any other federal agency ever received on a proposed rule. It had to back down.

The USDA label is a step forward, especially for the environment and our health, because it'll boost consumer purchases of organic food, prompting more farmers to shift from dousing their crops with the costly, highly toxic sprays pushed so relentlessly by the chemical corporations.

But the label is only the first step, and it will actually be a hindrance to the pure food movement if we stop there. The label defines organic merely as a technical process, rather than a structural concept that is centered on the culture of agriculture.

For example, under the USDA's definition, our nation's food supply would be considered organic even if (1) all of the production is controlled by General Mills, (2) it is produced seven thousand miles away on Chinese state farms using forced labor, and (3) sales are monopolized by Wal-Mart's supermarket division.

This is not a paranoid scenario. Indeed, corporations that ridiculed organic production only a couple of years ago now are grabbing for the green label—General Mills, Mars Inc., Tyson, ADM, Procter & Gamble, and Pillsbury are among the global players that have taken over such organic brands as Cascadian Farms, Horizon, Seeds of Change, Nature's Farm, Knudsen, and Muir Glen. Likewise, Wal-Mart, which has gone from a start-up supermarket a decade ago to now being the world's largest grocery seller, is bringing its labor-exploiting, farmer-squeezing management ethic to organic retailing. And firms in China already are applying for organic certification to sell their foodstuffs in the U.S.

Far from organic, this corporate grab is purely plutocratic, nothing but profiteering dressed up in a green suit. To be organic is to embrace and enrich the whole, not the few. It refers to a social organism with the complexity of a living thing in which the parts are unified, connected not only to each other but also to something larger—specifically to our democratic ideals. It's more about fairness and respect than it is about stock options and parts-per-billion of pesticide residues.

AMERICA'S NEW FOOD PIONEERS

Here again there is a cornucopia of good news. All across the country, grassroots pioneers are refusing to give in to the narrow, instead broadening America's organic possibilities by developing successful models for the common good.

Farmers

"Locally grown" is now developing the cachet of wholesomeness that "organically grown" once carried. These days, there's hardly a city of any size that doesn't boast of having somewhere between a handful and a few hundred farmers selling directly to local grocery stores, restaurants, or individual consumers. The primary appeal is the good-and-good-for-you freshness of having these local goods delivered to you right from the field at prime ripeness. But a close second in appeal is that you can know these farm families personally and know that buying from them makes you part of a local economic loop that sustains your community.

There's a wonderful example of this high-touch agriculture right here in my hometown of Austin, where Larry Butler and Carol Ann Sayle are true community treasures. Their five-acre Boggy Creek Farm (www.boggycreekfarm.com) dates back to the Texas revolutionary period of the 1830s, when the place was out in the countryside. Austin expanded, however, and the farm now finds itself smack in the middle of a city, but being on the poor side of town, this patch of deep, fertile bottomland never got developed.

Larry and Carol Ann came across it a decade ago, cleared it, and brought it back to life, creating a jewel of urban agriculture that turns out glorious organic produce, herbs, flowers, eggs, jams, salsa, and anything else that strikes the fancy of these two dirt geniuses. All of this is sold locally, delivered by them with the morning dew still on it. Their farm stand, open year-round, is a regular stop for Austinites, and restaurants vie to boast "Boggy Creek Tomatoes!" on their menus.

These city farmers are not only in Austin, they are immersed in it. When a person or group need help, Larry and Carol Ann are there with their big straw hats, big laughs, and big hearts. They help define the uniqueness of Austin and are all around more popular than any politician in our capital city.

When a storm crashed a tree into their restored farmhouse last year, chefs, customers, and friends spontaneously showed up from all across town with food, tools, and other donations, and plenty of this country's great barn-raising spirit to help make them whole. I don't think folks would do that for Wal-Mart.

I know of so many farmers like this—true pioneers in an entrepreneurial agriculture that's rooted in both economic and ecological reality. And they're having a ball!

For example, there's Joel Salatin, who calls himself a "grass farmer," because on only one hundred acres of well-nurtured pastureland in Virginia's Shenandoah Valley, he produces thirty thousand pounds of beef, sixty thousand pounds of pork, twelve thousand chickens, six hundred thousand eggs, one thousand rabbits, and six hundred turkeys each year! He does it by choreographing his various animals in an amicable, symbiotic waltz in which the cattle are allowed into a field to eat the long grasses, then moved out, after which chickens come in on a portable "eggmobile" and are turned loose to eat the shorter grasses and peck at the bugs, then are moved out so the sheep can get their turn . . . and so on, with each group doing its part to fertilize the grass for healthy growth and another feeding cycle. It has to be seen to be believed. His Polyface Farm (www.ecofriendly.com) is in rhythm with nature and is a wholly sustainable and profitable model that would boggle the dull, industrial mind of a Tyson executive.

Or check out the astonishing work of Eliot Coleman and Barbara Damrosch, who call themselves the "backwards farmers" (www. fourseasonfarm.com). "Backwards" because, as impossible as it seems, they farm only in the winter months in Maine. Yes, in the dark days of the brutal winters on Maine's Penobscot Bay, from October to May, they are gaily producing a bounty of organic greens and vegetables in three greenhouses, marketing all of their fabulous produce within forty miles of their remote and remarkable place. For thirty years, they've worked to perfect the science and art of cold-weather, sustainable greenhouse farming, and now they have a replicable model that can return an annual profit of more than $40,000 to farmers anywhere. Even in cities, they say.

Communities

Chicago is a city with a plan. Mayor Richard Daley is allocating tens of millions of dollars to make Chi-town the "Greenest City in America," and an innovative group of community activists and visionaries are developing a truly bold plan to make Chicago "The Land of Organic Opportunity." Far more than a few farmers markets, they're talking about a comprehensive regional organic food system that will encompass, involve, and enrich the area's whole extended community, ranging from farmers to community gardeners, chefs to the homeless, entrepreneurs to school kitchens.

Jim Slama, publisher of *Conscious Choice* and founder of Sustain, has been one of the key sparkplugs in launching a citywide planning process called the Local Organic Initiative (www.localorganic.org). LOI starts with the realization that, while organic sales are now about $8 million a year in the metro region, 97 percent of this food is being shipped in from California, Mexico, the Netherlands, and beyond—and Chicagoans are shipping out their organic dollars. So why not capture this growing market for the home folks, and get fresher food in the bargain?

Having inventoried the existing capacity to do this, LOI has recommended an effort to finance and build the necessary production, distribution, and marketing infrastructure:

- Increase the area's organic production by instituting a crash program to finance the training of farmers and their transition to organic methods; extend the Illinois growing season by teaching and financing greenhouse farming; expand and connect the many community gardens throughout Chicago; develop more urban production through vacant-lot and rooftop farming; encourage immigrants with farming skills to put their know-how to work, especially in the specialty crops of their home countries.

- Invest in local entrepreneurs, co-ops, and others to develop the trucking, warehousing, and management businesses to create a reliable, year-round distribution infrastructure.
- Finance organic food businesses, with an emphasis on enterprises located in and owned by inner-city entrepreneurs and co-ops, and businesses that pay good wages, provide good training, and offer growth opportunities for employees.
- Invest in markets, including opening more organic, locally supplied farmers markets throughout the area; creating a prominent, year-round market in Chicago's central commercial area; developing co-op buying clubs among both restaurants and consumers; developing a supply chain for schools, hospitals, jails, and other public institutions; educating the public about the benefits and availability of locally grown organic food, including teaching school kids about it.

Elements of this initiative are in place or under development at present, including some of the more innovative aspects. For example, Les Brown of the Chicago Coalition for the Homeless is spearheading a project called Growing Home (www.growinghomeinc.org) that will include gardens, greenhouses, and some processing facilities. It will grow organic food for homeless shelters, as well as to sell to restaurants and other outlets. It'll be staffed by the homeless, who'll get good pay, good skills, and a good chance to better their lives.

Marketers

Restaurants, grocers, co-ops, and direct farmer-to-consumers sales are bringing locally produced, organic goods within reach of nearly all of us these days. Alice Waters of Berkeley, California, was the pioneer restaurateur who, thirty years ago, first hit the back roads around the Bay Area to forage and scrounge among local farmers and food artisans, getting them to supply top-quality organic edibles for her seminal restaurant,

Chez Panisse (www.chezpanisse.com). Now it's common for cities everywhere to have restaurants that follow in Alice's steps, providing a growing market for more and more local producers.

One who has gone the extra mile is Nora Pouillon, whose Restaurant Nora in Washington, D.C. (www.noras.com), doesn't just serve locally grown, organic food—but the restaurant itself is certified organic, the first such in America. Essentially every ingredient is organic: "You know, the sugar, the salt, the chocolate, the butter, the milk, the flour, the bread, you know, everything," Nora says.

But you don't have to go to a high-dollar restaurant to get the goodies. Cafés, buffets, diners, breakfast joints, lunch spots, school cafeterias, and other everyday eateries are turning to locally produced and organic foods. In Barre, Vermont, for example, The Farmers Diner has a straightforward slogan: "Food from Here" (www.farmersdiner.com). From cranberries to cheese, sausage to syrup, lamb to lettuce, Tod Murphy's menu is provided by local farmers, with the fresh goodness of the products being the focus of preparation. Speaking of the diner's burger, made with local beef, Tod says, "We put salt and pepper on the meat and just stay out of the way." He sees this concept of good local grub working anywhere.

Nor is it necessary to eat out to enjoy the flavor of your own locale. Some 2,800 farmers markets are flourishing across the country (www.localharvest.org), with nearly twenty thousand farmers reaching hundreds of thousands of people in all kinds of neighborhoods.

The Japanese have a term, *teikei,* that means putting the "face of the farmer on the food," and farmers markets do just that. They link producers and consumers into the same social fabric and create a festive ambiance, while also offering a phenomenal variety of wholesome, just-harvested food at good prices.

Cities typically have a central market, then several neighborhood markets, and more and more are able to accept food stamps and WIC coupons, so low-income folks also can get better food at cheaper prices than supermarkets charge. The money we spend at these markets stays in our communities and keeps the farm economy vital. "What really saves our farms is that more people want local food," says Ken Migliorelli, who sells at some of the twenty-seven greenmarket sites in

New York City. "If it weren't for those farm markets in the city, I wouldn't be farming right now."

Workers

From the slaves of old to today's migrants, from rural poultry factories to suburban Wal-Marts, America's food economy has been built on exploitation of labor. Injustice cannot be part of an organic system, and here, too, change is coming, mostly led by activist unions that are organizing aggressively and forging coalitions with consumers, students, churches, responsible businesses, and others. An example is out in the apple country of Washington state, where some sixty thousand farmworkers toil for poverty wages and are treated abysmally in one of America's most dangerous industries.

For years, the workers and growers have battled each other, but the United Farm Workers union has recently taken another tack, saying to some of the farmers: Wait a minute, neither of us is getting a fair shake. "It's time to take on the retailers," says UFW's Lupe Gamboa. To do so, the union is reaching out to a large number of apple growers and local grocers to create a program called Fair Trade Apples.

As little as a nickel more per pound can make this system work. The retailers will agree to pay this nickel premium to any and all farmers who sign a contract with UFW, providing better wages, a pension, and safety protections for workers. In turn, the farmers will get a premium price. The nickel is a negligible sum for this high-volume, high-profit produce, and the grocers will get to sell an apple bearing the UFW's black eagle symbol, certifying to us con-

---

SLICING THE APPLE DOLLAR

Out of a dollar that we consumers spend for apples:

- The workers get only *4 cents.*
- The grower gets only *7 cents.*

Twenty-one cents goes to the wholesalers and transporters. But THE BIG HOG IS NOW THE RETAILERS (dominated by the likes of Wal-Mart, Kroger, and Safeway). *They take 68 cents of every apple dollar.*

sumers that these fruits are from labor and farmers who are getting a fair return. The bet is that you and I care about how we "vote" with our dollars and that we'll reach for Fair Trade Apples (www.ufw.org/ apple.html). They plan to have these apples in the markets next year.

Activists

Steadily, and sooner than the corporate powers thought possible, We the People are redirecting the food economy to fit our values and vision rather than theirs. Every step forward has come because we've demanded it and fought the powers. "We're not consumers, we're creators," says Andy Tembrill of the Center for Food Safety (www.organicandbeyond. com). Here are a few of the creators:

> Despite a relentless push by Monsanto and other genetic pol- luters, people around the world are saying no to these mak- ers of Frankenfoods and at least demanding that the genetic perversions be labeled (www.thecampaign.org); hundreds of prominent chefs have stepped forward on a range of pure food issues, from rejecting the use of genetically engineered salmon to supporting low-income gardens (www.chefnet. com/cc2000); organic farmers are organizing marketing co- ops to bypass monopolistic middlemen so they can sell their own brand-name milk, eggs, and other goodies (www. organicvalley.com); United Food and Commercial Workers is taking on the murderous treatment of thousands of people, largely immigrants, working in unspeakable condi- tions in meat processing plants (www.ufcw.org); and rural- urban coalitions are fighting to stop the loss of irreplaceable farmland (we lose two acres a minute), prevent sprawl, and keep farmers on the land by purchasing development rights from farm families (www.farmland.org).

There's a fantastic feistiness to the American people. Take Charlotte Ann Neely-White, for example. I don't know her, but I read about her wedding day.

A former school principal, she was out in her front yard in Mount

FAMILIES ARE FIGHTING MAD

Memo to Tom Ridge: It's Code Red here on the homefront!

While the Bushites worry about al Qaeda terrorist cells in the U.S., there are other cells not only terrorizing American families, but killing five thousand of us each and every year, with children being especially vulnerable.

These cells have names like *Listeria, E. coli,* and *Salmonella.* They are killer bacteria that have become epidemic in our food supply. Why? Because of one stupid reason: the filthy, contaminated, and essentially unregulated processing practices of such giant meat companies as ConAgra, Tyson, and Pilgrim's Pride. They speed up their processing lines for quicker profits, with the result that animal feces containing these bacteria routinely end up in Johnnie's hamburger, Suzie's hot dog, and that chicken you were going to serve tonight.

The body count: Fourteen unsuspecting Americans die *every day* from this meat contamination. Nearly nine hundred more are sickened and hospitalized each day

STOP has an answer: Stop it. Safe Tables Our Priority is an organization of families who have lost loved ones to meat profits. One member tells of Nicky, his two-year-old, "screaming nonstop for three days, and there was nothing I could do."

But Bush and the Congress can do something, which is to make the meat giants literally clean up their act or be shut down. Under current rules, recently "liberalized and streamlined" by the Bushites, companies can and do knowingly sell contaminated meat, even to the school lunch program, and get the USDA's seal of approval stamped on it.

Yet Bush sides with industry lobbyists and campaign givers (ConAgra alone gave some $600,000 to George in 2000, and three of the top aides to his agriculture secretary come from ConAgra or the National Cattlemen's Beef Association). The Bushites refuse to back legislation or rule changes supported by STOP to require ag officials to shut down, even temporarily, packing plants that repeatedly ship bad meat. They parrot the industry line that blames the victims for the problem: "The biggest issue is to get the consumer to cook the meat thoroughly," declares the National Meat Institute.

To help STOP stop the B.S., contact them at **www.stop-usa.org.**

Vernon, Missouri, on July 4th of 2002, when she was startled to see some guy screech to a halt in front of her house and come running up to her demanding that she turn over her pickup truck to him. He was quite agitated and insistent, threatening her by shouting, "There's a bomb in my car!"

Charlotte Ann, fifty-five, didn't take well to threats and was not about to surrender control of that pickup: "I said, 'No sir, you go ahead and set the bomb off. My house needs work anyway.'"

Then, like something out of a totally warped nightmare, the man commenced to attack her with a riding whip, whereupon Charlotte Ann hollered for her fiancé to bring out her .22 pistol, which he did. The assailant then stupidly grabbed for it, and, as she struggled with him, the gun went off, hitting him in the chest. Still, he managed to grab the gun, break a window of her truck with a piece of firewood, and get in. With the gun now pointed at her, Charlotte Ann finally backed off and he sped away. But having suffered mightily from his encounter with this formidable lady, he couldn't get far and was quickly arrested.

Three hours later, Charlotte Ann got married as scheduled. "It was a long day," she said simply.

Her story has nothing to do with food, but everything to do with the spunky quality of the American people. If we'll risk bodily harm for a pickup, we're damn sure not going to sit still for the corporate theft of our food supply.

CHAPTER 12

No Sweat

Pro golfer Nick Faldo once thanked a group of sportswriters "from the heart of my bottom."

That sentiment is what a couple of ex-Enron employees were reaching for when they started a humorous line of "pink-slip greeting cards." It included a special thank you card for former Enroners to send to Ken Lay and other top execs. The bosses had earlier locked the retirement funds of the employees into Enron's crashing stock, which was now worthless. Then the company itself was crashing and the execs were firing thousands. So to express proper gratitude the card said:

Thank You!
First you gave me the golden handcuffs,
And now you're giving me the boot.
And I didn't get you anything!

Worker attitude has been part of the job scene ever since the first boss started shoving people around. The straw boss, field boss, road boss, crew boss, big boss, boss hog—by whatever name, not much loved. There's a whole, rich genre of boss music that I grew up with, from Johnny Paycheck's "Take This Job and Shove It" to Jimmy Reed's classic blues: "Big boss man /Can't you hear me when I call / Well you ain't so big/ You're just tall, that's all."

These songs are popular for a reason, for most of us have experienced some so-and-so of a boss lording it over us as though he's King Tut and we're some mutt. But at least in these situations the boss has a name, a face (squinched up, beady-eyed, bloated, and blotched as it might be), a voice, a presence that we can . . . well, *hate* if we want to, or pity, or mock, or laugh at. There's a human focus for the late-night voodoo we practice (at least in our minds).

But I wonder about Wang Cei Hueng of Guangdong Province in China, or Matsietsi of Lesotho in southeast Africa. Whose faces do they conjure up in their moments of rage toward "The Boss"? They're both sweatshop workers. They could also be in Vietnam, Bangladesh, Saipan, the Dominican Republic, Guatemala, Russia—or Los Angeles, Dallas, Chicago, or New York.

All around our world, hundreds of thousands of workers are toiling right now in grinding poverty and abysmal conditions to make clothes, electronics, sports equipment, silverware, kitchen gadgets, toys, computer parts, tools, dishes, shower curtains, and other stuff for . . . whom? They don't know, no one bothers to tell them. They do know that most of it is for Americans. And sometimes they see names on boxes, such as Disney, Tommy Hilfiger, Wal-Mart, Barbie, Nike, Target, Abercrombie & Fitch, Toys "R" Us, Talbots, McDonald's, and Polo.

But who's their boss? The screaming, shoving, S.O.B. of a supervisor who's haranguing and harassing them every hour of every long day of endless weeks is the immediate boss, of course, but he or she is not the real boss. And they know the nondescript name of whatever factory or unit they're in, but these are subcontractors to "The Boss." Sometimes, one of the Nike or Disney or Gap people will sweep through on a product-quality inspection tour (the workers always know when these people are coming, for the place is spiffed up, fans are turned on, they're instructed to smile as they work, and the supervisor is nice for a day), but these inspectors aren't the boss.

The people hunched over doing the sweat labor don't know Michael Eisner at Disney (who was paid $6 million), Phil Knight at Nike ($3.3 million), Millard Drexlar at the Gap ($9.1 million), or any of the other real bosses who might as well live in outer space—and the bosses are equally removed from them, choosing never to visit the workers who are laboring for pennies to produce millions for them.

Toys of Misery

We could look at any of the sweatshop buyers, but why not the biggest . . . and the worst? Charlie Kernaghan of the National Labor Committee reports, "In country after country, factories that produce for Wal-Mart are the worst," adding that the bottom-feeding labor policy of this one corporation "is actually lowering the standards in China, slashing wages and benefits, imposing long mandatory overtime shifts, while tolerating the arbitrary firing of workers who even dare to question factory conditions."

Let's focus on toys. Wal-Mart does not want America's buying public—especially our children—to know that its famous low prices are the product of human misery, so while it loudly proclaims that its global suppliers must comply with a corporate "code of conduct" to treat workers decently, it strictly prohibits disclosure of any factory addresses that would allow independent sources to witness the "code" in operation.

However, Kernaghan's National Labor Committee, widely acclaimed for its factual reports on global working conditions, didn't wait for a corporate invitation (how rude!). In 2001, NLC's investigators visited several Chinese factories that make the playthings that Americans buy for their children at Wal-Mart. Seventy-one percent of toys sold in the U.S. come from China, and Wal-Mart now sells one out of five of the toys Americans buy. NLC interviewed workers in China's Guangdong Province who toil in factories making popular action figures, dolls, etc. sold at Wal-Mart and other stores.

Just before Christmas NLC issued a stunner of a report, titled "Toys of Misery." You might have missed it, since our diligent friends in the establishment media chose to ignore it, even though it was newsworthy, well-documented, timely, visually gripping, and had a great story hook to the holidays. (SMALL DIGRESSION: Is it too cynical of me to think that perhaps, just perhaps, the media conglomerates do not want to offend major advertisers with such unpleasantness, or perhaps that media conglomerates such as Disney [ABC], Viacom [CBS], GE [NBC], and AOL Time Warner [CNN] don't want to focus their cameras inside these sweatshops because—omigoodness—their own conglomerate's logos will be found on the boxes being filled by the workers? I hope I've not offended you with such a cynical turn.)

If it's "reality TV" that the media powers want, here's some reality NLC investigators found in Chinese factories under contract to Wal-Mart that make "hellhole" seem like a nice place:

- Thirteen- to sixteen-hour days molding, assembling, and spray-painting toys—8 A.M. to 9 P.M. or even midnight, seven days a week, with some twenty-hour shifts in peak season.
- Even though China's minimum wage is 31 cents an hour, which wouldn't begin to cover the basic subsistence-level needs of a person, these production workers are paid 13 cents an hour. That would be an abysmal $11.83 for a ninety-one-hour week, except that they are routinely cheated on wages: "No worker had any idea how their wages would actually be calculated," notes the NLC report, since piece rate, total production, and overtime are not listed on their pay stubs.
- Workers typically live in squatter shacks, 7' x 7', or jammed in company dorms with more than a dozen sharing a cubicle costing $1.95 a week for rent. They pay about $5.50 a week for lousy food. They also must pay for their own medical treatment and are fired if they are too sick to work. They have no money left for education, savings, or even a little entertainment.
- The work literally is sickening, for there's no health and safety enforcement. Workers suffer constant headaches and nausea from paint dust hanging in the air; the indoor temperature tops 100 degrees; protective clothing is a joke; repetitive stress dis-

A MESSAGE TO THE BOSS

Remember the old joke (or was it?) about getting a fortune cookie with a message that read: "Help, I'm being held captive in a fortune cookie factory"?

Well, in a twist on that, a Canadian couple got a startling message from a talking toy that they bought at Wal-Mart. Sold under the store's Kid Connection brand, the toy said in a tiny voice: "I hate you."

I hope the CEO got one of those.

orders are rampant; and there's no training on the health hazards of handling the plastics, glue, paint thinners, and other solvents in which these workers are immersed every day.

As for Wal-Mart's highly vaunted "code of conduct," NLC could not find a single worker who had ever seen or heard of it. These are not rogue factories in remote backwaters, but the plants of one of Hong Kong's top five exporters contracting with Wal-Mart, employing some twenty thousand workers, mostly young women and teenage girls.

Wal-Mart, renowned for its obsession with knowing every detail of its global business operations and for calculating every penny of a product's cost, knows what goes on inside these places. Yet, when confronted with the facts NLC uncovers, corporate honchos claim ignorance, feign outrage, blame the contractors, and wash their hands of the exploitation. Says CEO Lee Scott, *"There will always be some people who break the law. It is an issue of human greed among a few people."*

SWEATX

One day a couple of years ago, Susan DeMarco and I were doing our talk radio show, *The Chat & Chew,* on the topic of sweatshops, when a lady from Anniston, Alabama, called to say that whenever she goes into a store to shop for clothing, she seeks out the manager and asks: "Can you tell me where your made-in-the-USA section is?"

Good question. Check the labels at even such high-dollar stores as Nordstrom, Lord & Taylor, Neiman Marcus, Talbots, and Abercrombie & Fitch—and you'll find that many of these pricey goods are also made in China and other low-wage exits on the global highway. Just like Wal-Mart and the cheapie stores, the tonier salons pay a pittance to those "faraway people" who cut and sew the goods, which the stores sell for, say, $50, $100, or $1,000—the price bears no relation to the cost of making the thing. More than 80 percent of our clothing now comes from overseas plants, most from countries paying less than a buck an hour, and most likely made by a young woman or child.

But even a made-in-the USA label on your blouse or shirt doesn't

WHERE'S THE GOVERNMENT

You might recall the big sobbing saga of Kathie Lee Gifford a few years ago, when the National Labor Committee revealed that her line of clothing, sold at Wal-Mart, was made by children in Honduras getting paid pennies. Oh, the hue and the cry, oh, the tears from Kathie Lee, oh, the demands by politicos for reform, oh, the promises to clean up the scourge of sweatshops! Whatever happened to all that?

Well, Bill Clinton was the man in charge then, and he jumped on the issue like a gator on a poodle, loudly proclaiming his outrage. Then he did what he so often did: He talked about it at great length, created a committee to talk some more, then he went off to play golf. Nothing changed.

A Fair Trade Association was set up, but it was dominated by Ralph Lauren, Gap, Nike, and other industry bigwigs, so it has no credibility or clout. It issues *voluntary* guidelines for corporate codes of conduct, and if it makes any investigation, the FTA reports the results to the company, not the public.

The violators simply became the regulators . . . and nothing changed.

give the garment a gold star, because our Home of the Free and Land of the Brave has its own made-in the-USA sweatshops. *Beaucoup* of them. Only a couple of years ago the Department of Labor found that 63 percent of the garment companies in Los Angeles were violators of federal wage and hour laws.

In their book, *Behind the Label,* Edna Bonacich and Richard Applebaum dub L.A. "the sweatshop capital of the United States." About 140,000 people work in mostly small shops there cutting and sewing garments that ultimately sell for $28 billion a year. You can guess how much of that goes to the workers. Mostly immigrants, often illegal, these workers are not even paid the minimum wage, literally sweating out an income that averages $7,200 a year.

The change, as usual, is coming from the bottom. What the industry and their toadies in government don't seem to get is that people—especially the young—are appalled when they learn that sweatshops still exist and are so widely used by the barons of the industry. People view sweatshops as an absolute abomination, and there is growing success by such groups as UNITE (the garment industry union), National Labor Committee, United Students Against Sweatshops, Global Exchange, and others to spread the awareness and organize to stop this affront to our country's most basic values of justice and fairness.

THE MAINE WAY

On a trip to Deer Isle, Maine, I saw the truck of a local oil service firm that (I swear) is called Bandit and the Bitch.

Folks are pretty plainspoken up that way, and outspoken, too. One thing that a lot of Mainers have been outspoken about is their distaste for sweatshop products, and being a pragmatic sort of people, they're doing something about it.

For example, around the Penobscot Bay area, such towns as Bangor, Belfast, Blue Hill, and Bar Harbor have launched a Clean Clothes Campaign. It includes a "clean clothes inventory" that several shopkeepers have made of the clothing products in their stores, finding out from their suppliers whether the items have been certified by independent monitors as "sweatshop free." The stores highlight those items that are sweat free, and the salespeople are able to talk knowledgeably with customers about the whole issue.

Also, in Bangor, the campaign persuaded the city council to pass a purchasing policy to buy police uniforms, jailhouse sheets, soccer-league equipment, and so forth from no-sweat suppliers. Bidders for city contracts for these products have to certify that they are sweatshop free.

The campaign has gone statewide with the formation of the Maine Clean Clothes Alliance, which in 2001 got the state legislature to enact a landmark anti-sweatshop purchasing law. It sets standards for all state agencies buying goods, including a key provision that requires bidders to disclose the names and full addresses of all the factories they use to produce the goods that they want to sell to Maine taxpayers.

"We want the state to reward companies that choose to be ethical," says one Alliance leader. "We can attack the [sweatshop] problem with consumer power." At the time of passage, State Senator Peggy Pendleton added the thought that the new standards help Maine's small businesses in their bids for state contracts, for they "will no longer be subject to the unfair competitive advantage of corporations operating under exploitative conditions, paying substandard wages."

Other states, towns, and groups are working on doing it the Maine way in their area, and so can you. To get the Campaign Organizing Guide or their Shopping Guide, contact:

www.pica.ws

One place that's bringing change is the very place that this multi-billion-dollar industry most fears—the marketplace:

> "We were drinking coffee one morning in Vermont. There'd been an article in The New York Times about sweatshops that morning, and we were shaking our heads about it because it quoted some industry people saying, 'That's just the way it works, it's the economics of the industry, it's globalization, it's what it takes to compete.'
>
> "Well, we're business guys. We didn't know anything about the garment business, but it didn't make any sense to us that you had to run a sweatshop to make a profit. We thought that sounded like bullshit."

The "we" in this conversation was Pierre Ferrari and Ben Cohen. Pierre, whom I'm quoting here, has twenty-five years in the corporate world, having risen to the high post of V.P. at Coca-Cola. He was also on Ben's board of directors—Ben being the puckish entrepreneur, social activist,

SWEATSHOPS ARE GOOD FOR YOU

Taking the rosy view of sweatshops is Jonah Goldberg, a writer for the right-wing *National Review*. He criticizes us sweatshop opponents as antidevelopment and anticapitalist know-nothings, dismissing us as "dour feminists and moth-balled Marxists."

Indeed, this ivory tower observer (who clearly has not done much sweat labor himself) breezily asserts that "on the whole, what most opponents call 'sweatshops' are actually a good thing," adding cheerfully that "most of the 'exploitees' are happy to get these jobs."

The writer informs us that our American values of fairness and justice are alien to foreign cultures where sweatshops are common, so who are we to go sticking our noses where they don't belong?

"Take child labor: It may seem horrifying to Americans who treat their progeny as opportunities to display conspicuous consumption, but in much of the third world, it is natural to view your child as an economic asset."

No, Mr. Goldberg, it's natural everywhere to view your child as a child—a child who deserves more in life than being chained to a corporate loom.

marketing whiz, fine human being, and cofounder of Ben & Jerry's ice cream company. Rather than just having a cuppa joe, clucking their tongues about the problem, and going down the road as we sane people would've done, Pierre and Ben decided to look into it.

Ferrari immersed himself in the economics of garment production, reading, traveling, talking to people in the trade. Yes, it's a tough business, he learned, but not because of labor costs, which have practically *nothing to do* with the cost of the product, much less the price and profitability of the blouse or shirt you're wearing.

(I hate to do this to you, but it's going to be necessary to put forth the wee-est bit of math here, and, unfortunately, math often requires numbers, some of which I plan to use in the very next paragraph. I know it's scary, but it really won't hurt you, and you'll be a more informed, confident, and I daresay stronger person as a result of what you're about to learn. Let's try it, shall we?)

It takes an efficient worker about two and a half minutes to produce a T-shirt. Dividing this rate of production into the going wage in various parts of the world, here's the wage-cost of a T-shirt that you might buy at a Wal-Mart or Talbots or anywhere:

Asia	1¢
Latin America	4¢
Los Angeles sweatshop	16¢
U.S. minimum wage	21¢

Let's go with the high figure of 21 cents. That's what a U.S. minimum-wage worker gets out of a T-shirt that you'll pay somewhere between 10 and 20 bucks to buy. Working a year at minimum wage adds up to barely $10,000 gross pay—poverty.

So here's a question: What if that wage was *doubled*? Or even more? What if the workers were paid not 21 cents per shirt, but—what the hey, let's go crazy and throw in a whole extra quarter—paid 46 cents per shirt? This would mean the workers would be getting more than $20,000 a year! It's not a fortune, but it gets you out of abject poverty . . . it's a livable level of pay. And that extra quarter, which would mean so much to the workers and their families, would have no impact at all on your and my clothing budget.

"Come on," says Ferrari, "this industry has been exploiting people for a lousy 25 cents?" Yes.

Thus was born: TeamX. It's a new garment factory in Los Angeles, financed with an initial $1.2 million from the Hot Fudge venture capital fund of Ben Cohen. But this company is new in ways much more significant than its air-conditioned building and state-of-the-art equipment. It's new in approach. Its mission statement declares:

> *"TeamX seeks to change the lives of garment workers, both those that it directly employs, as well as the hundreds of thou-*

sands of other workers in this global industry, [by creating] a sustainable model that can be replicated worldwide."

How different is it from your run-of-the-mill garment business?

- It's a union shop, organized by UNITE.
- It's a co-op, owned by the workers themselves (five of the seven board seats are reserved for workers).
- It pays a living wage, starting at $8.50 an hour, plus good health care, a pension, profit-sharing, and vacation days ("I've been working in clothing for twenty years, and I never had a paid holiday before this," says Ana Acevedo, a Salvadoran immigrant and one of the founding co-op employees).
- It operates on the "solidarity ratio," which means that no executive can be paid more than eight times the pay of production workers.

There's one way, however, in which TeamX is just like any other garment business: It's out to make money. This is no little froufrou exercise in good works, but a profit-making enterprise that has drawn a small group of experienced managers and an exceptionally skilled and motivated workforce.

TeamX cranked up its operation in March of 2002 with eight employees, a vision, a plan, and a prayer. "We aim to put the lie to the myth that it's impossible to produce clothing at a competitive price and have a good quality of worklife," says Cohen. "Will we succeed? All I can say is, we'll see."

They have. With its snappy SweatX brand, the company was generating a profit by the end of its first year, and it now has fifty-five production workers turning out a stylish, top-quality line of everything from T-shirts to fleece jackets, baseball caps to blankets, sweatshirts to fashion tops.

Yes, but how can it keep up, how can it possibly compete with the morally bankrupt firms that are still using sweatshop labor? For one thing, TeamX pays its workers instead of paying celebrity endorsers (Nike is paying Tiger Woods $20 million a year for five years). That's $100 million of good money going to one already super-rich guy that could go toward fair pay and improved conditions for thousands of Nike sweatshop workers. Shifting payment from Tiger to workers would give Nike's swoosh a good scrubbing, put the company in a newly positive light with young people, create a global marketing windfall based on conscience, and eliminate any need to try hiding its corporate smarminess with costly celebrity masks. If you know anyone who knows Phil Knight, let the Nike honcho know that I'll let him have this marketing idea for free.

In fact, it's this "market of conscience" that TeamX is reaching out to—a huge and virtually untapped market of people (me . . . and you?) who'll gladly go for any brand that can assure us, without equivocation, that it contains *no sweat* (not to mention blood and tears), even if the no-sweat brand costs a few

BUY IT!

What a deal. A product that is made in the USA by union workers who own the company, is competitively priced, and is made of high-quality materials, including organic cotton. It's a piece of clothing so purely good you can damn near eat the thing.

If you know of groups that want such goodness in their garments, or if you'd be willing to approach a campus bookstore or other store about stocking SweatX clothes, contact these folks. They can also take individual orders through their website:

Toll free: 1-866-4SWEATX
www.sweatx.net /shop/
buy.html

Also contact them about materials for making a presentation to your church, class, or other group.

pennies more. TeamX doesn't have to sink itself with the huge weight of TV advertising, for a substantial part of the conscience market comes conveniently organized, reachable through such established networks as churches, campuses, and groups focused on environmental, women's, racial, and other issues.

Plus, unions. *Oh,* I hear people moan despairingly in my travels, *unions are so weak, only 13 million or so of the American population.* I

HOW YOU CAN PUT YOUR MONEY
WHERE YOUR MOUTH IS

Sweatshops can be stopped. Say that to yourself. (Go ahead, I'll pause here and wait.) There is no economic reason for them to exist. There certainly is no moral justification for such abuse. We, the American people, can stop sweatshops, because we are the market that finances them with our consumer dollars.

Use your dollar power not merely as a consumer, but as a citizen. You can change your own purchases so they're more thoughtful, withdrawing your money from the sweatshop spiral. But you can also have a larger impact by getting your church, your neighborhood school, your local clothing store, your book club, your civic organization, your bowling league, your political group (Come on Democrats, come on Greens, where are you buying your T-shirts?), your Sierra Club chapter, your public library, your softball team, your city council to come clean on the sweatshop issue by making more thoughtful group purchases.

Start small, wherever you're most comfortable. This doesn't have to be some huge, public crusade on your part. It begins with conversations—chances are you'll quickly find one or two other people who've been thinking about this, too, wondering what to do. Choose one group to try to influence. And get assistance.

Use the example of Harrell's, a local hardware store that I frequent here in Austin. It's always willing to talk customers through a project and even lend you a tool. The store has a slogan: "Together, We Can Do It Yourself."

That's the spirit. There are several groups that can help you do something yourself about sweatshops, offering information, ideas, tools, skills, and links. Here are a few. Please connect with them. **Sweatshops can be stopped.**

UNITE: www.uniteunion.org 212-265-7000
National Labor Committee: www.nlcnet.org 212-242-3002

United Students Against Sweatshops: www.usasnet.org 202-NO
   SWEAT
Global Exchange: www.globalexchange.org 415-255-7296
TeamX: www.sweatx.net 213-362-9001
American Apparel: www.americanapparel.net 213-488-0226
Behind the Label: www.behindthelabel.org
Sweatshop Watch: www.sweatshopwatch.org
Maine Clean Clothes Alliance: www.pica.ws 207-947-4203

look at the moaners in disbelief and say, You're whining about that?
Only 13 million? Sure, it ought to be more, and more people these days
are thinking union, but get real—that's a *lot* of folks! It's more than most
religious organizations can count as members, way more than the number of corporate executives and millionaires, and more than the supposedly "powerful number" of people tuning in today to the gaseous
leaf-blower of the airwaves, Rush Limbaugh. Add in their families,
neighbors, and friends, and you have a truly powerful number.

Also (here's the savvy of TeamX marketing), union members buy and
wear far more T-shirts than, say, your average country club member. Go
into any union hall, peek into the storeroom and closets, and you'll find
boxes upon boxes filled with T-shirts, knit shirts, sweatshirts, and others. They put their union logos and slogans on them for rallies, organizing drives, conventions—or just to wear to work or around the house.
It's a real market—and it's loving SweatX.

TeamX is only one company, but a lot of good has been done in this
old world by some *one* standing up to the B.S. of conventional wisdom
and saying, "That can't be right, there has to be a better way." As this first
factory succeeds, TeamX will expand to others, including an intention to
open factories abroad, in the face of global garment giants who claim
they "must" treat labor abysmally in order to be competitive. Competitive with whom? With each other, all of whom are sweatshop bastards.
TeamX offers some real competition.

CHAPTER 13

The Road to Privacy

My friend Molly Ivins and I have quite a bit in common: We're both former editors of the feistiest little mag in America, *The Texas Observer;* we live in the same neighborhood (literally as well as politically); we both write sociopolitico-humorosity books; we're both strikingly good-looking; and we both love to hoist a tall cool one, laugh, and swap great stories with folks.

It's this last one that got Molly and me all frustrated, cattywampus, and discombobulated once. While each of us does a great deal of speaking around the country, we're rarely on the same program together where we'd hear each other's speeches. A few years ago, though, we were back to back, and let me tell you it was unnerving, for as we spoke both of us were having to think about whether we were using each other's material—"Oh, geez," I thought as I headed off into a juicy story, "I think I got this one from Molly," and she'd think, "Oh rats, that was a Hightower line I just used."

It's supposed to be a trade secret, but I'll reveal it to you: We writer/speakers are shameless filchers, petty thieves, lifters of lines, stealers of stories. If you've got a good line that you want to keep as your own, don't use it in our presence—hide it like you'd hide a lamb chop from a coyote, for otherwise, it's ours.

There is, however, a code of honor among us thieves, a three-step ethical progression for converting material:

> *The first time* you use someone's line, you say:
> "As *Molly Ivins* once said . . ."

The second time, you say: "As *someone* once said . . ."
The third time, you say: "As *I've* always said . . ."

There's another theft taking place, however, that has no humor in it whatsoever. The thieves in this case are the relentless and remorseless kleptomaniacs who run CorporateWorld, and what they are stealing is you! By "you," I mean every scrap of data about your persona—they have your health records, bank and financial information, all of your purchases, employment history, records on your children, income and debt statements, court documents (from simple traffic tickets to jail time), credit ratings, property owned, taxes paid (or unpaid), college transcripts, travel history, divorces or family disputes, prescriptions, investments, retirement plans. . . .

It amounts to a virtual kidnapping—in corporate databanks all around the country, a little digital "you" has been hidden away, and they can pretty much do with it as they want, without the real you being notified, much less consulted, on what they're doing. This is in addition to the vast electronic dragnet that the Bushites (with the complicity of the Wobblycrats) are operating and largely opening up to private companies—much of the government's databases are run by corporate contractors, linked to corporate databases, and open to corporate use.

DON'T LOOK NOW, BUT THEY REALLY ARE WATCHING YOU

The London *Times* reports that our own George W leaned over to Tony Blair at an economics forum and confided, "The problem with the French is they don't have a word for 'entrepreneur.'"

George might not know it, but there is a French term that has swept across our country in the last decade or so that now defines our corporate culture more accurately than entrepreneurship. That word is "surveillance," meaning to watch from above.

Go into any Wal-Mart and most other big-name retailers and glance up at the dark, plastic, helmet-like fixtures mounted on the ceiling throughout the store—you're being watched and recorded. Look around

CHEF'S SURPRISE

Some of America's priciest restaurants have added a little *amuse bouche* to your dining experience, though they're not telling you about it, nor would you find it very amusing: They're watching you eat.

Using new, digital surveillance cameras, the kitchen can get remarkably clear pictures of your meal, table manners, footsie playing, or any other activities. The cameras have zoom lenses that can capture such fine details as what you're writing on your check. The rationale is that this peekaboo system allows the chefs to know how to pace your dinner—but the bottom line is that you're on candid camera.

In addition to the videos (one can easily imagine end-of-the-year staff parties featuring highlights of the Goofiest Customers of 2003), restaurant companies are building personal profiles on customers, putting your phone number, address, profession, eating habits, credit cards, drinking patterns, and more into their databases.

All of this turns what should be an intimate social outing into another corporate chance to watch, record, store, and use your private life—all without your knowledge or permission.

your workplace, including the employees' lounges and restrooms—someone's looking back and recording you at all times. Walk along the sidewalks and parking lots of shopping areas—you're being watched and recorded.

Much of the newer surveillance has nothing to do with shoplifting or other crime detection, which had been the chief excuse cited for this surreptitious monitoring of the marketplace. Rather, secret cameras and electronic devices are now being placed in stores to provide marketing research on us. This commercial snooping has even been given a pseudo-academic name: "retail ethnography." A more honest name would be "Stalking the Wild Consumer"—maybe it could run on Animal Planet, or on ESPN's hunting shows.

Instead, it runs in corporate marketing departments, which pay big fees to have us monitored clandestinely. As you move through some stores, hidden cameras and microphones are computerized to "track" you, identifying you by your body temperature and mapping your movements for later analysis. If you linger over a product, the camera can zoom in to catch your facial expression, which is thought to speak louder than words about whether or not you like the product.

There's so much monitoring that it's become a joke, albeit a very serious one. To call the public's attention to the constant eye in the sky, kids in various parts of the country have taken to staging "performances" in front of surveillance cameras in malls and stores and on sidewalks. Using handheld mikes and sometimes using a box as a stage, they'll sing, tell jokes, and do other routines, drawing a crowd while playing straight to the surveillance camera mounted up on a ceiling, wall, or pole. Security doesn't like it, but it's not against the law.

But if you really want to stir up security, do unto them what they're doing to you. A Canadian group has launched "World *Sous*veillance Day." Sousveillance is to watch from below, and that's what this band of roving imps do (and urge us to do), using their own camcorders as countersurveillance weapons.

The official World Sousveillance Day is Christmas Eve, when stores are filled with customers and surveillance is presumably at full tilt, though any day will do. These privacy guerrillas tilt their camcorders up to the corporate cameras and proceed to video the videoing, then they video the resulting scene when the corporate *gendarmes* (*sacrebleu,* George, there's another French word!) come spilling out of their hidden nests to demand the film and declare that it's illegal for us to record them recording us (yet another of life's ironies). All of this draws a crowd and helps to show people the absurd extent of our brave new snoopervision society.

Invasion of the Data Snatchers

Cameras are the least of what conservative columnist William Safire calls the "intrusion explosion," coming not from Big Government, but Big Corporations, including these tactics:

- Routine insistence on your giving up your Social Security number for the simplest transactions, such as obtaining cell-phone service, even though the law plainly says that this is your *private* number and you do *not* have to disclose it to anyone but the Social Security Administration and in a couple other cases of official business. Getting this number, however, is the key that allows any and all corporate data miners to unlock access to boodles of private info on you, so they constantly (and wrongly) assert that you must give it to them.

- Warranty cards that are longer than your arm. Buy a Sunbeam toaster, for example, and the company turns up the heat on you with a warranty card that asks you to reveal, among many other things, your income, marital status, ages and occupations of others in your home, what credit cards you use, whether you smoke cigars, the prescription drugs you take, whether you're a veteran, and whether anyone in your home suffers from angina, back pain, or thinning hair. In case you're disinclined to provide such a laundry list of personal data, Sunbeam's card warns: "FAILURE TO RETURN THIS CARD MAY AFFECT YOUR WARRANTY!" This is nothing but tosh and twaddle, for a simple store receipt qualifies you for a warranty (you can send back Sunbeam's card with a message to the CEO to shove it up his rump, and you're still covered). But the threat makes many customers think they must reveal all, including their thinning-hair problem, so Sunbeam gets scads of free data that it can package and sell.

- Selling you out. In addition to manufacturers like Sunbeam, such outfits as insurance companies, Internet firms, the phone giants, credit card companies, and so many others glean info on you as part of the business service that they provide—then they run a very profitable side business of selling that private information to marketers. Big chain pharmacies, for example, know what ailments you have and what brand of medicine you're taking for them. It's all in the chain's national database. Say that you're using Brand X to treat high cholesterol. The drug giant selling Brand Z will gladly pay big fees to get your pharmacy to send a letter to all Brand X users, suggesting they try Brand Z. Likewise, your Internet provider can make a bundle by selling not just your email address, but also your home address and phone number to marketing firms, meaning you'll get even more product hustles in your mail and from telemarketers.

Much of this mass invasion is coming at us not with jackbooted force, but in the softest, friendliest, and most soothing of tones, with corporate pryers and dossier developers wooing customers with amazing offers of rebates, discounts, and tons of free stuff if they'll just sign on the line—"All we need is your birth date, home phone, and, oh, put your Social Security number down there, too."

Then there's the extra convenience you'll get if you simply give them your index finger. Say what? Yes, not only are they digitally filing you away in their computers, but now the marketeers want to use your own digit to track your purchases. Kroger, McDonald's, and Thriftway are pioneering a system that, they coo, will save you the trouble of having to carry around a credit card. It's all about convenience, they say reassuringly, like a one-eyed cat squinting at the seafood store.

Here's how it works: They put your index finger on an image reader that digitally records thirteen unique points about your finger and stores this encrypted information in the central computers of a data management corporation. Henceforth, you needn't pay with a credit card, debit card, cash, or check—just run your own personal finger under the scanners at the checkout counter and the central database deducts the money directly out of your bank account or charges it to your credit card.

Oh, yes, there is that. In addition to your finger biometrics, you have to turn over your personal bank and credit card numbers to the database corporation, which gets a fee for every purchase rung up on your digit. The corporation also collects in its computers a record of everything you buy—compiling a very valuable database on you, via your own finger.

(WORRYWART ALERT: Finger-scanning also is sold to us on the basis of security: You no longer need to worry about having your credit card stolen, they say. But now, instead of mugging you for your credit cards, won't desperate criminals just grab you, chop off your finger, and go on a shopping spree?)

And now comes the ultimate in privacy invasion: VeriChip. In case you fear that this is a computer chip that gets implanted in your body, let me assure you here at the top of this story . . . YES, IT IS! This is Orwell realized, only instead of Big Brother implanting us, something called Applied Digital Solutions Inc. is doing it.

The chip is about the size of a grain of rice, and the idea for it is derived from technologies used to keep track of cows. Nice imagery, huh? The chip is encoded with information that can be read when someone runs a handheld scanner across the implant—yes, like a convenience store scanner reads the bar code on a bag of chips. More nice imagery.

Once again, this bit of technological progress is being pushed for our own good. The initial chips are being put in some Alzheimer's patients who might wander off. Good, I can see that. But, who's next . . . and next . . . and . . .

A.D.S.—the "solutions" outfit—says that its marketing profile is by no means limited to people with diseases, and that VeriChip has many possible uses (which is precisely what I feared they'd be thinking). The company plans to have a version soon that beams to satellites so A.D.S. or its clients can track you anywhere on the planet, anytime. Maybe you've got a bad credit rating—no need to write up a report on you. A.D.S. can track your every move. Maybe you've

> ### NICE TOUCH
>
> Part of VeriChip's marketing plan is to travel to senior-citizen centers in a "Chipmobile," implanting the old folks en masse, as if they were herds of cattle. *Moooo, Mooooooooo.*

got a jealous or suspicious spouse—no need to hire a private eye. A.D.S. knows where you are 24/7, as they say.

HOW TO POP THE PRIVACY INVADERS

When I was a mere tyke, my momma taught me at the supper table that if I wanted something, I shouldn't reach across the table and grab it, but ask for it—and ask politely, too.

I wonder if bankers had mommas. I wonder the same about all the corporate chieftains who now routinely reach out and grab our privacy without so much as a "pretty please." They are carelessly stiff-arming the Constitution, surreptitiously raking up every shred of the most personal information they can find on each of us and feeding this raw tonnage into the maws of their voracious mega-computers, which then spit out our privacy bit by bit, to anyone and everyone who will pay for it.

Oh, say the bankers, this is all legit. Didn't you know that Congress passed the Gramm-Leach-Bliley Act in 1999? Sure enough, GLB (properly pronounced GLUB for its drowning effect on privacy rights) expressly authorizes them to peddle our personal information. For example, a financial conglomerate like Citigroup (which led the lobbying effort) can hand your health records from their Travelers insurance subsidiary to their Citibank officers, or give your Citibank records to their Salomon Smith Barney investment house—without asking for your OK.

Also, they can sell your personal records to anyone as long as they have notified you somewhere back in the fog of time about their "privacy policy." These corporate policies are gems of obfuscation, usually written in such indecipherable legalese that you either ignore the damned thing or pass out trying to read it.

Hey, retort the bankers, we're more than fair because our lobbyists specifically (and rather magnanimously, we'd add) wrote into the GLB a provision allowing you to (JARGON ALERT, JARGON ALERT!) "opt out." What this provision means is that if you really, really, really don't want these privacy peddlers selling your personal information:

> *First,* you must somehow be aware that this obscure law lets you choose to have your information deleted from the "for sale" list of the banks, insurance companies, etc.—a customer choice that is not heavily advertised by the corporations.
>
> *Second,* you must take your time (which corporations consider worthless) to figure out the various procedures the companies have for "opting out"—and, again, they do not go out of their way to inform you about these procedures.

Third, you must then take off a few days from work to try to locate someone in each of the corporations' global empires who knows and will give you the number of the person in charge of "opting out"—and then you enter corporate hell. You will get wrong numbers, endless busy signals, painful Muzak (interspersed with company ads), and tortuous voice mail systems before finally reaching Ingrid in Latvia, who promptly disconnects you.

Fourth, you must be gullible enough to believe that after going through all of this, the company actually removes your name and data file from its for-sale list.

BUSH OPTS OUT OF OPT-IN

"I'm for 'opt-in,' " George W said firmly when asked during the 2000 campaign about the privacy of our medical records.

Way to go, W!

But he soon weaseled. In 2002, he reversed a mild Clinton rule that required hospitals to get the written consent of us patients before handing over our medical records to insurance companies, employers, and others. In other words, the first chance he got, he killed "opt-in."

Speaking for the Bushites, Health Secretary Tommy Thompson snorted at patients: "You never did have federal privacy rights."

Excuse me for being persnickety, but even if the corporations explicitly informed all customers about "opt-out" and made the process as simple as one-two-three, this is still not the way to treat We the People, who have a Fourth Amendment *right* to be free of any such intrusion. The language and the spirit of the Fourth Amendment is as clear as my momma's early instructions to me: Ask before you grab.

If you want to compile a computerized dossier on me and sell any part of my personal life, the burden is on you to get my informed, written consent in advance every time you do it. It's called—and this is our WORD OF THE DAY— "opt-in."

Yes, you might say, *I support that concept of consent, but lord have mercy, Hightower, surely you're not suggesting that we can beat the bankers, insurance giants, and all those other corporate powers who've rigged these privacy rules against us. Are you?*

Charlene Beats the Bankers

In 2001, Charlene Nelson, a stout believer in the Fourth Amendment, learned that a cabal of bankers, legislators, and the governor of her state of North Dakota was trying to undo a good state "opt-in" law requiring banks to get permission before selling their customers' financial data. The cabal claimed that this pesky permission provision had to be altered to bring North Dakota into compliance with GLB.

Nelson, a mother of three young boys who lives west of Fargo, considers herself a conservative; she had never been much of a political activist, but she knew political horse manure when she sniffed it—and this claim was seriously stinky.

In fact, the bankers lied. GLB does not require states to conform— indeed, it specifically allows states to provide more privacy protection for their citizens. Offended by the lie, Charlene wrote her legislators, assuming they would respect the wishes of citizens like her. They didn't. "I was just stunned when it passed," she says, and she went from angry to activist.

About a dozen friends and neighbors met, came up with the punchy acronym POP (Protect Our Privacy), decided to petition for a binding referendum to reverse the legislators' action, and set out to collect signatures to put the issue on the ballot.

The Powers That Be scoffed, believing that these were rank amateurs and asserting that North Dakotans didn't care about the privacy change. But POP hit the streets, the phones, and talk-radio shows, creating quite a stink of their own. They rallied hundreds of volunteers to collect signatures and shocked the cognoscenti by getting more than enough signers in only six weeks—unheard of in North Dakota. Along the way, they also built a right-left coalition ranging from the Constitution Party to labor unions, from the Farm Bureau to the ACLU.

Now the chase was on, and the Big Boys resorted to their usual arse-

ZAPPING ZAPME!

Especially offensive is the corporate invasion of the classrooms, sneaking out with personal data on children, which is then sold to marketeers . . . or whomever.

One of the top name brokers, for example, is American Student Lists, which brags: "To help you reach this highly lucrative market, ASL has over 12 million names of children between the ages of 2 and 13, representing Pre-K through the 8th grade."

Another classroom snoop is ZapMe!—an Internet provider backed by Microsoft, Dell, and other giants. It provides computers and services to some six thousand schools—for free! Good deal . . . but what does ZapMe! get?

The schools must promise that the students will use the computers at least four hours a day—and ZapMe! sells ads that flash at the kids as they use the machines.

Worse, however, the company collects the names, ages, gender, addresses, and other personal data of the students, without any limits on how the information can be used or to whom it can be sold.

This was being done without the knowledge or consent of the parents . . . until parents found out and raised a hellstorm of protest! *Their grassroots outrage forced Congress to pass a law in December 2001 requiring parental consent before any corporation can extract personal information from schoolchildren.*

For more information, contact the watchdog group Commercial Alert:

www.commercialalert.org
503-235-8012

nal of money, lies, and raw ugliness. "All we had was grassroots folks and the issue," says Nelson, who directed POP's campaign from her kitchen table.

The bankers put up $150,000 (five times what POP could collect), hired professional flacks, and launched a television assault. First they tried to buffalo voters with the odd assertion that North Dakota banks don't sell their customers' information, so there's no need to worry. North Dakota might be a rural state, but the people aren't rubes—if bankers don't plan to sell people's privacy, why did they change the law?

Oh, right, conceded the bankers, who then shifted to the old ruse that passage of the referendum would cause corporations to flee, jobs to be lost, and the state to dry up and blow away. This ridiculous pitch became the bankers' featured campaign theme, complete with an absolutely hilarious television ad that had all the credibility of a 1950s monster-from-outer-space movie.

The ad began with a peaceful scene of a bridge leading into North Dakota. As a voice-over begins to warn of the dark economic consequences of POP's privacy referendum, viewers see a big stone wall moving from the left side of the screen until it completely blocks the bridge, sealing the state's borders from outside commercial intercourse. The punch line comes in the form of a metal shield rising in front of the bridge with the ominous words: CLOSED FOR BUSINESS!

As Napoleon once advised, "Never interrupt your enemy when he is making a mistake."

Then the PR henchmen of the industry went from stupid to mean, turning on Nelson herself, assailing her as some sort of right-wing wacko—a tactic that North Dakotans, a very decent people, did not find amusing. The amazing thing is that the bankers and the politicos thought any of these ploys would work. As a writer for the *Fargo Forum* put it, "In the end, the biggest wall was the one blocking the bankers' view of the electorate."

They got what they deserved, which is an old-fashioned drubbing from the voters, who sided with POP by 73 to 27 percent in last year's election.

By daring to stand up, Charlene and her grassroots rebels tapped into a public anger that is seething all across our country. The privacy thieves think they're getting away with it, but they are despised by the people (polls consistently reveal 70 to 90 percent opposition to their various tactics and thefts), and whenever people are given the chance to pull a lever, as Charlene gave the people of North Dakota, they respond in huge majorities.

This is a realignment issue for American politics, with people of all

CAMPAIGN CONTRIBUTIONS IN THE PRESIDENTIAL AND CONGRESSIONAL RACES OF 2000 AND 2002, BY THE FINANCIAL INDUSTRY ALONE:

$507.7 million

LOBBYING EXPENSES BY THE INDUSTRY 2000–2002:

$101.5 million

Source: www.opensecrets.org

ideologies (except corporatism and authoritarianism—a decidedly narrow base in our land) wanting to stop the thievery and force the thieves to spend the rest of their lives going from county fair to county fair, where they'd be required to sit all day in dunking booths marked PRIVACY THIEF—25 CENTS A SHOT. They'd be dunked so often their skin would have a permanent pucker.

What we have here is another failure of our country's corrupt political leadership. How corrupted is it? So totally that neither the Republican nor the Democratic Party will reach down to pick up this big, juicy, rich, and ripe political gift laying on the ground right in front of them. Neither party has the guts or gumption to rankle the powerhouse corporate contributors—who happen to be the privacy thieves.

Charlene Nelson says she and the other POP-ers got "a crash course in civics," and they are staying in the fight. Not only are they being vigilant and noisy about ongoing sneaky banker efforts to punch loopholes into North Dakota's "opt-in" requirement, but she's also organizing in her hometown against the privacy-crushing provisions of Bush's PATRIOT and Homeland Security acts. She believes we all need to stand up, and she's willing to share with anyone the lessons she's learning in her kitchen table rebellion: r.cnelson@702com.net.

CHAPTER 14

Don't Be an Idiot

Did you know that:

- In San Francisco, it's a crime to pile horse manure more than six feet high on a street corner. (Apparently, up to six feet is fine, but a quarter-inch more, no—I wonder, do S.F. police carry measuring tapes?)
- In Oklahoma, it's a crime to get a fish drunk. (There must be some *very, very* lonely people in Oklahoma.)
- In Oneida, Tennessee, it's a crime to sing the song "It Ain't Goin' to Rain No Mo'." (Actually, I'm OK with this and would even add that anyone singing more than five verses and choruses consecutively is subject to lethal injection, and I'd add that anyone even starting to sing "One Hundred Bottles of Beer on the Wall" in a public place may legally be shot dead on the spot.)

But the greatest offense against our society these days is not any one law or a particular assault on our freedoms. Rather, it is the persistent, insidious effort by those who shape our culture to reduce the American citizenry to idiots. From corporate advertisers to political sermonizers, from boards of education to the entertainment programmers, their goal is idiocy.

By "idiots," I'm referring to more than the constant charge that we're all a bunch of dummies. *(Hey, Biff, didya hear the report on TV that kids today can't even name the capital of Lithuania? I mean, what is this country coming to?)* That's just manufactured media fluff. Far from being a nation of numbskulls, Americans (and especially young folks) are smarter than ever. But to what end?

The original Greek word *idiotes* referred to people who might have had a high IQ but were so self-involved that they focused exclusively on their own life and were both ignorant of and uncaring about *public* concerns and the common good.

Such people were the exact opposite of the Athenian democratic ideal of an active citizenry fully involved in the civic process, with everyone accepting their responsibilities to each other and all of humankind. This is the ideal that Jefferson and Madison built into our own nation's founding documents, the ideal that Lincoln embraced when he spoke of striving for a "government of the people, by the people, for the people," the ideal that Justice Louis Brandeis was expressing when he wrote that "the most important office" in our land is "that of a private citizen."

Far from calling on you to measure up to this high democratic ideal, however, the Powers That Be quite prefer that you be an idiot.

Be an involved citizen? Forget about it, Jake. Don't waste your time. Get a job, keep your head down, play the lottery, don't be different, take a pill, watch "reality TV," buy things, play it safe, live vicariously, don't make waves, prepay your funeral. Oh, and on those big questions—such as economic fairness, going to war, "rebalancing" that liberty/security equation, and the shrinking of democracy itself—don't hurt your little gray cells by focusing on them, for there's not a lot you can do about them, we know more than you do, and don't worry . . . we'll take care of you. Go about your business—be a good idiot.

THE OPPOSITE OF COURAGE IS NOT COWARDICE, IT'S CONFORMITY

Come on, America, that's not us! Don't let BushCo, the Wobblycrats, and the Kleptocrats steal our country and trivialize We the People as being nothing more substantial than passive consumers who can even be made to cower in duct-taped "safe rooms" whenever the governing authorities shout "Code Orange!" out their windows.

America was built not by conformists, but by mutineers—we're a big, brawling, boisterous, bucking people, and now is our time!

Our democracy is being dismantled right in front of our eyes—not by crazed foreign terrorists, but by our own ruling elites. This is a crucial moment when America desperately needs you and me to stand as full *citizens,* asserting the bold and proud radicalism of America's democratic ideals.

Who said this?

> *It is not that we see democracy through the haze of optimism. We know that democracy is a jewel that must be polished constantly to maintain its luster. To prevent it from being damaged or stolen, democracy must be guarded with unremitting vigilance.*

That's not Patrick Henry or Abe Lincoln, but Aung San Suu Kyi, the inspirational and courageous democracy fighter of Burma. Her life literally is on the line every day, for she's the leader of the popular opposition to the ruthless military dictatorship that usurped this beautiful country's democracy in a bloody coup. In 1990, her National League for Democracy won 82 percent of the vote in a democratic election, but the military and the economic elites stepped in and invalidated the people's choice, and they have ruled through iron-fisted repression, murder, and armed force ever since.

You think democracy asks a lot of us—too many meetings, too much risk of getting your name on Ashcroft's database, too much confrontation with authority? Try walking a few miles in the shoes of Suu Kyi. Burma's military thugs would love to kill her, and the threat of this is a constant reality in her life, but for now they know that they could not withstand the popular explosion that would follow such a murder, for she's the symbol of the people's suppressed democratic yearnings. Instead, they held her under house arrest for seven and a half years, and though she was officially released last year, she is hounded, harassed, monitored, and followed everywhere she goes in an effort to intimidate her and Burma's other democracy activists. They wish she would leave, but she wouldn't even go to Stockholm to accept the Nobel Peace Prize she won in 1991, because she feared she would not be allowed to re-enter her country.

Use It or Lose It

Maybe you're thinking: *Well, Hightower, sure, if a dictatorship was imposed here in the US of A, then, by golly, you can bet your boots that I'd stand up!* Too late, mañana patriot.

A military coup is not the only way to slip the plush rug of America's democracy from beneath your motionless feet. A few tugs here and a couple of hard yanks there . . . and it's gone. And they've been tugging and yanking furiously of late, taking scores of actions that would cause Paul Revere to mount up again, including: Ashcroft's ruling that the FBI can secretly infiltrate and spy on political and church meetings without a warrant (yes, *your meetings*, not just the meetings of Muslims or dark-skinned, foreign, "terrorist-looking" people); the federal judge's ruling that New Yorkers could be denied their constitutional right to march in protest of Bush's war plans, instead relegating them to a ten-thousand-person "rally pen" where they "could be adequately policed"; Ashcroft's PATRIOT Act II, which would provide advance immunity for federal agents who conduct *illegal* surveillance at the behest of top executive branch officials (a provision that would have protected Nixon's illegal wiretappers).

This undermining of our basic civil liberties and imposition of antidemocratic police power are in addition to other maneuvers that are steadily strangling our people's democracy:

- The Supreme Court's 1976 ruling that campaign money is "speech" effectively negates the value of your vote and electoral participation, while giving a handful of corporations and wealthy interests far more "speech" than the rest of us and also putting the possibility of holding public office beyond the reach of ordinary Americans. Nothing has been so destructive of our nation's promise of democratic representation as has this totally un-American decree—which neither political party challenges.
- The unheralded provisions of NAFTA, the WTO, the forthcoming FTAA (Free Trade Area of the Americas), and other arcane trade schemes that allow global corporations to wield veto power over your local, state, and national laws, usurping our people's right to self-

government—a theft of power that has been pulled off without the people knowing it, much less agreeing to it.

- With a massive infusion of campaign donations, a half-dozen conglomerates have gotten Congress and the FCC to rush through a radical rewriting of the rules so that they now control our public airwaves, making a mockery of our "Freedom of the Press" and restricting the mass-media debate to corporate-approved topics and viewpoints.

Don't expect these political, corporate, media, and other money powers to alert you to the fact that big chunks of your democracy, right here in the US of A, already have been seriously damaged or stolen—and they're certainly not going to rally us to the essential cause of repairing and retaking our democracy. That's up to us.

Of course, BushCo is hoping we're idiots, and to help keep our minds from wandering to what's going on with democracy here in The Homeland, they have us riveted on color-coded threats from afar, warning sternly that millions of the world's people hate us—indeed, as George so eloquently put it, "They hate our freedoms."

Bullfeathers! Start with this, George: The world's people are perfectly able to discern the difference between the American people on the one hand and America's corporate and military force on the other.

What they hate is that our government, corporations, and military storm around the world in betrayal of every democratic value that the American people hold dear. Bush poses grandly as the noble spearpoint for democracy, yet he (like his predecessors) is a willing accomplice of brutal dictators and global corporate powers that oppress the world's people, impoverish them, and plunder their resources. Through his perpetual war agenda, his oil buddies, the World Bank, the arms dealers, his defiance of environmental and human rights treaties, and dozens of other actions, George W (and our Congress) is an enthusiastic supporter of global-scale theft and thuggery.

> *"Educate and inform the whole mass of the people. . . . They are the only sure reliance for the preservation of our liberty."*
>
> —Thomas Jefferson, Letter to James Madison, 1787

Perhaps he thinks (whoops, back up, that's too strong of a concept for him, so let's start over). Perhaps it doesn't cross his mind that the people who are being run over can clearly see America's economic, governmental, and military might behind the thievery and thuggery. Aung San Suu Kyi damned sure saw it. When the generals threw out Burma's elected government and installed themselves in power, the U.S. did nothing in support of democracy. Worse, our government turned its back as Unocal, Texaco, and Halliburton cut deals with the new junta (which had given itself the Orwellian moniker of SLORC, the State Law and Order Restoration Council) to develop gas fields there and build the billion-dollar Yadana pipeline across the country. The pipeline partnership stole land from farmers, displaced entire villages, uprooted sections of rain forests, and conscripted locals who were forced at gunpoint to help construct the pipeline. Unocal, based in California, is still in partnership with these dictators, who daily hound and harass Suu Kyi.

Such upstanding American corporations as Disney, Eddie Bauer, Levi Strauss, Liz Claiborne, Macy's, and PepsiCo

DICK DEFINES CORPORATE MORALITY FOR US

Our very own veep, Dick Cheney, was at the helm of Halliburton when it defied human rights activists and the Burmese democracy movement by signing a deal with Burma's totalitarian rulers to build the Yadana gas pipeline. This pipeline now delivers up to $400 million a year in gas revenues to the dictators, helping to keep them in power.

Asked about the morality of participating in a forced-labor project with some of the worst human rights abusers on earth, Dick offered this insight into his corporate soul:

"You have to operate in some very difficult places and oftentimes in countries that are governed in a manner that's not consistent with our principles here in the United States."

Have to, Dick?

also made business deals with the devils of Burma—though grassroots boycotts and political pressure back here in the U.S. and elsewhere finally forced them to withdraw (www.freeburma.org).

It is this investment by our oil giants and other corporations that has given the generals the wherewithal to build and maintain a police state that boasts 300,000 armed forces deployed to stifle democracy and keep the dictatorship in power. This is the face of America that much of the world sees—the faces of executives from Unocal, Halliburton, Disney, and others, standing side by side with the SLORCs of the world.

Yet Suu Kyi does not hate you and me. She knows the difference between us and our corrupt leadership. She knows and shares our egalitarian values, and she is sacrificing her comfort, happiness, and quite possibly her life to try to extend to her country the very values that you and I cherish. She and oppressed people throughout the world love freedom, and they look to the American people as a beacon of the democracy that they seek.

The irony is that she is more aware of what we're at serious risk of losing here than most Americans are.

MAKE YOUR MARK

I've always liked the way George Carlin thinks. It's clear that his plumb lob doesn't go quite perpendicular, but in this crazy time, that strikes me as just about right. At least he asks provocative questions: "If black boxes survive air crashes—why don't they make the whole plane out of that stuff?"

I like his ingenuity, too—his ability to make a lot out of very little, which I think is one of the terrific enterprising traits of the American people. Here's George:

> "In some hotels they give you a little sewing kit. You know what I do? I sew the towels together. One time I sewed a button on a lampshade. I like to leave a mark."

That's the spirit! Instead of just going along with the hotel's authorized amusements (watch the telly, order room service, read the Gideon

Bible, or suck the minibar dry), George blazed his own path . . . and set an example for all of us. (No, the message is not to go around sewing buttons on lampshades, but to defy the official order every now and then—make your mark.)

If you do, you'll have plenty of company, for millions of Americans are already out there in the cities, neighborhoods, towns, and country-side—in the fight, in the face of power, leaving their marks.

Water Wars

With astonishingly little public notice from the media, a handful of global behemoths are moving rapidly to seize the people's most essential public resource: our water supplies. They are determined to turn this necessity of life into just another commodity for traders and specula-tors—a private plaything for personal profiteering.

And if you're xenophobic, get ready to have your eyeballs explode: The Big Three water grabbers are foreign! Where's Tom Ridge? Where's John Ashcroft? Code Red, Code Red!

Mon dieu, fraulein, it's Suez Lyonnais of France, Vivendi Universal of France, and RWE of Germany that now have the water systems of such cities as Houston, Indianapolis, Lexington, Jersey City, Milwaukee, Washington, D.C., and dozens of other cities in their grasp.

The promise of water privatization has been golden, the delivery leaden. In city after city that has succumbed to the golden promises, lo-cals have seen their monthly bills skyrocket, service crumble, water quality stink, and democratic control evaporate. For example, Suez's 1999 takeover of Atlanta's system has been a disaster—in 2002 alone, residents were given five "boil water" alerts for unsafe contaminants coming out of their taps, fire hydrants have been dry and useless for months, leaking water mains went unrepaired for weeks . . . and Suez's response was to run to the city screeching that it was not making a profit, so it demanded millions more in tax subsidies.

The corporate grab has led to a spreading water war that makes the old battles of the Wild West look like badminton tournaments. Battles are raging in New Orleans, Stockton, Laredo, and elsewhere. People are speaking out, organizing, doing petition drives, holding referendums, going to court, and doing whatever else it takes to stop the corporate heist of their water supply. In Atlanta, the people were so fed up that in early 2003 they up and fired Suez, taking their water back into public control. Jacksonville has done the same, Lexington is battling for its freedom from RWE, Indianapolis is beginning to fight Vivendi, and other communities are also in rebellion.

This is one of the biggest, most widespread (and most unreported) struggles taking place in America (and throughout the world, as Ghana, Bolivia, Canada, and other nations also battle the water giants)—and it's also a struggle that can be won, as people are showing. One more thing: It's worth the fight. This is our water, for goodness sake! As an Atlanta city council member, Clair Muller, put it, "Water is the worst thing to privatize. It's what we need to live. I think that's key to the whole debate—are we going to lose control over functions that are essential to life?"

YOU'RE NEXT

Think the privatizers won't hit your town or city? Their lobbyists have slipped a stick of dynamite into a bill in Washington called the Water Investment Act. The overall bill is needed, for it would provide the funds that cities must have to upgrade and expand our public water systems.

But the water hustlers put in a provision that would *force your city* to consider privatizing your water supply . . . or be denied any public funding. Also, for the first time, your federal tax dollars could be used to finance the corporate takeover of your water.

Public Citizen can help you fight back:
www.citizen.org/cmep/water
212-546-4996

Is this a private fight,
or can anyone join in?

—Old Irish saying

Be my guest. *Unfortunately,* there is no shortage of fights to join these days. *Fortunately,* however, we're a country of democracy fighters, and you can join one or more wherever you are . . . or start your own! I don't mean to fight for fighting's sake, but fight to take our country back.

Join Global Trade Watch to stop the latest sovereignty-choking glob of global greed called Free Trade Area of the Americas, which "frees" corporations to privatize everything from schools to postal services in your city or anywhere else in the Western Hemisphere, whether we want it or not (www.tradewatch.org).

Join the millions of people working in cities all across our country to stop Ashcroft and Ridge from getting local police to assist in federal surveillances, interrogations, and other autocratic actions that violate our civil liberties and constitutional rights (www.bordc.org).

Join a growing number of grassroots organizations daring to confront the very heart of corporate power by challenging the absurd notion that a corporation is a "person"—a fiction that, ironically, gives these paper structures more power than a real person has, or, as we've seen, more power than an entire nation of actual living, breathing persons (www.reclaimdemocracy.org).

Join the fight for living wages in your city, the fight to reclaim our public airwaves, the fight to make public schools work again, the fight to stop redlining and predatory lending, the fight to let patients and doctors decide about medical marijuana without the police intruding, the fight for public funding of your local and state elections, the fight to [FILL IN YOUR FAVORITE HERE]: _____

Don't wait on "heroes" or national leaders. Be your own hero—everyone can do something, everyone makes a contribution. I think of a story told by a fellow named Bernard Mechlowitz. He was in a New York City restaurant in 2002 and says:

> I noticed a husky, very athletic-looking man seated at a table behind me. A short time later, two people came over and took his picture. I was certain he was some well-known football player, though I didn't know which one. As I was leaving the restaurant, I asked the waiter if he knew who the V.I.P. was.
>
> "Oh, yes," he said. "He's the bus driver for a group of tourists eating here."

As far as I'm concerned, being a bus driver in New York City certainly qualifies you for hero status!

Everyone who does any heavy lifting in the democratic cause is a hero. As writer Elbert Hubbard noted a century ago, "God will not look you over for medals, degrees, or diplomas, but for scars."

The important thing to know is that you are wanted. You are needed. You are important. You are not only what democracy counts on, you are what democracy *is*.

Thomas Paine saw in America something breathtaking, which he expressed as the opportunity to *"start the world over again."* Paine and others got America off on the right foot, but our leaders have stumbled badly of late. That's why we have to step in now. You and I have the chance to bring our great country back to the ideals that launched it, ideals that remain gently nestled in our hearts.

Live your ideals.

IV. EPILOGUE

CHAPTER 15

Bob Runs for President

A Drama in One Act

"Hi, my name's Bob," he said, "and I want to be your president. But I'm not willing to mortgage my soul to get there, so you might as well know right from the start where I stand on things."

Bob wasn't announcing his White House run in front of national TV cameras. Hell, he hadn't even formed a Bob for President Exploratory Committee to test the waters. Besides, the media didn't know him from a tall radish. Neither did we. He just showed up one morning at the Chat & Chew Café and startled us regulars by turning toward us from his counter stool, clearing his throat, and launching right into his presidential announcement. It was uninvited, but then again, who exactly invited George W or Gibberish Joe Lieberman or Ol' Long Face John Kerry to offer themselves up?

Naturally, Bob had to be nuttier than a sack of goobers, but he didn't seem to be any kind of dangerous nut. Said he was just a guy who'd been going up and down the road all across America and had learned a lot about our country. He called it a "great country, way better than the greedheads and boneheads who're running it—and doing their damnedest to ruin it." Well, we all had to nod at that.

For a man on the road, Bob seemed to clean up pretty well, and he wasn't ranting or asking us for spare change or doughnut money, which is more than you can say for most practicing politicians. Anyway, we were getting a little weary of our own B.S., so, with a couple of winks around the room, the regulars decided he could have the floor. "Go ahead on," I said to Bob. "Give us your best shot."

And so he did.

"Last year, I saw a bumper sticker on a pickup truck here in Texas," Bob began. "It said:

WHERE ARE WE GOING?
And what am I doing in this handbasket?

"Well, that's exactly our problem," Bob said, thumping the countertop. "The big shots who run the corporations, the government, the media, and everything else in today's system have loaded America into their little red-white-and-blue, jet-powered handbasket and, without so much as a by-your-leave, they've headed you, me, and our *great country* hellbent in a direction we never chose."

When Bob said "great country," it didn't sound like some pus-filled polyp of a speechwriter's cliché like it does when those Congress Critters rise up on hind legs to tell us peasants how fortunate we are to live in such a "GREAT COUNTRY." Out of their mouths, it sounds all brassy, like something farted out of a tuba in an oompah-pah band. Out of Bob's mouth, it sounded modest, respectful, even kinda affectionate. It's a small thing, I guess, but right off, it made me like this guy.

"Without us even realizing it," Bob declared, leaning out to us from his stool, "you and I have let a tiny, powerful elite in our society take control." His hands were in motion now, like a gardener pulling carrots: "Group by group—working stiffs . . . small farmers . . . Main Street business . . . consumers . . . the middle class as well as poor folks . . . retirees . . . immigrants . . . taxpayers . . . you name it—we've been plucked from America's rich democratic soil.

"The fundamentals have changed. It's not a matter of a couple of policies or of a little economic downturn. While we weren't watching, the basics of our democracy—I mean the gut-level values that everyone sitting in this room believes in, like fairness, justice, equality—have been shoved aside by the money powers. Have you noticed? The CEOs, the politicians, the media, and the rest don't even bother talking about these values anymore, much less act on any of them. Far from it. They're grabbing everything they can for themselves while staying busy in Washington ripping up all the rules and laws that have brought our America so far since 1776 and have given some muscle to those ideals of fairness, justice, and equality. What we're experiencing is more than just another case of the rich getting richer. They're altering the *moral underpinnings* of our democracy, assaulting our understanding of what it is to be American."

There were a lot of surprised looks and even a few hesitant heads bobbing in quiet agreement. This was not the kind of talk we were used to hearing from politicians, so the small, crowded room quieted down some. "I'm guessing that most of you, in your private moments, realize that this has happened, that something big has slipped away from us in the past thirty years. Let me put it to you like this: Do the people in power really give a damn about folks like you and me anymore? Start with your own government—the lawmakers down at city hall, in your state capitol, or up in Washington. Do your opinions really matter to them . . . or do they just go with the big money?"

At this, a couple more people shifted in their chairs toward Bob, and I noticed that Louise, the World's Worst Waitress (Triple W, we call her, though we shortened that to Trip), was tuning in with half an ear as she stacked coffee cups behind the counter. Big Ed Wheeler, sitting at a table to the right of the speaker, kept his back squarely to Bob, arms crossed tightly over his chest. But, then, we wouldn't expect either more or less from Ed, who, the story goes, went into a grumpy funk when Ronnie Reagan couldn't run a third term.

"And that's just the government," Bob continued. "At least with government you get to vote, but the real power has been grabbed by corporate executives whose names are never on a ballot, whose decisions affecting you are made in secret, and whose butts you can't even find to kick. Whether it's the laws passed, the water your kids drink, the future of your neighborhood, or what's allowed in your news feed every day— We the People don't have much to say about it."

Ellie Lowen, a retired librarian of tender sensibilities, piped up in her best much-offended voice, "Fires, car wrecks, floods, and police raids, that's all they show on the local news. Gets everyone as nervous as a cat on hot asphalt."

Bob smiled sympathetically at Ellie, just as most people do, and continued: "A handful of guys with limousine lifestyles are sitting in soft leather chairs up in faraway skyscrapers deciding our futures. They don't know you, won't ever visit your town, and don't give a ding as to how their decisions impact you. Their values stop at what's good for their company's stock value. Us? We're just bugs on their windshield."

At this, out of the corner of my eye I saw Eddie Vasquez pump a fist in the air. He got laid off a few months back after twelve years with the same company. The New York owners 'shipped his job—and seventy-five others—off to someplace in the south of India. He's been pretty hangdog ever since, and I noticed that after he shoved his fist up, he dropped his head down, fork dolefully pushing refried beans around the plate.

Bob pushed ahead: "I'll give you an example of what I mean: Has the electric company raised rates here?"

"Doubled 'em in two years," said Tyrone Bledso, a regular with his own small dry-cleaning business.

"Did you have a say or even get a reason that made a lick of sense?" Bob asked. Guffaws. "I'll bet that increase put a squeeze on a lot of you." Heads really bobbing up and down now

Then Bob fires off a few quick questions we hadn't asked ourselves but realized as he popped 'em at us that we probably should've been asking them all along:

"Who owns this electric company?

"Where're they headquartered?

"How much money do they haul out of here each month?

"Who turned them loose to make a killing off you?"

Now he was on a roll. "These are all questions you have a *right* to ask. It's your town, your money—why should they get to rig the rules and pick your pocket? Speaking of money," Bob said without even taking a breath, "I saw the big bank buildings downtown as I came in. Had names like Citibank and Wells Fargo. None local. How do they treat you?"

"Like we're cockroaches at the country club buffet," came a disembodied retort, fired like a shot through the pass-through window of the kitchen. It was Lupe Garza, who owns the Chew. He's also the day cook and "chief of stuff," as he puts it. He's always busy back there in the kitchen, so we hardly ever see him, but he always seems to know what's going on out front. "I went to every bank in town for a lousy $30,000 loan for those new booths you're sitting in and a little expansion back here in my kitchen. I couldn't find anybody with a pulse," Lupe shouted out to us.

Lupe's head suddenly appeared in the frame of the window, dark eyes blazing. Jack Orlock, a plumber and recent addition to us Chew regulars, audibly gasped, "Wow, so that's Lupe." Lupe wasn't done. "Loan officers were all twenty-five years old, just moved here, didn't know me from Zapata's horse, and told me they don't do business loans under five million." The head disappeared.

"That's the kind of thing I'm talking about—and want all of us to start talking about," Bob responded to the now vacant service window. He spun on his stool back to the room and rose to his feet. "It's time to move from small talk to big talk in our conversations, to start asking basic questions about fairness. Here's one for you—when they put in a toxic waste plant, why's it always on the poor side of town and never on Hob-Nob Hill?"

"Oleander Heights," I heard myself say without thinking.

"Sir?" Bob asked.

"That's where the Mc-mansions are. And, no, there's no waste dump or factory or creosote plant or anything like that anywhere near Oleander Heights."

"Right," Bob continued. "And when Bush and Congress go to cutting taxes, why's it always the taxes of Exxon and of the privileged people they know, people with offshore bank accounts and $6,000 shower curtains? They never seriously cut taxes on businesses like the Chat & Chew here, or on your and my payroll taxes. Then there's war. They say 'we've' got to go to war, and they strut around like a bunch of red roosters full of their own cock-a-doodle-doo—but notice that none of their kids ever have to go to their wars. And don't even get me started about NAFTA, WTO, IMF, FTAA, and all those other initials that, if you mixed them all up, spell GLOBALONEY. When did we have an election to surrender our democratic power to multinational corporations?"

Here, Bob leaned back on the counter, took a deep breath, and reached for his coffee.

For one long moment, no one moved or said a thing. Then Trip began to clap her hands slow and loud from behind the counter, grinning with delight at the morning surprise that had come from out of the blue and landed, pretty as you please, right there at her station. Murmuring and whispering broke out. A low voice behind me said to someone across the table, "He's making sense, you know," and the other one said back, just as low, "Yeah, but you can't run for president talking like that, can you?" This is when a gravelly bark of a question ripped through the room: "Who the hell *are* you?" Big Ed demanded, his back still turned, hands gripping the tabletop.

"I'm you," Bob said, real quiet like. "I'm all of you in this café, and all the people you know. I'm a regular Joe, who's just been trying to make a go of it and gotten a snoutful of being treated like a stray dog in my own land.

"Sure, I've got a background I could tell you about, a résumé, a family picture album, a personal story—but that's not the important thing. What's significant is that my song is essentially the same as yours. We've all got a few different verses, a little different beat, and different starting points, but it's one big song that so many people know by heart these days, of being left out and kicked about by so-called leaders who are betraying the spectacular, breathtaking possibilities offered by democracy and embodied by you . . . and you . . . and you," he said, pointing around to various coffee sippers.

"I'm everybody who thinks there's a big hole in America today, that we've lost something that really matters. I want my country back. Probably you do, too. But who's going to bring it back for us? Republicans? Democrats? Wall Street? Corporate executives? Media pundits? Or any of those other wax dummies sealed in their glass cages?"

Bob looked searchingly around the café, and all we could do was look back in a sort of group sigh. "Might as well hope the coyotes return your chickens," snorted Letty, who'd grown up on a ranch and was fluent in animal sayings.

"That's why we've got to quit waiting on them," Bob said, hoppin' to his feet with a new jolt of energy, like he'd swallowed a perky pill in his coffee. "Instead of getting down, let's get up.

"It came to me when I was working a job out West. At the end of the day, I was sipping a cold one at an outdoor café, taking in one of those extreme sunsets with all the sweeping colors that make you wonder why

painters even bother trying to capture nature on a canvas." Bob spread
his arms, asking us to imagine it. "Got me to thinking about the hundreds of glorious sunsets I'd been lucky enough to see in my rambles,
and as my mind wandered down memory lane, it flashed on another
beauty I've encountered again and again, one I had to admit ranks right
up there with a sunset."

Dramatic pause. The man obviously knew something about talking
in public. Curiosity rippled through the café.

"I'm talking about that spark that's deep inside all of us, urging us to
keep going, to be bigger than the sum of our parts, to keep reaching for
something better, richer, more meaningful and satisfying than what is—
or what we're told can be. I'm talking about *The Human Spirit*. This
spirit's our natural democratic impulse that tells us to rebel against the
no-good powers that keep shoving past us, stepping on our feet, telling
us to get outta the way."

"Well, I for one am pissed," Linda Carlson stated in a flat tone of suppressed anger. Linda had struggled to go back to school so she could
upgrade her computer skills, and now that she had graduated, the
economy was in the tank, and she was having a hard time finding any
kind of job.

"It's part anger," Bob admitted, "but the bigger part is hope, a small
but constant flicker of belief that we really could create a place, a society
I mean, that practices what it preaches. And sometimes, the harder they
try to push us back, the brighter that little flicker gets inside us, until it's
fueled by enough anger and hope that it becomes a hot flame, and we
begin to push back. That's what's pretty special about America—the human spirit has a chance here."

There was something about the way Bob said all this, a kind of earth-
iness in his voice and steadiness in his eyes, that made fuzzy stuff like
"human spirit" go down easy with me. It wasn't woo-woo, if you know
what I mean, but something solid and honest. I've gotta say, every now
and then I feel that thing he was talking about. For me, it's an ache, a
welling up of white-hot passion for something bigger than another day
of work, paying the bills, or going golfing, for godsake. When's the last
time any politician reached out to tap that caring part of us?

One thing for sure, what started out as a little hoot for us at the Chew had turned into something else. I hadn't seen this bunch of mutts sit still for any one talker longer than a couple of ticks of the clock (except for the time Malvina had that incident with the squirrel). Here we were, fifteen minutes after Bob had cleared his throat, and no one was switching topics, jumping up to go, or wanting him to go. In fact, they were settling in, really interested in where this peroration was going to end up. Trip moved around the tables with more coffee, Sheepskin (we call him that because he's always reminding us about his Ph.D.) ordered a second plate of Lupe's rancheros, and Bob went on.

"I know about that spirit, about its power, because as I roam around from place to place, I see it sparking just about everywhere. Of course, it doesn't get any press, but it's happening all the same.

"Did you know that the people in states like Maine and Arizona, and now in North Carolina, too, have passed laws that take corrupt corporate money out of their state elections? They've provided public funding so politicians don't have to sell out to the Big Money boys—plus this public election fund means that someone like you, just regular people who have a lot more ideas than money, can draw from the fund, giving you a chance to run for office and beat the establishment.

"And let me tell you about this little town in Wisconsin, called New Haven. Perrier—you know, the fancy water from France—this company came steamrolling in and cut backroom, sweetheart deals with the mayor and the governor to let it haul off the area's pure spring water for its own profit—water that the small farmers and other locals use. Perrier gave $20,000 to the town of New Haven and thought the deal was done. But the people rose up, organized, launched a referendum, and voted 3 to 1 to send Perrier *away*," Bob exulted, swooshing his arms like he was tossing something out. "But that's not all," Bob almost shouted with excitement. "They also had a recall election on that mayor who'd taken Perrier's $20,000. They voted him out by 3 to 1, too, then gave back the money! How about that?

"Then there's this issue of our wonderful low-wage economy, where you work your butt off, do extra hours and weekends, but still can't get ahead. Congress keeps talking about raising the wage floor—and talking and talking, but doing nothing. Guess what, though? Congress did sneak through *pay raises for itself in four of the past five years*—did you know that?" Groans welled up from all around the room. "But, wait, 'cause here's the good news. In more than a hundred cities and counties across America, people have gotten together and passed what's called 'living wage' laws, setting local wage floors high enough so these corporations can't come in and steal from us. This gives hardworking people a shot at the middle class, a chance to better themselves and to lift up their whole community. See, we don't have to wait on Congress to—"

With that the door swung open and in barrelled Margie Rogers, just off the 11–7 shift in the hospital emergency room. "Damn, it is going to be a scorcher—just heard it on KNOW—like these geniuses think there might be another possibility in July," she said, laughing. "You believe those guys get paid . . . what . . . what did I say?" Margie asked, mystified at the impatient faces that had turned toward her at the noise of the door slamming shut. Trip waved Margie to a table, put an iced tea in front of her, and asked, "The usual?" Margie said yeah and cocked her head to the side with a curious "What's going on, guys?" expression. We turned back to Bob.

"I can go on and on with road stories of people standing up to the grasping greedheads. Here's one. I don't know how it is here, but there's a growing rebellion against local politicians who bilk us taxpayers to build new sports palaces for the rich owners of sports teams. It's all about them wanting luxury skyboxes they can—"

"I'll tell you what it's about," exploded Big Ed, so loud it sounded like a grenade had hit us. All heads jerked toward the explosion and saw Ed's torso twisting around so he could face Bob. "It's about graft, is what it is. This one rips my shorts. We've got a baseball owner here with more money than the pope's got in Rome, yet we're supposed to build him a stadium? He backed our new mayor, see, and now the mayor's saying we need to pay another quarter-cent sales tax so this guy can have a $300 million ballpark. Says it'll make us a 'world class' city. My ass—world-class suckers is what we'd be."

Ed glared at the rest of us, defying us to contradict him. "I've seen the plans. They're gonna raise ticket prices, charge six bucks for a small beer, take out the bleachers, and put in a line of $100,000 suites for the high rollers. If this bunch was any hoggier, we'd have to talk to them in Pig Latin.

"But they're running things, not us," Ed said, winding down and waving a hand weakly at the room when he said "us."

"But that's my point," Bob retorted, closing in on Big Ed. "They're only in charge if we do nothing. That's the purpose of my presidential campaign."

"Oh, stuff it," Ed snapped back. "You're not gonna be president, you're not even making a real run. Even if I think you're right about some things, if all of us here think you're right, you've got no money, no name, no connections, no backing, no nothing. What're you running on, the Bob Party? You're wasting our time!"

"Well, we could do worse than a Bob Party. But I assure you, I'm not wasting your time, not if you're really wanting to shake things up so people like us matter and so this system of ours is a whole lot fairer for folks."

Bob took a deep breath, looked around at us, smiled, and said in a softer voice, "I know that this is not the kind of change you can get done in a one-shot, hotshot run for president. Never has been. What I'm talking about is bigger than that—it's got to be built patiently and steadily expanded, reaching out to people who then reach out and involve others, so that over time it becomes not just another campaign, but a democratic movement that spawns and wins lots of campaigns. That's what democracy asks of us."

As if on signal, Sheepskin rose to his feet, straightened his bow tie, and launched into a history lesson: "This is how we got our United States. The American Revolution didn't just pop up in 1776. It was a movement that was gradually spread from head to head and place to place, and in its early stages, it was widely scoffed at as futile, even when Thomas Paine penned *Common Sense* and when Thomas Jefferson drafted the Declaration. It had to build at its own pace."

Bob nodded with approval (Bob didn't have to deal with Sheepskin day to day). The rest of us rolled our eyes and suggested he sit his butt down before his eggs got cold.

Picking up on Sheep's theme, Bob added, "Look at all the other movements that've expanded our democracy—from abolition and suffrage to labor and civil rights. They spread just like I'm talking about, with people like you in spots like this Chat & Chew getting together and getting serious about making changes. The only way to combat Big

Money is with organized people. None of those movements waited on someone who could get elected president.

"That's what hit me while I was soaking up sunsets out West and thinking about the human spirit: We've got to quit acting like consumers of politics and become creators again. Sure, it seems foolish for a nobody to run for president, but I'm running for the long haul, trying to get all of us nobodies running again—I'm not 'The Candidate,' I'm 'A Catalyst.'

"By 'running,' I mean that I can come in here and maybe get some of you folks talking about where we are as a country and where we ought to be—and what America *can be* if we all work together. Build from what we've got, from the ground up, understanding what we've got in common, and especially understanding that we are *not* alone—that fact gives us strength. Of course we can't win the presidency in '04! But if we don't start running now, we won't be able to win in '12 or '16 either. And, meanwhile, I'll bet you could beat that mayor and his stadium in the next election.

"Wouldn't be the first mayor who served only one term," Mack Martinez announced with rough humor in his voice. Then he gave Big Ed a thumbs-up! Shocked me. I'd never seen Mack even speak to Ed. Given their political differences, they usually avoided each other with that careful two-step people do when they have to share the same space.

"Let's make connections, invite some people from across town to have discussions with you here at the Chew over coffee or beers, team up on some local issues, and begin to build your own world. We have to push our own vision and values forward to counter those of the elites, giving people a clear choice. Get uppity where you have to, make demands, make plans, question authority, then question the answers, realizing that you are the only true authority. After all, it's our country, and we have the kids and grandkids to think about." Bob's voice was packing a preacher's punch now.

"I look around at you and I get such hope. You might think, 'Well, we're so few, we can't do anything.' But it's like they say about apples: You can count the seeds in an apple, but you can't count the apples in a seed. Corny, I guess, but the greatness of our country has come from the seed of ordinary people producing extraordinary things."

With that Bob abruptly quit the floor, saying he had to move on. I don't think he convinced Big Ed that any of this would work, but even Ed shook Bob's hand. Trip came around and asked Bob for his card, saying she wanted to get involved, but Bob said he didn't carry any cards, and besides, the place to get involved was where she was—and she could be one to help get it started. Sounded like she might, so I told her I'd give her a hand if she wanted. Lupe shouted out that Bob's coffee was on the house, but Bob, who was already out the door, had left money by his cup, including a tip that'll give Trip a big head for a month.

Interesting fella. Maybe we can turn our complaining into action. Now wouldn't that be something!

CONNNECTIONS

A man ain't no good alone.

—TOM JOAD

The greatest compliment I've ever received came from a young guy named Jay. He was a waiter in a Cajun café here in Austin. He'd heard me speak and been reading my stuff, and he said: "You give power to my voice. Before, it was just volume, but now I have information and connection."

That's awfully nice to hear, for that's exactly what I hope my modest work might amount to—giving strength to others so *together* we can do what needs to be done.

Of course, I too draw my strength, ideas, information, and inspiration from others. The Powers That Be want you to feel alone, weak, and hopeless, but that's nonsense—not only do we progressives have the numbers, but we also have tremendous activist resources to draw on, inform us, and—most important—connect us.

Here are some of the great public-interest and grassroots groups that I turned to for material in this book, and I urge you to connect with them:

ACORN
Living Wage Resource Center
1486 Dorchester Avenue
Boston, MA 02122
617-740-9500
www.livingwagecampaign.org

AFL-CIO
815 16th Street, NW
Washington, DC 20006
202-637-5000
www.aflcio.org

Agribusiness Examiner
Corporate Agribusiness Research
    Project
P.O. Box 2201
Everett, WA 98203-0201
425-258-5345
www.ea1.com/CARP

Alliance for Democracy
681 Main Street
Waltham, MA 02451
781-894-1179
email: peoplesall@aol.com

Alternative Radio
P.O. Box 551
Boulder, CO 80306
1-800-444-1977
www.alternativeradio.org

AlterNet.org
77 Federal Street
San Francisco, CA 94107
415-284-1420
www.alternet.org

American Civil Liberties Union
125 Broad Street
18th Floor
New York, NY 10004
212-549-2500
www.aclu.org

American Independent
Business Alliance
1510 Fifth Street
Boulder, CO 80302
303-402-1575
www.amiba.net

American Library Association
50 East Huron
Chicago, IL 60611
1-800-545-2433
www.ala.org

Bioneers
Collective Heritage Institute
901 West San Mateo Road, Suite L
Santa Fe, NM 87505
1-877-246-6337
www.bioneers.org

Business Alliance for Local Living
    Economics (BALLE)
www.livingeconomics.org
National Coordinators:
    Michelle Long
    360-303-7779
    Michelle@LivingEconomics.org
    or
    Derek Long
    360-303-7776
    Derek@LivingEconomics.org

Campaign for America's Future
1025 Connecticut Avenue, NW
Suite 205
Washington, DC 20036
202-955-5665
www.ourfuture.org

Carol Trevelyan Strategy Group
    (CTSG)
1718 Connecticut Avenue, NW
6th Floor
Washington, DC 20009
202-448-5200
www.ctsg.com

Center on Budget and Policy
  Priorities
820 1st Street, NE
Suite 510
Washington, DC 20002
202-408-1080
www.cbpp.org

Center for Community Change
1000 Wisconsin Avenue, NW
Washington, DC 20007
202-342-0567
www.communitychange.org

Center for Public Integrity
910 17th Street, NW
7th Floor
Washington, DC 20006
202-466-1300
www.publicintegrity.org

Center for Responsive Politics
1101 14th Street, NW
Suite 1030
Washington, DC 20036
202-857-0044
www.opensecrets.org

Center for Study of Responsive Law
Ralph Nader
P.O. Box 19405
Washington, DC 20036
202-387-8030
www.essential.org

Center for Voting and Democracy
6930 Carroll Avenue
Takoma Park, MD 20912
301-270-4616
www.fairvote.org

Center on Wisconsin Strategy
  (COWS)
University of Wisconsin—Madison
1180 Observatory Drive
7122 Social Science Building
Madison, WI 53706
608-263-3889
www.cows.org

The Century Foundation
41 East 70th Street
New York, NY 10021
212-535-4441
www.tcf.org

Citizens for Tax Justice
1311 L Street, NW
Washington, DC 20005
202-626-3780
www.ctj.org

Commercial Alert
4110 SE Hawthorne Boulevard #123
Portland, OR 97214-5426
503-235-8012
www.commercialalert.org

Committee for the Study of the
  American Electorate
421 New Jersey Avenue, SE
Washington, DC 20003
202-546-3221

Common Cause
1250 Connecticut Avenue, NW #600
Washington, DC 20036
202-833-1200
www.commoncause.org

Communication Workers of America
501 3rd Street, NW
Washington, DC 20001-2797
202-434-1100
www.cwa-union.org

Conscious Choice
920 Franklin Street #202
Chicago, IL 60610
312-440-4373
www.consciouschoice.com

Consortium for Independent
    Journalism
2200 Wilson Boulevard
Suite 102-231
Arlington, VA 22201
www.consortiumnews.com

Consumers Union
101 Truman Avenue
Yonkers, NY 10703-1057
914-378-2000
www.consumersunion.org

Co-op America
1612 K Street, NW
Suite 600
Washington, DC 20006
1-800-58-GREEN
www.coopamerica.org

Critical Mass Energy and
    Environmental Program
1600 20th Street, NW
Washington, DC 20009
202-588-1000
www.citizen.org/cmep

Democracy Now!
DCTV
87 Lafayette Street
New York, NY 10013
212-431-1990
www.democracynow.org

Economic Policy Institute
1660 L Street, NW
Suite 1200
Washington, DC 20036
202-775-8810
www.epinet.org

Electronic Privacy Information
    Center (EPIC)
1718 Connecticut Avenue, NW
Suite 200
Washington, DC 20009
202-483-1140
www.epic.org

Fairness and Accuracy in Reporting
    (FAIR)
112 West 27th Street
New York, NY 10001
212-633-6700
www.fair.org

Farm Aid
11 Ward Street, Suite 200
Somerville, MA 02143
617-354-2922
1-800-FARM AID
www.farmaid.org

Free Speech TV
P.O. Box 6060
Boulder, CO 80306
303-442-8445
www.freespeech.org

Global Exchange
2017 Mission Street #303
San Francisco, CA 94110
415-255-7296
www.globalexchange.org

Global Trade Watch
215 Pennsylvania Avenue, SE
Washington, DC 20003
202-546-4996
www.tradewatch.org

Granny D
P.O. Box 1492
Dublin, NH 03444
www.grannyd.com

Grassroots Solutions
1954 University Avenue, Suite 12
St. Paul, MN 55104
651-645-2433
www.grassrootssolutions.com

GreenpeaceUSA
702 H Street, NW
Suite 300
Washington, DC 20001
202-462-1177
1-800-326-0959
www.greenpeaceusa.org

Independent Media Institute
77 Federal Street
San Francisco, CA 94107
415-284-1420
www.alternet.org

Independent Press Association
2729 Mission Street #201
San Francisco, CA 94110-3131
1-877-INDYMAG
www.indypress.org

Institute for Agriculture and
    Trade Policy
2105 First Avenue South
Minneapolis, MN 55404
612-870-0453
www.iatp.org

Institute for Policy Studies
733 15th Street, NW
Suite 1020
Washington, DC 20005
202-234-9382
www.ips-dc.org

Jobs With Justice
501 3rd Street, NW
Washington, DC 20001
202-434-1106
www.jwj.org

Moveon.org
P.O. Box 9063
Berkeley, CA 94709-0063
www.moveon.org

Multinational Monitor
P.O. Box 19405
Washington, DC 20036
202-387-8034
www.multinationalmonitor.org

The Nation
33 Irving Place
New York, NY 10003
212-209-5400
www.thenation.com

National Farmers Union
400 North Capitol Street, NW
Suite 790
Washington, DC 20001
202-554-1600
www.nfu.org

National Labor Committee
275 Seventh Avenue, Suite 1503
New York, NY 10001
212-242-3002
www.nlcnet.org

National Priorities Project
17 New South Street, Suite 302
Northampton, MA 01060
413-584-9556
www.natprior.org

Natural Resources Defense Council
40 West 20th Street
New York, NY 10011
212-727-2700
www.nrdc.org

New Dimensions Radio
P.O. Box 569
Ukiah, CA 95482
707-468-5215
www.newdimensions.org

The New Rules Project
Institute for Local Self-Reliance
1313 5th Street, SE
Minneapolis, MN 55414
612-379-3815
www.newrules.org

Organic Valley Family of Farms
CROPP Cooperative
507 West Main Street
LaFarge, WI 54639
1-888-444-6455
www.organicvalley.com

People for the American Way
2000 M Street, NW
Suite 400
Washington, DC 20036
1-800-326-7329
www.pfaw.org

The Program on Corporations,
    Law & Democracy (POCLAD)
Box 246
S. Yarmouth, MA 02664-0246
508-398-1145
www.poclad.org

The Progressive
409 East Main Street
Madison, WI 53703
608-257-4626
www.progressive.org

Progressive Majority
1025 Connecticut Avenue, NW
Suite 205
Washington, DC 20036
202-408-8603
www.progressivemajority.com

The Progressive Populist
P.O. Box 150517
Austin, TX 78715
512-447-0455
www.populist.com

Progressive Strategies, LLC
1224 M Street, NW
Suite 201
Washington, DC 20005
202-628-7771 phone
202-628-7773 fax
www.progressivestrategies.net

Public Campaign
1320 19th Street, NW
Suite M1
Washington, DC 20036
202-293-0222
www.publicampaign.org

Public Citizen
1600 20th Street, NW
Washington, DC 20009
202-588-1000
www.citizen.org

ReclaimDemocracy.org
P.O. Box 532
Boulder, CO 80306
303-402-0105
www.reclaimdemocracy.org

Rocky Mountain Media Watch
P.O. Box 18858
Denver, CO 80218
303-832-7558
www.bigmedia.org

Rolling Thunder Down-Home
   Democracy Tour
c/o Carol Trevelyan Strategy Group
116 New Montgomery Street
Suite 237
San Francisco, CA 94105
415-267-0888
www.rollingthundertour.org

Social Ventures Network (SVN)
P.O. Box 29221
San Francisco, CA 94129-0221
415-561-6501
www.svn.org

Sojourners
2401 15th Street, NW
Washington, DC 20009
202-328-8842
1-800-714-7474
www.sojo.net

Sprawl-Busters
Strategic Planning—Field Operations
21 Grinnell Street
Greenfield, MA 01301
413-772-6289
www.sprawl-busters.com

TeamX/SweatX
807 Mateo Street
Los Angeles, CA 90021
213-362-9001
www.sweatx.net

Tides Center
The Presidio
P.O. Box 29907
San Francisco, CA 94129-0907
415-561-6300
www.tidescenter.org

TomPaine.com
1636 Connecticut Avenue, NW
Suite 30
Washington, DC 20009
202-332-2881
www.tompaine.com

True Majority
191 Bank Street, 3rd Floor
Burlington, VT 05401
802-860-6882
www.truemajority.org

Union of Needletrades, Industrial
   and Textile Employees (UNITE)
1710 Broadway
New York, NY 10019
212-265-7000
www.uniteunion.org

United for a Fair Economy
37 Temple Place, 5th Floor
Boston MA 02111
617-423-2148
www.stw.org

United Food and Commercial
   Workers Union (UFCW)
1175 K Street, NW
Washington, DC 20006
202-223-3111
www.ufcw.org

United Steel Workers of America
   (UWSA)
5 Gateway Center
Pittsburgh, PA 15222
412-562-2400
www.uswa.org

United Students Against Sweatshops
888 16th Street, NW
Suite 303
Washington, DC 20006
202-NOSWEAT
www.usasnet.org

U.S. Public Interest Research Group
   (PIRG)
218 D Street, SE
Washington, DC 20003
202-546-9707
www.pirg.org

Utne Magazine
1624 Harmon Place
Minneapolis, MN 55403
612-338-5040
www.utne.com

Wellstone Action
P.O. Box 14386
Saint Paul, MN 55114
651-251-7550
www.wellstone.org

Working Assets
101 Market Street, Suite 700
San Francisco, CA 94105
415-369-2000
www.workingassets.com

INDEX

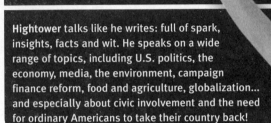